Early Childhood Education Series

Leslie R. Williams, Editor Millie Almy, Senior Advisor

Understanding Quantitative and Qualitative Research in Early Childhood Education
WILLIAM L. GOODWIN & LAURA D. GOODWIN

Diversity in the Classroom: New Approaches to the Education of Young Children, 2nd Ed.
FRANCES E. KENDALL

Developmentally Appropriate Practice in "Real Life": Stories of Teacher Practical Knowledge
CAROL ANNE WIEN

Quality in Family Child Care and Relative Care
SUSAN KONTOS, CAROLLEE HOWES, MARYBETH SHINN, & ELLEN GALINSKY

Using the Supportive Play Model: Individualized Intervention in Early Childhood Practice
MARGARET K. SHERIDAN, GILBERT M. FOLEY, & SARA H. RADLINSKI

The Full-Day Kindergarten: A Dynamic Themes Curriculum, 2nd Ed.
DORIS PRONIN FROMBERG

Experimenting with the World: John Dewey and the Early Childhood Classroom
HARRIET K. CUFFARO

New Perspectives in Early Childhood Teacher Education: Bringing Practitioners into the Debate
STACIE G. GOFFIN & DAVID E. DAY, Eds.

Assessment Methods for Infants and Toddlers: Transdisciplinary Team Approaches
DORIS BERGEN

The Emotional Development of Young Children: Building an Emotion-Centered Curriculum
MARION C. HYSON

Young Children Continue to Reinvent Arithmetic–3rd Grade: Implications of Piaget's Theory
CONSTANCE KAMII with SALLY JONES LIVINGSTON

Moral Classrooms, Moral Children: Creating a Constructivist Atmosphere in Early Education
RHETA DeVRIES & BETTY ZAN

Leadership in Early Childhood: The Pathway to Professionalism
JILLIAN RODD

Diversity and Developmentally Appropriate Practices: Challenges for Early Childhood Education
BRUCE L. MALLORY & REBECCA S. NEW, Eds.

Understanding Assessment and Evaluation in Early Childhood Education
DOMINIC F. GULLO

Changing Teaching, Changing Schools: Bringing Early Childhood Practice into Public Education–Case Studies from the Kindergarten
FRANCES O'CONNELL RUST

Physical Knowledge in Preschool Education: Implications of Piaget's Theory
CONSTANCE KAMII & RHETA DEVRIES

Caring for Other People's Children: A Complete Guide to Family Day Care
FRANCES KEMPER ALSTON

Family Day Care: Current Research for Informed Public Policy
DONALD L. PETERS & ALAN R. PENCE, Eds.

The Early Childhood Curriculum: A Review of Current Research, 2nd Ed.
CAROL SEEFELDT, Ed.

Reconceptualizing the Early Childhood Curriculum: Beginning the Dialogue
SHIRLEY A. KESSLER & BETH BLUE SWADENER, Eds.

Ways of Assessing Children and Curriculum: Stories of Early Childhood Practice
CELIA GENISHI, Ed.

The Play's the Thing: Teachers' Roles in Children's Play
ELIZABETH JONES & GRETCHEN REYNOLDS

Early Childhood Education Series titles, continued

Scenes from Day Care: How Teachers Teach and What Children Learn
ELIZABETH BALLIETT PLATT

Raised in East Urban: Child Care Changes in a Working Class Community
CAROLINE ZINSSER

United We Stand: Collaboration for Child Care and Early Education Services
SHARON L. KAGAN

Making Friends in School: Promoting Peer Relationships in Early Childhood
PATRICIA G. RAMSEY

Play and the Social Context of Development in Early Care and Education
BARBARA SCALES, MILLIE ALMY, AGELIKI NICOLOPOULOU, & SUSAN ERVIN-TRIPP, Eds.

The Whole Language Kindergarten
SHIRLEY RAINES & ROBERT CANADY

Good Day/Bad Day: The Child's Experience of Child Care
LYDA BEARDSLEY

Children's Play and Learning: Perspectives and Policy Implications
EDGAR KLUGMAN & SARA SMILANSKY

Serious Players in the Primary Classroom: Empowering Children Through Active Learning Experiences
SELMA WASSERMANN

Child Advocacy for Early Childhood Educators
BEATRICE S. FENNIMORE

Managing Quality Child Care Centers: A Comprehensive Manual for Administrators
PAMELA BYRNE SCHILLER
PATRICIA M. DYKE

Multiple World of Child Writers: Friends Learning to Write
ANNE HAAS DYSON

Young Children Continue to Reinvent Arithmetic–2nd Grade: Implications of Piaget's Theory
CONSTANCE KAMII

Literacy Learning in the Early Years: Through Children's Eyes
LINDA GIBSON

The Good Preschool Teacher: Six Teachers Reflect on Their Lives
WILLIAM AYERS

A Child's Play Life: An Ethnographic Study
DIANA KELLY-BYRNE

Professionalism and the Early Childhood Practitioner
BERNARD SPODEK, OLIVIA N. SARACHO, & DONALD L. PETERS, Eds.

Looking at Children's Play: The Bridge from Theory to Practice
PATRICIA A. MONIGHAN-NOUROT, BARBARA SCALES, JUDITH L. VAN HOORN, & MILLIE ALMY

The War Play Dilemma: Balancing Needs and Values in the Early Childhood Classroom
NANCY CARLSSON-PAIGE
DIANE E. LEVIN

The Piaget Handbook for Teachers and Parents: Children in the Age of Discovery, Preschool–3rd Grade
ROSEMARY PETERSON
VICTORIA FELTON-COLLINS

Teaching and Learning in a Diverse World: Multicultural Education for Young Children
PATRICIA G. RAMSEY

Promoting Social and Moral Development in Young Children
CAROLYN POPE EDWARDS

Today's Kindergarten
BERNARD SPODEK, Ed.

Supervision in Early Childhood Education
JOSEPH J. CARUSO
M. TEMPLE FAWCETT

Visions of Childhood: Influential Models from Locke to Spock
JOHN CLEVERLEY & D. C. PHILLIPS

Starting School: From Separation to Independence
NANCY BALABAN

Young Children Reinvent Arithmetic: Implications of Piaget's Theory
CONSTANCE KAMII

Ideas Influencing Early Childhood Education: A Theoretical Analysis
EVELYN WEBER

The Joy of Movement in Early Childhood
SANDRA R. CURTIS

For Marilyn - Happy reading!
Laura Goodwin
William Goodwin

Understanding Quantitative and Qualitative Research in Early Childhood Education

William L. Goodwin
Laura D. Goodwin

Teachers College, Columbia University
New York and London

Published by Teachers College Press, 1234 Amsterdam Avenue, New York, NY 10027

Library of Congress Cataloging-in-Publication Data

Goodwin, William Lawrence, 1935–
Understanding quantitative and qualitative research in early childhood education / William L. Goodwin, Laura D. Goodwin.
p. cm. – (Early childhood education series)
Includes bibliographical references (p.) and index.
ISBN 0-8077-3548-5 (cloth : alk. paper). – ISBN 0-8077-3547-7 (pbk.)
1. Early childhood education—Research—Methodology. I. Goodwin, Laura D. II. Title. III. Series.
LB1139.23.G86 1996
372.21'07—dc20 96-23110

ISBN 0-8077-3547-7 (paper)
ISBN 0-8077-3548-5 (cloth)

Printed on acid-free paper
Manufactured in the United States of America

03 02 01 00 99 98 97 96 8 7 6 5 4 3 2 1

Contents

Preface

Our purpose in this book is to describe the research process and to facilitate the reader's understanding of the process and its products. We examine both quantitative and qualitative research methods. While some authors present these two general approaches as opposing methodologies, we emphasize ways in which they can be used together to fully study a given phenomenon or topic. Each methodology has unique strengths to bring to bear on the generation of new knowledge. Thus we view them as complementary and promote their joint use.

Throughout the book, we present research concepts in straightforward terms so that the reader can easily gain an understanding and appreciation of the diverse array of research procedures that are available. The book contains many examples of research investigations; in most cases, we have drawn these examples from the field of early childhood education. The examples, we believe, help bring the various methods "to life" for the reader. They were carefully chosen from hundreds of available articles in numerous professional journals, as well as selected books, to illustrate the particular methods we discuss.

This book could be used as the principal text in a research methods course that aims to help professionals understand the research endeavor. For example, we plan to use it in a seminar that considers the domain of early childhood education research. After studying and discussing the processes involved in quantitative and qualitative research, each student will prepare a seminar presentation on some specific topic; the presentations focus on extant research they have judged to be sound. The book could also be used in a supplementary way in various other courses in which research methods and early childhood education intersect. Another potential role for the book would be by early childhood professionals who wish to update their knowledge of research methodology and its uses in the field.

We wish to acknowledge and thank many persons who have helped in the writing of this book. The many students in our classes have taught us much. We have learned from their struggles to understand certain concepts, their insightful comments, and their suggestions about better ways to present material after they have mastered the essence of what we were trying to convey. The outstanding guidance and editorial assistance provided by Susan Liddicoat at Teachers College Press was sincerely appreciated, as was help from Karl Nyberg and Peter Sieger. Our thanks are extended, too, to Catherine Blakemore, who did an excellent job helping us locate and review potential examples of research studies, and to Susan and George Zacharkiw, who provided wonderful assistance in preparing the figures and tables. Finally, we express our great appreciation to our son, Matthew. He tolerated (usually graciously) the writing of this book, which often took time away from him. His entire childhood has reminded us daily about the thousands of interesting questions that research has yet to answer about young children. As he just now enters his teenage years, the list of unanswered questions seems to have increased exponentially! With thanks and love, we dedicate this book to Matthew.

PART I

FUNDAMENTAL ELEMENTS IN RESEARCH

Chapter 1

Research and Its Role in Early Childhood Education

"The inquiring mind wants to know!" So goes the advertising slogan for a supermarket tabloid in the United States. While we do not intend to endorse that paper in any sense whatsoever, we must admit that we like the statement's sentiment. Having spent most of our adult lives in and around universities—first as students and now as professors—we hold knowledge that exists and the creation of knowledge as very important in the grand scheme of things. Therefore, the "inquiring mind" is a delight to us, whether observed in our students, our colleagues, or ourselves.

Further, we believe that knowledge from research can help us all perform better. Suppose you as a preschool teacher have been assigned to "quarrel patrol" by your more experienced colleagues. We think research can help place your task in perspective. Over half a century ago, Dawe (1934) analyzed 200 quarrels of nursery school children. She found most of them to be short (only 13 of the 200 lasted over a minute), to be a struggle for possessions, to be solved by the participants themselves, and to be followed usually by renewed playing with little residual bitterness. More recently, others have extended Dawe's work. For example, Laursen and Hartup (1989) observed conflicts between 53 preschoolers across 10 weeks. They found a majority of the conflicts to be short (less than 10 seconds), to concern behaviors more often than possessions, to be solved by the participants themselves often via one child's insistence, to be nearly universal (only one child had been in no quarrels), and to result in continued interaction and playing after the episode, especially by older children. Thus, with knowledge of this research, you might decide to approach quarrel patrol in a fairly laid-back manner since most often such quarrels are short and self-solving. Your plan might be to address only those quarrels of longer duration that involve aggression and to help younger children who are quarrel-prone to develop social skills for resolving disputes. In our view, research is a friend to us all.

In this book, our principal purpose is to describe the research endeavor and to provide the means by which the reader can understand both the research process and its products, especially as they pertain to early childhood education. Research is a pervasive phenomenon, crucial in any number of ways for different groups in society, and important in a great number of fields. In the past, agricultural research dramatically improved the capability of societies to produce food. Present fields with high research visibility include medicine and technology. Medical research continues to supply the world with drugs, devices, and procedures to eliminate or ameliorate the debilitating effects of many diseases and conditions. Largely due to research, infant mortality has been reduced dramatically this century, while life-span expectancies have gradually increased. In the United States there is a clear increase in the proportion of people over 65 years of age, with a larger number of persons living past 100. (And, as George Burns once noted, he would have it made once he made it to 100, since one hardly ever hears of anyone over 100 dying!) In technological fields, research has triggered massive changes in society. Communication links now allow transmission of words and images instantly between most populated points on the globe. Computers, continuously enhanced through research and development, have served as catalysts for massive changes that have affected all of us.

Profound issues, if not dilemmas, for society often surround research undertakings. For example, medical interventions with infants born very prematurely often can "save" the infants' lives, but issues arise concerning the quality of life then possible, as well as the extraordinary costs of such procedures. Research has made abortion a relatively safe procedure, but the intensity of disagreement over the ethics of abortion shows no sign of abatement. At the other end of the continuum of life, society also is struggling with issues related to the "artificial" prolonging of life, such as the "right to die." Issues involving the "advances" in weaponry made possible by research are ongoing and sobering. At the same time, present and past research has been a key element in stimulating advances in numerous and diverse fields that have bettered the lives of all of us.

In this book, our research playing field and area of focus is early childhood education. For our purposes here, we have defined "early childhood" as encompassing the ages from birth to 8 years (with some greater attention in our examples to children ages 3 to 6 years). We use "education" in a very broad sense to include settings with formal educational objectives (e.g., intervention-oriented programs at centers or hospitals, preschools, and kindergartens), settings with typically less formal educational expectations (e.g., homes and child care sites), or settings and activities intending to nurture young children's development in general (e.g., books, television shows, play, and games).

We consider it important to state "up front" our particular view that, in general, there are neither best nor worst research methods and procedures. Rather, each research method and technique has its own strengths and weaknesses. Any subject under investigation can be approached from a host of different directions using a range of research methods. Of course, good methods may be used improperly by poorly trained investigators. In this book, our intent is to present most of the many research methods with an even and impartial hand. If it appears to you that we are unduly favoring or criticizing a particular method, then it represents our clumsiness at using words for full and accurate expression. We truly believe that there are neither good nor bad research methods, but rather an arsenal of methods with differing capabilities for addressing a research problem.

DEFINING RESEARCH AND ITS LINKAGES

In a general sense, *research* means finding out. While there are numerous ways to slice the research pie—that is, many types of research have been identified, as will be made explicit in Chapter 2—the types or methods have in common the *generation of knowledge* at varying levels of detail, sophistication, and generalizability. Research results in the creation of knowledge to solve a problem, answer a question, and better describe or understand something. In all these instances, producing new knowledge highlights the research process aimed at finding out.

Three terms closely related to research also require definition: measurement, statistics, and evaluation. *Measurement* is a process defined as "determining, via observation or testing, an individual's behaviors or traits, a program's characteristics, or the characteristics of some other entity, and then assigning a number, score, or rating to that determination" (Goodwin & Driscoll, 1980, p. 1). As such, measurement involves numbers, scales, constructs, validity, and reliability. Measurement is at least as old as civilization. More modern emphases on measurement in education are often traced to Thorndike's (1918) dictum that anything that exists, exists in some amount and thus can be measured. Today, the array of measures available, both standardized and not, is truly vast. Still, available instruments are distributed unevenly across all the types of characteristic of young children and their families that one might desire to measure (more on this in Chapters 4 and 6). The linkage between measurement and research is direct, substantial, and crucial. In the process of conducting virtually all research, some measurement is involved. The quality of the research that results is vitally dependent on the quality of any measures that were used in the research effort.

Statistics are techniques used to analyze, summarize, interpret, and present numerical data. Two major branches of statistics can be identified, descriptive and inferential. In an earlier work (Goodwin & Driscoll, 1980), we noted that *descriptive statistics* are used to describe a set of data, such as a class's average performance and variability on a measure. In contrast, *inferential statistics* are employed when taking outcomes from a given set of data and generalizing to a larger group. Data are drawn from a *sample* of persons or objects thought to be representative of a much larger group, or *population*, of persons or objects. Descriptive statistics such as the mean or average are calculated for the sample; then, using inferential statistical techniques based on probability theories, statements are made about the likely nature of the entire population. Thus, statistics relate to research both by helping describe and present data assembled during the research enterprise and by supporting inferences made related to the research problem area. Note, too, that less quantitative types of "data" are generated in qualitative research as we describe in Chapters 5 and 6, and somewhat analogous procedures are used to assemble, describe, and interpret such data.

Evaluation, the third process linked importantly to research, is variously defined. For example, Worthen and Sanders (1987) identified six evaluation approaches or orientations—objectives, management, consumer, expertise, adversary, and naturalistic-participant; those espousing each orientation define evaluation somewhat differently. However, for Worthen and Sanders, and for us, the essence of evaluation "is judging the worth of something—often in terms of its costs, adequacy or effectiveness" (Goodwin & Driscoll, 1980, p. 2). Therefore, it involves needs, values, measurement, criteria or standards, and cost analysis. Programs, educational products or procedures, and individual performance are often evaluated in early childhood contexts. Besides the shared reliance on measurement, evaluation relates to research in that it often uses many research-linked procedures. For example, one way to determine the worth of a new curriculum for young children would be to compare its effects on children with the effects of a competing curriculum using controlled procedures "borrowed" from research.

THE VALUE OF CONDUCTING AND UNDERSTANDING RESEARCH

Conducting research properly can be a costly venture in terms of resources expended such as time and money. While there is obviously great variability in the complexity and therefore the cost of research, there is no escaping the legitimacy of the question "Why conduct research?" The answer is that the research process is the most reliable means that we have to generate knowledge.

Kerlinger (1986), building on the work of the philosopher Charles Peirce (Buchler, 1955), presented a quartet of ways that we have of "knowing." In the *method of tenacity*, persons hold firmly to the truth, and they know the truth to be true because they steadfastly hold to it. Under such a method, "knowledge" essentially has a life of its own and can outlive even strong evidence to the contrary. Via the *method of authority*, established beliefs constitute knowledge. If a particular idea has the weight of tradition and public opinion, it must be so; at the same time, such a method can be unsound at times. The *a priori method* claims to be a more effective means to determine knowledge in that it is based on propositions that "agree with reason," and that persons should be able to reason and reach the truth through vigorous communication. Of course, the difficulty is whose reasoning is to be trusted—"it stands to reason" is seen as a weak defense when persons disagree.

Kerlinger agreed with Peirce that the *method of science*, the fourth approach, held greatest promise as a means of knowing. Via this method, rigorous procedures are used to generate knowledge independent of one's particular opinion about that knowledge. Importantly, the scientific method has built-in checks in order to create dependable knowledge. For example, even if a hypothesis appears to be supported in an initial study, the investigator should test alternative plausible hypotheses that might also explain the outcomes observed; such testing must be open for the inspection of other professionals and the public.

While the scientific method is held in high regard among scientists and most persons in higher education, there are naysayers who believe that research too often is an expensive, time-consuming means to demonstrate something trivial or obvious. Not too many years ago, a U.S. senator, William Proxmire, established the Golden Fleece Award; he periodically singled out a research study he considered to have been a shameful waste of tax dollars in terms of its trivial or unnecessary nature. More recently in Illinois, state legislators balked at continuing to fund a researcher who was studying owls' eating habits by collecting and analyzing their vomit. On a less formal basis, we hear such criticism on a Denver news-only radio station, which often reports results of this or that research undertaking. Frequently, one of the announcers will chide the study's results, suggesting that no elaborate research was needed since the outcomes were predictable if not obvious. In the current vernacular of Matthew, our 12-year-old son, such pedestrian research results would be greeted with a derisive "Big whoop" or a sarcastic "Cool!"

Relatedly, Kaestle (1993) interviewed 33 key federal officials and researchers to discern their impressions of educational research over the past quarter century. A view expressed frequently was that such research had an "awful reputation" as federal legislators opined that many expensive studies at best resulted in outcomes that they had known since their own life experiences in fourth grade—and they had all been through the fourth grade. This view, four years more advanced but otherwise reminiscent of Fulghum's (1988) *All I Really Needed to Know I Learned in Kindergarten,* was "legitimized" by legislators' personal experience in education—but could not be applied to fields like medical or space research. Clearly such attitudes are a restatement of the obviousness argument.

This issue has been formally summarized and deftly countered by Gage (1991). Citing doctoral dissertations completed at Stanford (Baratz, 1983; Wong, 1987), he denoted how well-educated persons—and very likely others, for that matter—typically regarded research findings as "obvious." The essential approach used by both Baratz and Wong was to present research "findings" to subjects to be rated on a four-point scale, "extremely obvious," "obvious," "unobvious," and "extremely unobvious." *Obvious* was defined as self-evident, that is, that the research outcomes found certainly were to be expected. Subjects consistently tended to rate the "findings" as obvious. Subjects were unaware, however, that still other subjects were presented with findings for the same studies stated in exactly the opposite direction—these latter subjects also judged the contrary findings to be obvious. The central point, then, was that subjects *always* rated the outcomes as obvious, whether they reacted to the actual outcomes of the study or to outcomes just the reverse of what was actually found. When told the outcomes of a study, one's natural tendency appears to be to consider the results predictable and, thus, in a certain sense, trivial. It follows, then, that much research needs to be focused on determining whether the obvious is true or merely "obvious." Said differently, certain of the less reliable ways of knowing, detailed by Peirce (Buchler, 1955) and Kerlinger (1986), produce "knowledge" that requires verification through the use of the scientific method.

Farley (1993) identified a related concept, "street science," which differs from professional science's formal knowledge structure. Street science appears in media clips, sound bites, and news stories, and consists of

> that less understood, less respected, less coherent patchwork of general utterances and speculations in lay forums about how things work, what might be "at the bottom" of human and natural events, why people are the way they are and behave the way they do. (p. 11)

Popular views of psychology—and Farley suggested that virtually all of us are self-anointed psychologists—were deemed important for the general public's support of the discipline. While noting the responsibility of scientists to advance professional science, Farley (similar to the American Association for the Advancement of Science) also advocated their accepting the charge of enhancing the coherence and quality of street science. Scientific psychologists were encouraged "to take up the pen of popularization." Such a populist practice by the hundreds of psychologists who do research on young children, their families, and their education and care would undoubtedly both create considerable popular support for the discipline's research and enlighten and inform many persons' interactions with young children. In a similar vein, Berliner (1992) recommended that educational researchers increase their skill at "telling the stories" of their studies' outcomes. By conceptualizing and reporting research findings in narrative form, often identifying real teachers and students, he believed that researchers would be understood and very influential with practitioners. Indeed, narrations and stories are becoming an increasingly popular reporting format for educational researchers. Examples include *The Play's the Thing* (Jones & Reynolds, 1992) and *Developmentally Appropriate Practice in "Real Life"* (Wien, 1995).

Overall then, high-quality research is needed to generate reliable knowledge. In turn, that knowledge assists those trying to understand and guide a field and also provides a secure base on which to construct positive changes for a field. Professionals in early childhood education need to have the skills to allow them to understand research that pertains to young children—their nature, development, and learning. Regardless of one's current skill at nurturing the development and learning of young children, his or her ability will be elevated by reading and acting on sound research in the field. Understanding research stimulates professionals, invigorating their personal growth and increasing their effectiveness.

THE NATURE OF RESEARCH IN EARLY CHILDHOOD EDUCATION

Research involving young children and their families is extensive. While the following survey is far from comprehensive in scope, we note some areas that have witnessed considerable research activity in the recent past. Many of these areas of investigation have their roots in societal trends and issues.

The apparent effects of growing up in nontraditional family structures is of considerable interest to researchers currently. The impact of divorce on young children has been studied for the past quarter century. Over the same span of years, researchers have frequently asked questions and framed hypotheses centering on the possibility of deleterious effects on young children of child care received outside the home or within the home from other than the child's parents. Extensive research has examined the nature of developmental delays and other exceptionalities in young children, as well as the effectiveness of interventions designed to assist children in such regards. Quite recently, studies have been conducted on child abuse and the potential effects of violence on young children and their families. A related issue under study, crossing research and measurement boundaries, concerns the reliability of young children as witnesses in legal proceedings.

The foregoing might leave you with the impression that research focuses primarily on society's problem areas. While a substantial amount does, all research does not. For example, considerable recent research has targeted children's language development; of particular interest to educators has been the development of literacy in young children. Other areas of active research document the impressive attainments of young children, such as their capabilities to think, solve problems, cope, establish friends, and learn in several fields of knowledge. Developmental characteristics of children in the cognitive, affective, and psychomotor domains are frequently studied, as well as cross-domain topics such as gender development. Additional areas of inquiry currently of note include parent/family involvement, issues related to diversity and multiculturalism, and computers and young children.

The Research Community and Organizations

Who conducts research on young children? By and large, persons with advanced degrees, typically the doctorate, conduct such research. The majority of these persons are housed in universities and colleges. Others work for institutions whose major mission is to conduct research, or for government agencies set up to do research; these organizations are often affiliated with universities.

A crucial element often is obtaining the requisite funding to conduct research—that is, who pays for it? A number of less costly investigations are conducted by professors as part of their professional responsibilities; being an active researcher and publishing frequently is an expectation of higher education faculty in a majority of institutions, especially those with graduate-level programs. Many colleges and universities have small grant programs in which professors competitively seek funding; if obtained, such grants help offset the cost of research. More elaborate research undertakings in this country typically are funded by government agencies, especially federal and to some extent state agencies. Via government Requests for Proposals (RFPs), researchers at universities and other public and private agencies design and submit competitive proposals intended to address the issues raised in the RFP. The proposals then are judged by review panels, with the better-regarded ones eventually funded. Private foundations also fund a lesser, but significant, amount of research.

Building a sense of community among researchers is important in early childhood education, as it is in all fields, and organizations have appeared to meet this need. Several professional organizations particularly focus on young children and, to varying degrees, on research. The Society for Research in Child Development (SRCD) is a pivotal organization in both regards. The society was founded in 1933 to advance child development research, to encourage interdisciplinary attention to substantive and methodological problems related to child development, and to stimulate the dissemination of research findings via child development courses. National meetings are held every other year by SRCD. The 1995 meeting presentations give an excellent overview of the breadth of SRCD; they were categorized under 20 topics, such as infancy—cognition and communication; children at risk; language; educational issues; social development and behavior—prosocial behavior, aggression, and play; affect; family and kinship relations; and public policy issues.

Other important organizations for communicating early childhood education research include the Association for Childhood Education International (ACEI), the Division for Early Childhood (DEC) of the Council for Exceptional Children (CEC), the National Association for the Education of Young Children (NAEYC), and Zero to Three. Other national organizations contain researchers who study young children and their families, such as the American Anthropological Association (AAA), the American Educational Research Association (AERA), the American Psychological Association (APA), the American Psychological Society (APS), and the American Sociological Society (ASA). These organizations are broadly based and often include special groupings that focus on young children and research. For example, AERA has its Special Interest Group of researchers and practitioners in Early Childhood/Child Development, and APA's Divisions 7, 15, and 37 are Developmental Psychology, Educational Psychology, and Child, Youth, and Family Services, respectively. Across these organizations, tens of thousands of persons are represented as producers and/or users of research; for instance, SRCD alone had about 5,000 members in 1995.

Research-oriented Journals and Publications

Both producers and users of research often desire to locate research on a given topic. Reports of research can be classified as archival or fugitive, and also as primary or secondary (Smith & Glass, 1987). *Archival* collections exist in published journals and books, and are accessible in academic libraries. *Fugitive* reports, so called because they are more difficult to locate, consist of papers presented at national organizations' conferences, theses, unpublished research reports, and technical papers. *Pri-*

mary sources are reports of research drafted by researchers themselves. *Secondary* sources, on the other hand, report and often synthesize the results of a number of research ventures, and include research review articles, textbooks, and handbooks.

Journals represent the largest primary archival source of research studies. The number of journals being published, in this country and internationally, has increased substantially in the past several decades. Since there presently is no end in sight to the frequently touted "knowledge explosion," we expect the initiation of many more journals. While electronic means for storing and transmitting information have become increasingly sophisticated, our guess is that journals will continue to be a prime means of communicating research for some time to come.

Which journals should one consult to examine the research studies that have been published on early childhood education? While not wanting to seem flip, we might answer "almost all of them." Fortunately, computer retrieval systems with keyword descriptors linked to your topic of interest now make it possible to locate relatively quickly numerous articles from "mainline" sources, as well as the occasional early childhood study that might appear in a journal not typical for such articles. In addition, we frequently direct our students to journals that we know are likely to serve as either primary or secondary sources of research in early childhood education, as shown in Table 1.1 (entries are coded in terms of their usual nature as primary or secondary sources of research, or both). The list there derives from our personal experience, as well as the work of others (e.g., Dorsey, 1992; Henson, 1995; Lukasevich & Summers, 1986), and the list of journals received for possible annotated entries in *Child Development Abstracts and Bibliography*, a publication of SRCD that in itself serves as an excellent avenue to relevant research. Other abstracts and indexes—such as *Current Index to Journals in Education*, *Education Index*, *Resources in Education*, *Psychological Abstracts*, and *Sociological Abstracts*—are available at academic libraries and speed and expand the search for primary literature. Of special note is *Resources in Education*, published by the Educational Resources Information Center (ERIC), as it indexes and abstracts thousands of documents pertaining to education. One of its 16 clearinghouses is named Elementary and Early Childhood Education; it is housed at the University of Illinois, Champaign-Urbana.

Several secondary sources should also be noted. The *Encyclopedia of Early Childhood Education* (Williams & Fromberg, 1992), the *Handbook of Research on the Education of Young Children* (Spodek, 1993), and the *International Handbook of Early Childhood Education* (Woodill, Bernhard, & Prochner, 1992) are particularly relevant. Many disciplines frequently publish handbooks or reviews. Some handbooks focus on research—for

TABLE 1.1 Significant Journals for Early Childhood Education Research

American Educational Research Journal (P)
American Psychologist (S)
Anthropology and Education Quarterly (P, S)
Australian Journal of Early Childhood (P, S)
British Journal of Developmental Psychology (P)
British Journal of Educational Psychology (P)
Child Development (P)
Childhood Education (S)
Day Care and Early Education (S)
Developmental Psychology (P)
Early Childhood Development and Care (P, S)
Early Childhood Research Quarterly (P)
Early Education and Development (P)
Educational Evaluation and Policy Analysis (P)
Educational Leadership (S)
Educational Researcher (P, S)
Elementary School Journal (P)
Exceptional Children (P, S)
Family and Child Mental Health (P, S)
Family Relations (P, S)
Gifted Child Quarterly (P, S)
Harvard Educational Review (P, S)
Infant Behavior and Development (P)
International Journal of Early Childhood (P, S)
International Journal of Qualitative Studies in Education (P, S)
Journal of Abnormal Child Psychology (P)
Journal of Applied Behavior Analysis (P)
Journal of Child Language (P)
Journal of Early Intervention (P, S)
Journal of Educational Psychology (P)
Journal of Educational Research (P)
Journal of Experimental Child Psychology (P)
Journal of Experimental Education (P)
Journal of Genetic Psychology (P)
Journal of Pediatric Psychology (P)
Journal of Research in Childhood Education (P)
Journal of Social Psychology (P)
Merrill-Palmer Quarterly (P)
Monographs of the Society for Research in Child Development (P, S)
Phi Delta Kappan (S)
Play and Culture (P, S)
Psychology in the Schools (P)
Reading Research Quarterly (P)
Review of Educational Research (S)
Teachers College Record (S)
Topics in Early Childhood Special Education (P, S)
Young Children (S)
Zero to Three (S)

Note: P = Primary research source   S = Secondary research source

example, Spodek's offering cited above, the *Handbook of Research on Teaching* (Wittrock, 1986), and the *Handbook of Qualitative Research* (Denzin & Lincoln, 1994). There are dozens of fruitful secondary sources of research (for a full review, see McMillan & Schumacher, 1993).

PLAN OF THE BOOK

In Chapter 2, we present additional fundamental elements related to research, as well as a schematic of the principal types of research currently in use. General procedures or steps in conducting research are considered there, along with the determination of research topics, hypotheses, and variables. Ideas involving sampling and site selection also appear in Chapter 2.

Part II contains information on, and examples of, quantitative research, especially as it occurs in early childhood education. Types or methods of quantitative research are described in Chapter 3, as well as procedures for users to critique such research. Measurement in quantitative research forms the nucleus of Chapter 4, and data analysis methods are briefly described; the scope of this book unfortunately does not permit a comprehensive treatment of many of the statistical procedures used.

In Part III qualitative research is examined. In general, the framework utilized in Part II is repeated, but in a somewhat different pattern. That is, in Chapter 5 different types of qualitative research are presented. Instrumentation and analysis in qualitative research, and guidelines for critiquing such research, form the nucleus of Chapter 6. The critique guidelines are considered last because the merit of qualitative research rests heavily on its entire process, including any integral analytic procedures used enroute.

In Part IV the seventh and final chapter focuses on the integration of quantitative and qualitative research in efforts to generate knowledge in early childhood education. We consider this "merger" highly appropriate and effective. Emphasis is placed on the complementary nature of both orientations and their measurement and analysis procedures.

In debating what to include in this book, we decided to emphasize understanding the general nature of the research enterprise. Thus, our goal is to enable the reader to make informed judgments about the quality of a study and to appreciate the important contributions made by high-quality research. Throughout, we use research examples from the field of early childhood education. We develop the thesis that both quantitative and qualitative research—separately and in combination—can generate knowledge of great value to children and those who guide them in their early years.

Chapter 2

An Overview of the Research Endeavor

In this chapter, we take you through some general yet important elements of the research process. The first stop on this journey is a general examination of the research process, essentially the actions taken by the researcher. Then typical classifications of research, as well as an array of types or methods of research, are presented. An important decision for the investigator is which methodological emphasis or combination of methods to employ. The next stop concerns the determination of research topics or questions, hypotheses, and variables in the study. Our overview journey concludes with the researcher's consideration of sampling and site selection.

THE RESEARCH PROCESS—IN GENERAL

All research—whether in early childhood education or any field—begins as an idea in the mind of the investigator. If sufficiently compelling, a possible research topic then can stimulate the completion of a series of steps or activities. While the order in which these steps are taken might vary for different types of research (as will be noted), as well as the speed with which they are completed, they constitute a process by means of which knowledge is generated. Let us present a typical series of steps prior to noting some exceptions.

1. *Conceptualizing a topic area to research.* The researcher might identify a topic linked with a current societal problem (e.g., the experiencing of violence by young children and their families) or something that has piqued his or her curiosity (e.g., children's different styles of "convincing" other children to share their snacks). Or the topic may be more developmental in nature (e.g., whether younger and older children in a mixed-age preschool spend equivalent amounts of time in various activity centers), or of a cause-and-effect nature (e.g., the

effect on parent participation of different approaches to eliciting involvement in their children's education). Of course, there is an unlimited number of topics that might capture the researcher's interest. The topic that persists after meeting other criteria—such as reasonable cost, availability of appropriate subjects or sites, and suitable measures—frames the next stage of the process. Depending on the type of research contemplated, this step can involve statements of hypotheses to be tested and key questions to be answered.

2. *Reviewing the extant literature on the topic.* As noted in Chapter 1, computers and focused abstract collections now speed the identification of research and other writings related to the topic. There are "how to" chapters concerning literature reviews in most major research methods texts. If not already examined, available theory that underpins the topic also should be reviewed at this point; in some cases, existing theories may have been major stimuli in the original selection of the topic in step 1. The literature contains what other researchers employed in terms of measures and procedures.
3. *Designing the procedures of the study.* In light of the literature surveyed and the investigator's own ideas, the details of the investigation are laid out. These include: identifying the prime variables and the sample or sites for the study (discussed later in this chapter); determining the means of gaining access to conduct the study and of protecting subjects' rights; working out the many issues related to data generation (e.g., who will be collecting what using which methods and instruments); and contemplating how data will be analyzed.
4. *Collecting data.* The procedures crafted in step 3 are placed in motion. After subjects and sites are identified and access is obtained, data collection begins. This stage can take from a few hours to months or even years, depending on the specific topic of investigation and the methods used. Data must be both carefully assembled and meticulously stored for later analysis.
5. *Analyzing data.* Numerous techniques exist for the analysis of data, as Chapters 4 and 6 will reveal. Researchers have to choose those analysis techniques that are technically appropriate and that will best reveal patterns in the data. Determining the former can be quite complex, and expert statistical or analytic advice is often sought.
6. *Interpreting the data analyses.* In this step, hypotheses are tested and questions are answered, at least in preliminary form. This stage is crucial. After an investigator or research team has invested heavily in time and money to initiate and implement a study, it is important to examine the analysis results to derive as much meaning from the

data as possible. Past experiences of the researchers come into play at this point, as does their familiarity with research literature and theories relevant to the topic studied. Parsimonious explanations of the data and their analyses are sought.

7. *Reporting results.* This element involves sharing the outcomes of the research with a wider audience or, in some cases, with multiple groups. Reporting is an art. The researcher must denote the problem and the background literature, detail the procedures and measures used, display the results, and interpret and discuss the significance of the knowledge generated in the study. Common means for reporting include publication in journals (such as listed in Chapter 1), monographs, and books, and presentations at meetings (e.g., most professional organizations meet annually or every other year).
8. *Replicating the study.* A key final element in establishing the credibility of research, replication concerns repeating the study by the original researcher or others to establish the stability of the results and, therefore, of the knowledge created. While seeing this as an important concluding step, we realistically must note that it is rare in the social sciences for a study to be replicated exactly as initially done. Lessons learned during the original undertaking usually are reflected in some changes when and if the research is redone. At the same time and much too often, studies are published and not directly replicated by anyone.

The eight-step sequence above is typical of quantitative studies, as defined in the next section of this chapter, for they follow a deductive investigatory pattern. Most qualitative research, on the other hand, is inductive in character. While the first step and the last two steps in the sequence occur in the same order in qualitative research, they are different in character. That is, step 1 for the qualitative researcher involves selecting a general or working topic that may change over time and possibly identifying individuals or groups of special interest; reports in step 7 are usually narrative rather than numerical; and step 8 is usually conceptualized as reproducibility of the concepts and theories generated, rather than as the replication of quantitative results. Step 2 is often only briefly addressed by most researchers early in a qualitative study, so step 3 (involving the study's design) next takes center stage. Steps 4, 5, and 6 often occur interactively and concurrently in qualitative research; that is, they influence one another. Ideas emanating from these steps and the actual data collected frequently prompt the investigator to consult the literature (step 2 in the sequence above) in greater depth at this point. Final analyses then precede steps 7 and 8, reporting and reproducibility. Even though the sequence of steps, and indeed the nature of the steps themselves, varies in quantitative and qualitative inquiries, the prime purpose of each is the generation of knowledge.

TYPES OF RESEARCH

There are many ways to slice the research pie. One common classification scheme has three groups: basic (also termed fundamental or pure), applied, and evaluation research; this scheme concerns the purposes of the research and the generalizability of the knowledge produced. Following Best and Kahn (1993), Graziano and Raulin (1993), Kerlinger (1979), and McMillan and Schumacher (1993), *basic research* is conducted to test theory and to study phenomena and their relationships. Little attention is given to applications of the knowledge generated to practical problems; rather, knowledge is generated for its own sake. On the other hand, *applied research* uses many of the same techniques as basic research but is focused on the solution of practical and often pressing problems in applied settings. A typical, but not exclusive, pattern is for basic research findings to inform and stimulate applied research. Since educational research frequently seeks knowledge that permits generalizations about the teaching-learning process and other instructional elements (e.g., materials, settings, motivation), much of it is considered applied. Even more applied, *evaluation research* concerns the determination of the merit and worth of a given practice at a selected site or multiple sites; quite concrete, it uses systematic procedures to add research-based knowledge concerning the practice and to facilitate local decision making. While not a focus in this book, *action research* is related to evaluation research in that practitioners and others study a topic of local interest with readily available subjects for direct application, say, to the classrooms of the teachers taking part (but probably not generating knowledge of wide applicability). Increasingly, authors have suggested that teachers approach teaching as active investigators and researchers in their own right (e.g., Eisenhart & Borko, 1993; Hopkins, 1993; Hubbard & Power, 1993). Also recently, universities have been offering numerous related courses such as Research for Teachers and Teacher Inquiry.

Another approach to carving up the research pie is to consider quantitative and qualitative research. We have chosen to emphasize this delineation in this book for several reasons. First, while quantitative research has been predominant in education, qualitative research has increasingly been in evidence during the past quarter century. Second, important compatibilities exist between qualitative research and the field of early childhood education, though historically less so for early childhood special education (Odom, 1988). Third, and centrally, we view quantitative and qualitative research as complementary and mutually supportive (see Chapter 7).

Quantitative research generally derives from a logical-positivist philosophical position that holds that a single objective reality exists that can be discerned through scientific research. Thus, such research strives to be value-free and deductive, to determine relationships (often causal) between variables, and to report outcomes in numerical, statistical form. It assumes that "there are facts with objective reality that can be expressed numerically. Consequently, there is a heavy reliance on numbers, measurement, experiments, and numerical relationships and descriptions" (McMillan, 1996, p. 9).

Qualitative research claims its roots in a naturalistic phenomenological philosophy that contends that multiple realities exist and must be recognized by giving attention to group and individual constructions and perceptions of reality. Therefore, this research seeks to understand phenomena via induction; to emphasize process, values, context, and interpretation in the construction of meaning and concepts; and to report findings in narrative form. "Qualitative research is a particular tradition in social science that fundamentally depends on watching people in their own territory and interacting with them in their own language, on their own terms" (Kirk & Miller, 1986, p. 9). In addition and as will soon be noted, certain analytical forms of research can be thought of as qualitative.

Table 2.1 contains a series of characteristics on which quantitative and qualitative research generally can be differentiated. As can be noted in the table, both theoretical and academic bases for quantitative and qualitative research vary substantively, with the former attempting to generate knowledge from an objective detached perspective (i.e., etic) and the latter seeking a naturalistic or personalized orientation (i.e., emic). The purposes and design likewise differ, quantitative methods being deductive, predetermined, and specific, while the qualitative approach is inductive, emergent, and less specified, especially at the onset. The researcher's role is notably different also, as one would expect. The two orientations vary with regard to the instruments used to generate data. Though both use interviews and observations, quantitative investigations tend to utilize highly structured forms of each, while qualitative studies use open-ended formats. Inspection of the data-analysis procedures and reports emanating from each type of research likewise reveals differences, with quantitative reports more likely numeric and deductive and qualitative reports more often in narrative form and inductive. A number of these variations are more finely detailed in the following chapters.

Yet another classification scheme involves the particular type of research method that predominates in a given study. Our choice in Table 2.2 is to

TABLE 2.1 Features of Quantitative and Qualitative Research

Feature	Quantitative Research	Qualitative Research
Theoretical bases	Logical positivism Behavioralism Etic (outsider's point of view)	Phenomenological Naturalistic Emic (insider's point of view)
Academic linkages	Psychology, economics, sociology	Anthropology, sociology, history
Purposes	Determine relationships between variables, often causal Test theory Establish single, objective reality Predictive	Construct portrayals Develop meaning and understand perspectives Develop grounded theory Describe multiple realities Interpretive
Design	Predetermined Detailed, structured Formal	Emergent, evolving General, flexible Intuitive
Sample	Probability Often large Random selection	Purposeful Often small Nonrepresentative
Procedures, methods	Experimental Correlational Seeks consensus, norm	Analytical Ethnographic, fieldwork Seeks pluralism, complexity
Researcher's role	Detached, objective Impartial, distant Subject as subject	Participant observer Immersed, close Subject as friend
Instruments, data sources	Measures, questionnaires, scales, tests Structured interviews, observations	Field notes, documents, tapes, photographs Ethnographic interviews, observations
Data analysis, reporting	Quantitative, numbers Statistical, numeric Hypothesis testing Typically at study's end Context-free generalizations Deductive, from theory	Descriptive, words Thematic, conceptual Search for patterns Ongoing throughout study Context-bound generalizations Inductive, grounded theory

Note: Adapted from Bogdan & Biklen (1992); Glesne & Peshkin (1992); McMillan (1996); McMillan & Schumacher (1993).

TABLE 2.2 Primary Types of the Research Method

Quantitative		Qualitative	
Non-experimental	**Experimental**	**Naturalistic**	**Analytic**
Descriptive (survey & developmental)	True experimental	Ethnographic	Historical study
Correlational	Quasi-experimental		Legal study
Causal comparative	Single subject		Policy study

Note: Adapted from McMillan & Schumacher, 1993.

link these specific methods to the umbrella categories of quantitative and qualitative research just introduced. In part, the table represents an oversimplification in that certain of the methods overlap, especially in actual practice. While it contains the more common types of research, it is not exhaustive. The quantitative methods are divided into nonexperimental and experimental. The former are characterized by structured activities to generate knowledge without using procedures that involve manipulation of, or interventions with, subjects; findings typically are reported in numerical formats. The experimental designs, also quantitative, usually do involve manipulations in their quest of cause-and-effect relationships. On the other hand, the qualitative methods tend to result in the generation of knowledge that most often is reported in words and narratives. The naturalistic approach that this book will focus on is ethnography, with its numerous linkages to anthropology. In terms of analytic qualitative methods, limited attention will be given to historical, legal, and policy studies. Table 2.2 serves as a schematic of available research methods and also as a preview of the organization of Chapter 3 and Chapter 5, where each method will be defined and elaborated.

KEY COMPONENTS OF RESEARCH STUDIES

All types of research require initiation and advance planning. In this section, we examine some of the principal elements of research that must be addressed, although in different ways in quantitative and qualitative investigations. Considered are research topics, hypotheses, and variables.

Research Topics or Questions

The first step in the research process described in this chapter's opening is the conceptualization of a research topic. The reasons underlying the selection of a particular topic are varied. Possibly the researcher is aware of a particular theory that she or he would like to do research on or of a gap in existing research (e.g., suppose research has been done on the health concerns expressed by school-age children, but not those stated by preschoolers). Or perhaps the investigator is naturally curious about something, say children's humor, and therefore selects that as an area for study.

Frequently the stimulus that leads to the identification of a research topic is a problem perceived as needing at least attention, if not solution. Kerlinger (1986) addressed research problems quite formally. He wisely noted, "If one wants to solve a problem, one generally must know what the problem is. It can be said that a large part of the solution lies in knowing what it is one is trying to do" (p. 16). He also opined that simple, straightforward problems were preferable in research and that questions had the virtue of framing problems directly. For example, suppose a problem area is identified as increased amounts of violent behavior among 3- to 7-year-old children, both in school and in play settings. A question might be asked to further define the problem area, such as: What is the relationship between types of television program watched by young children and the amount of violent behavior exhibited toward each other in school and at play?

Consider a real-life example of the birth of a research topic. One of our students, a primary grade teacher, noticed in his own and other classrooms dramatically different behavior by children and teachers toward the class pets, such as gerbils, fish, and rabbits. He watched behaviors such as handling, feeding, cleaning the animals' spaces, and determining their diet. Sometimes the behaviors were appropriate and sometimes not. His literature search turned up remarkably little prior research in this area. The teacher selected the treatment of classroom pets by children as his topic. He then designed a training program to be used with some children and not others to see if it affected their attitudes and behavior toward classroom pets; this is similar to action research as defined earlier. He also hoped to gauge whether having pets at home influenced the impact of the training program. While he has designed an attitude-toward-pets questionnaire, he has not had the opportunity to conduct the study. This example shows the emergence of a research topic, and its further development.

The impetus for what has become quite a well known research topic was a clever "flipping of the coin." Research in this and other countries since, say, the 1960s has made it very clear that certain categories of children are at risk in the areas of normal development and positive mental health. A host of risk factors were identified, both biological—such as low birth weight, congenital defects, prematurity, and the like—and environmental—such as unstable homes, poverty, parental alcoholism and mental illness, and other stressful events. Some researchers flipped this well-established coin of vulnerability by becoming interested in children who beat the odds, so to speak, in that they experienced many of these potentially debilitating factors and yet thrived. Werner and Smith (1982) were among those targeting this research topic, and they dubbed these survivors "resilient children." As a result of their qualitative longitudinal study (children were followed from pre-birth to their twenties), they found Hawaiian children's resiliency to be associated with their generally positive orientations toward their families and toward school; their ability to gain positive attention from others; their proactive approach to solving daily problems; their doing required acts of helpfulness; their tendency to perceive even painful experiences constructively; their internal loci of control; and their confidence in the predictability of the environment and in surmounting obstacles that arose.

In quantitative research, the typical pattern is to define the problem quite precisely at the start of the investigation. Conversely, qualitative research often is initiated with a general area for the study—quite often related to the personal life experiences of the researcher—and possibly a "working" problem as discussed earlier in the chapter.

Hypotheses

In general, we all have hypotheses. For example, one of us might "hypothesize" that enrollment at the Comfy Cozy Child Care Center is increasing because the center's reputation of providing high-quality, developmentally appropriate care is becoming better known in the community. Someone else may believe or hypothesize that her 10-year-old's continuing struggle to spell accurately was caused by allowing and praising too much his "inventive" spelling during his early years in school. As such, these hypotheses are educated guesses or hunches.

In research, this notion of a hypothesis as a guess or a hunch also applies. At the same time, several varying, yet more precise definitions of hypotheses used in research are available. McMillan (1996), for example, viewed a hypothesis as "the investigator's prediction or expectation of what the results will show. It is a conjectural statement of the researcher's expectations about how the variables in the study are related" (p. 46). (We define variables in the next section.) Borg, Gall, and Gall (1993) added that hypotheses should be explicit, linked to theory, and succinct. Kerlinger (1986) stressed that hypotheses are the working instruments of theory and must be testable.

Two specific types of hypothesis—research and statistical—deserve mention because of their frequent use. The *research hypothesis* is a statement in words of the results an investigator expects to find in a study. An example of a research hypotheses would be "Children who receive a literacy-oriented whole language program will exhibit higher reading comprehension than children experiencing a phonics-based basal reader program." On the other hand, *statistical hypotheses* are statements using symbols that can be tested statistically. In a given study, statistical hypotheses include the *null hypothesis*, a conjectural statement of no difference or relationship between variables, and the *alternate hypothesis*, which typically matches (using symbols) the investigator's research hypothesis (see Chapter 4).

The preceding material describes hypotheses as exemplified in quantitative research. Recall that in qualitative studies, the researcher uses an inductive process by means of which concepts emerge or are discovered over time. The researcher may at some point hypothesize about why certain events had occurred or were occurring, or about how certain concepts were related or had gained prominence in the study. At the same time, this use of hypotheses is more informal and quite different from their overt functioning in quantitative investigations where they are stated early, precisely, and–in the case of statistical hypotheses–in testable form.

Variables

A *variable* is an established entity or characteristic that varies. In research, it is necessary that a variable have at least two values, although having many values is typical. Thus, if females and males serve as subjects in a given study, gender can be a variable with two values. In the same investigation, if scores on a mathematical problem-solving test are to be determined, the test scores likewise serve as a variable. If the study involves separate groups of subjects being taught to solve problems by either Approach A or Approach B, then approach likewise serves as a variable with two values. Recall step 3 in the research process noted earlier in this chapter; one key element in designing a study's procedures is specifying variables and how they will be operationalized (defined and measured).

While variables can be classified in numerous ways, probably the best known differentiation is as independent and dependent. An *independent variable* is the presumed cause in a study, while the *dependent variable* is the presumed effect. To illustrate, assume that infants in an impoverished region are divided into two groups; one group of infants is designated to receive their "normal" diet for the first two years of life and the second group is to be given a protein-rich diet. After two years, all the infants are weighed and also rated by pediatricians on a scale of general health. Recalling that a variable must have at least two values, we identify type of diet—normal or protein-rich—as the independent variable (that is, one variable at two levels or values). Type of diet serves as the presumed cause of variations observed in the two groups in terms of weight and healthiness. The latter two measures are the presumed effects of variations in the independent variable of diet; hence, weight and health status function in this study as dependent variables. Note that there still would have been a study with just a single dependent variable, say, health status, or if there had been more than two dependent variables. In the description of a study, dependent variables are among the easiest to identify as they are measured at the conclusion of the study.

In the example just above, diet was an independent variable that was actively manipulated by the researcher; that is, the investigator's assignment of infants to groups determined whether a normal or an enriched diet would be received. This variable is thus more accurately referred to as an *active independent variable.* It is also possible to have one or more independent variables measured and built into a study, rather than being manipulated. We prefer to term these, following Kerlinger (1986), *attribute independent variables.* In our sample study above, the researcher could have decided to include gender as an attribute independent variable by "measuring" each infant (i.e., determining the gender of each). This information is then built into the study by assuring that female and male infants were divided equally among the two diet groups. Note that with this inclusion, the researcher can examine *interactions* between the active and attribute independent variables, for example, whether the protein-rich diet appeared to have similar effects with male and female infants. Other writers use different terms than attribute independent when referring to this type of variable, terms such as measured independent, assigned, moderator, organismic, status, and personological.

For us, the definitions of active independent, attribute independent, and dependent variables fit best true and quasi-experimental research (as will be defined in the following chapter). Thus, in the sample study, type of diet is the manipulated, presumed cause and the active independent variable. The group receiving the protein-rich diet is designated the *treatment* group and the "normal" diet infants serve as the *control* group. Gender can be measured and built into the study as the attribute independent variable, with weight and health status of the infants at 2 years of age functioning as dependent variables. In other types of research, independent and dependent variable classifications are also made but, in our view, with some strain. For example, some writers apply the independent and dependent variable terminology to correlational research. In some correlational studies, we tend to prefer the designations of predictor (for independent) and predicted (for dependent) variables. In correlational studies where prediction is not involved (i.e., where relationships are examined with no potential cause-and-effect linkage or chain of influence proposed), we favor identifying the variables involved as "symmetric" (Smith & Glass, 1987), rather than labeling each differently. Additional information relative to these distinctions is presented in Chapter 3.

Variables as presented above are distinct and important components in quantitative research. In qualitative research, little attention is given to predetermining variables for the investigation that follows. Rather, the methods used are broadly naturalistic and inquisitive with elaborate data collection via observation, interviews, document review, and the like (see Chapter 5). Then an inductive analytic process follows, oriented toward discovering unifying concepts and generalizations. While the "discoveries" at times may be stated in terms similar to how one might describe a variable, qualitative research in general is not characterized by any systematic approach to identifying, varying, or measuring variables.

SAMPLING AND SITE SELECTION

An important component in any research undertaking is determining which persons and, sometimes, which sites to study. The researcher often seeks to generalize the study's findings beyond the immediate group studied. Still, the degree of accessibility of subjects and sites is clearly an issue; reaching less accessible subjects usually increases the costs of conducting the study. We now examine some procedures and issues related to sampling and selecting sites for a research study.

A *population* is a defined group of cases or items—individuals, events, or objects. The population is pertinent and of interest in a research context, as it is the group to which the investigator hopes to generalize the results of the study. While there is a temptation to typically think of populations as people, note that a defined population could be inanimate (e.g., all Head Start centers in the United States) or event-related (e.g., all cases of measles reported in the world in the year 1995). Many years ago, one of us advised on a study in which the population of interest was all rabbits in rural Wisconsin.

A defined population most often is too large to study in its entirety, so the researcher must decide how to select a portion of the population to actually study. This portion is termed a *sample*. The sample is studied in depth, and its characteristics (or statistics such as the sample mean) are determined. Based on these findings, inferences are made about the population's characteristics (or parameters, such as the population mean). While there are numerous ways to select a sample from the population, the researcher's main concern is to select a sample that is as representative of the population as possible. With representativeness, the investigator gains an enhanced ability to generalize the study's results to the population of interest.

A number of *probability sampling* techniques exist. Since they are based on probability, their degree of representativeness can be estimated. The best known and simplest of these is *simple random sampling,* in which each member of the population has an equal and independent chance of being selected to be in the sample. Population members are listed by number; this list of members is known as a *sampling frame.* The sample then is selected randomly using a table of random numbers or a computer program. The key is that the sample chosen in this fashion is as representative of the population as one would expect due to chance—no human decisions or biases are involved in selection. A related procedure is *stratified random sampling.* In this, members of the population are first divided into subgroups based on a stratifying variable, then a random sample is selected from each resultant stratum. To illustrate, suppose an investigator is interested in young children's social competence and has identified all kindergarten children in Los Angeles as the population of interest. Rather than selecting a simple random sample, the researcher decided to use gender as a stratifying variable, divided the population into females and males, and then randomly drew equal numbers of each sex to study.

Two other procedures using elements of random selection are systematic and cluster sampling. In *systematic sampling,* the population members are ordered in some known fashion (like an alphabetical list of names). Assume that a researcher has a list of 2,000 kindergarten children in the population and desires to select a sample of 50 children. The population is divided by the sample size (i.e., 2,000/50 = 40). The researcher then randomly selects a number between 1 and 40; say the number 21 is drawn. The 50 children selected for the sample are those numbered 21, 61, 101, and so forth. While faster than simple random sampling, this method should not be used if the researcher believes that the children have been listed in some biased fashion—such as alternately by gender.

In *cluster sampling* (also known as area sampling), the population typically is very large geographically or one for which no list of population members exists or both. To conserve resources, a multistage random sampling procedure is followed. For example, if all kindergartners in the United States were the identified population, the researcher might first randomly select five states, then within those states randomly select five school districts, and within the districts randomly select five kindergarten classes for the study. The resultant sample of 125 classes is not randomly representative and thus lowers the investigator's precision in estimating the accuracy of the population parameters. Still, the generated sample statistics are far more trustworthy than had the researcher simply selected kindergartners at one site to represent all those in the country.

In contrast to probabilistic random procedures (simple, stratified, systematic, and cluster), a number of *nonprobability sampling* procedures can be identified. In *quota sampling*, the researcher sets quotas of different types of subjects thought to be representative (such as in terms of gender, ethnicity, age, type of community—urban, suburban, or rural—and so forth). Then those collecting data—interviewers or poll takers or whoever—seek subjects of the various types preset in the quota. In *convenience sampling*, the researcher uses as subjects persons who are convenient and readily available (some prefer to call this accessible or even accidental rather than convenience). One variation of convenience sampling is *snowball sampling*, where the present subject "nominates" additional persons for the researcher to use in the study. (For some reason this reminds us of the time-honored technique used by some salespersons, say of vacuum cleaners, who sell you their product and then offer to reduce your cost by a few dollars for each friend's name you provide for their subsequent sales presentations.) Another phenomenon closely related to convenience sampling is the use of *volunteers* as subjects in a study. By the simple act of volunteering, the subjects constitute a group different from those who do not volunteer; generalizing from volunteer samples is problematic.

The concern with nonprobability samples is that the representativeness of the sample is unknown and cannot be estimated. The resultant sample, therefore, is *biased* in unknown ways and limits the researcher's ability to generalize the results obtained. We usually get a pretty good chuckle in our classes when we note that substantial amounts of research dealing with learning and motivation used either rats or college sophomores as subjects. Both of these "groups" represent convenience samples. However, most researchers realize that the prohibition of convenience sampling would markedly reduce the number of studies conducted, for such samples usually are less costly and time-consuming to obtain. If using nonprobability samples, the investigator needs to provide full description of the subjects used, use more cautious interpretations of the data analyzed, and subdue claims for the generalizability of results.

Of course in real life, researchers sometimes alter these sampling strategies or combine more than one sampling strategy, or even use nonprobability and probability procedures in a single study. A recent example of the latter involved the "Cost, Quality, and Child Outcomes in Child Care Centers" (1995) study. California, Colorado, Connecticut, and North Carolina were selected as the states in which to conduct the study due to their regional, demographic, and early childhood education program diversity (even though a national perspective was being sought). This nonprobability procedure was then paired with a probability technique, stratified random sampling. That is, within each of the four states, strata were formed of nonprofit and for-profit child care centers, and 50 of each type were randomly selected. In spring 1993, the researchers visited each center, conducted interviews, observed two randomly selected "classrooms," and distributed questionnaires to directors, teachers, and parents. They also collected developmental outcome data on children in summer 1993. Among other findings (purported to apply to the entire country), the study found child care at most centers to be poor to mediocre, estimated that only 1 in 7 centers provided a level of child care quality that promoted healthy development and learning, and noted that lower wages were paid by lower-quality centers, on average.

In qualitative research, "sampling" takes a form quite different from anything probabilistic or nonprobabilistic as described above. As indicated in Table 2.1, terms typical in describing samples in qualitative endeavors are *nonrepresentative, small in number* (maybe even only one case), and *purposeful*. Initially selecting a site, or sites, in which to conduct the study is deliberate, with emphasis on places thought likely to yield rich material pertinent to the general topic of interest or working-problem area. The qualitative investigator makes a sequence of ongoing decisions about what information to seek and from whom, when, and where in the case of persons, documents, policies, and the like. Each subsequent decision is in part based on what was just learned. This evolving method of identifying and harvesting fertile data sources is termed *purposeful*. Since this approach to acquiring "subjects" and data is an integral part of the qualitative research process itself, we will describe it in greater detail in Chapter 5.

SUMMARY

The research process results in the production of knowledge. Eight general steps in that process are conceptualizing a topic, reviewing pertinent literature, designing the study procedures, collecting data, analyzing data, interpreting the outcomes, reporting the results, and replicating the investigation. While there are numerous ways to categorize research methods, the principal scheme adopted here is to differentiate, generally, between quantitative and qualitative—both use the research steps above, but with some variations in the nature of each step. Research topics are generated in light of societal issues, personal interests, and other forces. In quantitative research, the topic then leads to defining variables operationally, specifying procedures, and, eventually, testing hypotheses; in qualitative research, much less predetermination occurs. Sampling involves determining who or what is to be studied, with quantitative researchers favoring probabilistic samples to achieve known representativeness. Qualitative researchers, conversely, seek purposeful samples. In Part II we focus on quantitative research, with a discussion of methods and presentation of examples of their use in early childhood education contexts given in Chapter 3.

PART II

QUANTITATIVE RESEARCH

Chapter 3

Types of Quantitative Research

Numerous methods for conducting research are quantitative in nature. That is, they generally follow a deductive approach to the generation of knowledge using highly structured procedures and measuring instruments. Also, data analyses and reports of results from this type of research usually are quantitative in nature, involving numbers, tables, and graphs.

In this chapter, we describe the better known and more commonly used quantitative research methods. We review the key features and typical uses of the following types of research: descriptive, including survey and developmental; correlational; causal-comparative; experimental, including pre-, quasi-, and true experimental designs; and single-subject. Examples of each of these research methods, drawn primarily from early childhood education, are presented. The chapter concludes with guidelines for critiquing quantitative research.

DESCRIPTIVE RESEARCH: SURVEY AND DEVELOPMENTAL

The purpose of descriptive research is to generate knowledge that describes something—the opinion of an identified group, the characteristics typical in 3-year-old children, the usual parent-child interactions during "reunions" as children prepare to leave preschools or child care centers. A view frequently expressed by writers and professional researchers is that research is either descriptive, correlational, or experimental. While it is true that qualitative research, particularly ethnography, is descriptive, we consider it separately in Chapters 5 and 6. Here, prior to reviewing correlational and experimental research, we examine descriptive research—survey and developmental—that is mainly quantitative.

Basic Design Elements and Primary Uses

In *survey research*, the investigator typically uses structured interviews or questionnaires to ask questions of persons in the sample. Less common, observation of the subjects may occur to avoid the hazards of self-report via questionnaire or interview (such as faking or giving a "socially desirable"—or possibly, these days, the politically correct—response rather than the view actually held). The steps involved in survey research, adapted from Graziano and Raulin (1993), Jaeger (1988), and Kerlinger (1986), and amplified at times, are noted below:

1. State the problem to be investigated and the information to be sought in clear, specific terms.
2. Identify the target population (that is, the entire population of interest) and the sampling procedures to be used. From Chapter 2, recall that random and stratified random samples permit more confident generalizations. The merit of the sampling procedures directly affects the quality of the results obtained. A sample made up of volunteers is especially troublesome.
3. Select the type of instrumentation needed—questionnaire, phone interview, personal interview, or observation. This is far from a trivial decision. We have ordered these choices in terms of our view of economy and effort. That is, questionnaires tend to be most economical and require least researcher effort in administration, with observation being least economical and most labor-intensive. At the same time, the more personal methods (personal interview and observation) have advantages, such as opportunities for probing by the investigator and in-depth responses; observation avoids the difficulties associated with self-report measures.
4. Choose or construct the needed measures—observation schedules, interview protocols, or questionnaires.
5. Pilot test and refine the measures. Usually, this involves administering them to a small group of (one hopes representative) respondents. Estimates of relevant types of reliability and validity are obtained. If one is using observation or interviews, training the observers and interviewers is essential.
6. Collect the data.
7. Analyze the data. Descriptive and inferential statistical techniques are used, as briefly noted in Chapter 4.
8. Report the results. If there are multiple audiences for the survey results, different reporting formats may be used, such as journal articles, executive summaries, and oral reports.

This brief listing of steps should not connote that survey research is simple or easy to conduct. Well done, it has the advantages of amassing considerable data relatively quickly and of enabling the researcher to estimate sampling error. Further, descriptive research can be used in the early understanding of a phenomenon or characteristic, thereby establishing a knowledge base from which other forms of research can be conducted. Disadvantages frequently mentioned include its lack of depth (especially if done by questionnaire), the considerable expense in time and money, and the frailties of self-report.

Note that there is no manipulation of variables by the researcher in descriptive research. It is effective for answering questions of the "what is" variety. A good example of survey research using probability sampling and interviewing is the annual Gallup national poll on public attitudes toward education, including early childhood. For example, most of the 1,306 adult respondents believed that preschool programs would help low-income children perform either "a great deal" (39%) or "quite a lot" (34%) better in public school (Elam, Rose, & Gallup, 1992). A year later, most subjects gave a "very high" (41%) or a "high" (48%) priority to the national goal of having all children start school ready to learn by the year 2000 (Elam, Rose, & Gallup, 1993).

We have also singled out *developmental research* as a type of descriptive research, given its pertinence to early childhood education. Many descriptive studies chart and report developmental characteristics of infants and young children. These quantifications provide important comparison data on normal development and behaviors for children of given ages.

Studies in the developmental category vary in a significant way: whether they are longitudinal or cross-sectional. In *longitudinal* research, certain characteristics of the same subjects are studied over time. A major advantage of this approach is that individual differences among subjects do not play a major role; a key disadvantage is the expense and frustration of keeping track of subjects over time. In *cross-sectional* research, the characteristics of interest are measured simultaneously in subjects varying in age. Its limits and merits are generally the reverse of those for longitudinal designs.

Research Examples in Early Childhood Education

In this chapter, as well as in Chapter 5, we describe actual examples of each research method. Our intent is to "bring the method to life" for the reader. We also should note that many investigators combine more than one method in a single study.

In terms of descriptive survey research, we have already mentioned some examples. In discussing sampling in Chapter 2, the "Cost, Quality, and Child Outcomes in Child Care Centers" (1995) study was described. A central question addressed in that research was what the quality of child care is in centers in the United States. This question was answered through the use of interviews and questionnaires with center directors, teachers, and parents, as well as some observations in centers. While much variability was noted, the average quality of care was found to be mediocre and poor to the point of interfering with children's intellectual and emotional development. A second survey research example—the annual Gallup poll of public attitudes toward education—was noted earlier.

In their research, Rothlein and Brett (1987) wondered about children's, parents', and teachers' perceptions of play. Over 100 preschoolers, 2 to 6 years old, and lesser numbers of parents and teachers in Florida, were surveyed using open-ended questions about play. When children were asked "What do you think of when I say the word *play*?" they most often mentioned outdoor play activities (e.g., running, swinging, riding tricycles and bikes), closely followed by activities involving dramatic play and housekeeping. Parents and teachers generally had similar views of play, with teachers more likely to note play's relationship to social and cognitive development. While all teachers indicated that they included play in the curriculum, only one-fifth of them identified play as an integral part of the school day. More common was a circumscribed notion of play—with specific periods set aside for free, outdoor, or indoor play.

Peck, Carlson, and Helmstetter (1992) used the descriptive survey method to study parent and teacher perceptions of the outcomes that typically developing children experienced from attending integrated or inclusionary early childhood programs (that is, settings for both typically developing children and children with disabilities in the same room). The researchers first enlisted the assistance of a small group of teachers and parents of typically developing children to construct a questionnaire on expected outcomes for their children from attending integrated preschools and kindergartens. Once the survey was designed, it was distributed to 44 integrated early childhood programs in Washington State—to all teachers in blended classrooms and to five randomly selected parents of typically developing children in each program. Teachers and parents generally agreed about the probable outcomes for typically developing children. For example, they believed that attending the integrated settings was a positive experience, that children showed an increased tolerance for human differences and an elevated sense of other children's needs, and that discomfort and stereotypes toward persons with disabilities and those who behaved and looked differently were reduced.

Yet another descriptive survey study, by Peet (1995), concerned parental perceptions of which data sources they utilized for information about their child's development. Subjects from a midwestern community were 60 mothers and 60 fathers in intact families with an oldest child 3 years of age (in all, 30 girls and 30 boys). Via a structured interview, mothers and fathers independently revealed their preferences for 28 information sources on child development. Mothers identified physicians, magazines, and preschool teachers as their primary external sources, followed closely by their own mothers, books, other families, observing others, spouses, and friends (of note is that mothers-in-law were only about half as likely as to be utilized as a source as one's own mother). Fathers listed spouse, magazines, and books, with physicians and observing others next. They too were more likely to use their own mothers as a source than their mothers-in-law, but by a narrower margin than was true for mothers. Least often selected as external sources were ministers, priests, and rabbis; community agencies; radio; and astrology. Interestingly, about half the mothers and fathers reported using internal sources, that is, their own childhood experiences (especially true for fathers), intuitions (particularly for mothers), and religious beliefs. Another finding was that parents relied on their own internal sources of information most often in regard to their child's development in the social, rather than in the cognitive or motor, domain.

Turning from surveys to descriptive developmental studies, an imaginative study by Chandler, Fritz, and Hala (1989) is noteworthy. Their research was directed at determining at what age children displayed some theory-like understanding of other people's minds. They reasoned that such an understanding was present if the child could deceptively lead others into false beliefs. Titling their work "small-scale deceit," they used 50 2-, 3-, and 4-year-olds as subjects. After practicing a game of hiding a small treasure bag of "gold coins and jewels" in different colored plastic containers on a washable white playing surface, subjects were instructed to help a puppet, "Tony," hide the bag so that a second experimenter could not find it. Tony, however, was designed to leave inky footprints on the white surface, making his route during the hiding of the treasure quite obvious. Deceptive strategies, in order of their perceived thoughtfulness, were wiping up Tony's tracks; lying directly about the true location of the treasure; laying false trails by helping the puppet walk toward—and leave footprints leading to—empty containers; and being doubly deceptive by both wiping up the true trail and laying down false ones. Chandler and his colleagues found a range of deceptive strategies used by most of the children, even the youngest; they concluded that very young children were able to lead others to false beliefs and, therefore, had an operative theory of mind.

Trawick-Smith (1992) videotaped five preschoolers in a developmental study aimed at describing persuasive preschoolers. From the videotapes, attempts to influence the behavior of others, and responses to these initiations, were transcribed and analyzed. Persuasive preschoolers were identified as those who successfully got others to comply with requests, using requests and friendly demands frequently and agonistic tactics such as force or threats relatively less often. In general, such children did not comply regularly with directives of others, made only moderate use of extremely friendly or extremely aggressive techniques, and attempted to influence others more often using a broad array of strategies. For example, one child identified as persuasive wanted to use a play telephone already controlled by a second child. He first convinced the second child that the phone was theirs jointly, and then proceeded to take and use the phone to complete a call to the police that he described as in their mutual best interest. In another instance, the same persuasive child literally "sweet-talked" another child into compliance by calling her "Sweetie."

Our final descriptive developmental example is a favorite of ours, possibly because we realize how difficult research involving very young children and the affective domain can be. An important but hard-to-measure milestone is the development of self-recognition. Lewis and Brooks-Gunn (1979) had mothers "secretly" apply a spot of rouge to their infants' noses while pretending to wipe their children's face. Then the mothers placed their infants before a mirror. If the infants recognize the mirror image as themselves, logic requires that they should see the red spot and then reach for or wipe their own noses. This "rouge test" was given to infants 9 to 24 months old. The youngest children displayed no self-recognition, but a few of the 15- to 17-month-olds and a majority of the 18- to 24-month-olds did; this research helped establish the time during development when self-recognition occurs.

CORRELATIONAL RESEARCH

Correlational research examines the extent of relationship between variables. As presented in Chapter 2, a variable is an entity or a characteristic that varies. It is possible to consider two variables simultaneously, such as the weight and height of a class of preschoolers, in terms of how they relate to each other. In this example, one would expect a positive relationship between the two variables, that is, generally they would "move together" or in the same direction, with heavier children being taller and lighter children being shorter, on average. On the other hand, one might expect a negative relationship—high values on one variable associated with low values on the other—between the speed with which kindergartners printed their names and the legibility of the names, that is, slower printing producing more legible names and vice versa. The calculation and interpretation of correlational indices known as coefficients are described in Chapter 4. Here we review correlation as a research method.

Basic Design Elements and Primary Uses

The purpose of correlational research is to determine the relationship between two or more variables. As in survey research, the investigator manipulates no variables—rather, variables are identified and measured as they exist.

Considerable premeditation is required of the investigator doing correlational research. Three areas require particular attention. First, the variables to be related must be selected carefully as worthy of exploration and items on which the sample probably will vary. Low variability in subjects on a selected variable—called *restriction of range*—results in correlations closer to zero than is likely to be true in fact. Second, the sample of subjects must be carefully selected for the study, as it will frame the generalizability of the results observed. Third, how well the variables are measured becomes a crucial concern. The researcher must strive to select or develop measures with good psychometric credibility in terms of validity, reliability, and other crucial properties (see Chapter 4). For example, measures low in reliability result in correlations closer to zero than is true in fact, a phenomenon known as *attenuation*.

Two general types of correlational research have been identified. In *relationship* or simple correlation studies, the focus is on better understanding phenomena represented by variables. How the variables are related is determined via a series of steps. First, the variables of interest for a given group or context are identified; two variables are denoted in the simplest case. Next, appropriate measures of each variable must be obtained and the sample identified. The sample is then measured on the variables and correlational analyses of the resultant data are completed. Finally, the researcher interprets the analyses in terms of the original question asked and the research findings of others. Consider a simple example. The director of a child care center might decide to examine the relationship between the age of the child and the ease of separation from the adult bringing the child to the center. The first variable, age, is expressed to the nearest month, while the ease of separation variable is rated on a 5-point scale by an observer (very smooth and positive, mostly smooth and positive, neither positive nor negative, mostly rough and negative, and very rough and negative).

Some relationship studies measure and interrelate a large number of variables. When done thoughtfully with a good basis in theory and past research, these investigations result in a correlation matrix that contains considerable information about the linkages between each of the variables. When done recklessly with little forethought, the generation of numerous correlations in the hope that some of them certainly will be significantly large (that is, different from zero; see Chapter 4) is looked on with disdain by the research community as a "shotgun" approach (McMillan & Schumacher, 1993) or a fishing expedition.

The second type of correlational research involves *prediction* studies. Here the researcher is interested in how well a variable obtained now can predict a future outcome. The design steps are essentially the same as for relationship studies, except that here the outcome or predicted variable is collected later in time. Recall from Chapter 2 that we preferred to think of variables in this correlational context as predictor and predicted, because independent and dependent variables suggested cause and effect to us. Consider an example of this type of study in early childhood. During their last months of kindergarten, young children might be rated by their teachers in terms of their apparent "literacy development." Let's imagine a 6-point rating scale: extensive, substantial, above average, below average, poor, and barely emergent. This rating serves as the predictor variable. Then, 2 years later, the same children are rated by their new teachers in terms of their general reading ability—this later rating serves as the predicted variable. Finally, a correlational analysis yields the relationship between the predictor kindergarten ratings and the reading ratings obtained 2 years later, and these results are interpreted. Note that different predicted variables might have been used, such as end of grade 2 reading achievement test scores or the children's ability to explain a passage they had just read.

Prediction studies can be elaborate. Sometimes the researcher wants to combine a number of variables in a weighted fashion to best predict some subsequent outcome. These efforts are termed *multiple regression* studies and result in the determination of a multiple regression coefficient symbolized as "R." To illustrate, assume an investigator wished to predict the risk of serious cognitive developmental delay at age 4 years. Variables used in the prediction equation might include birth weight, age of mother, protein in diet during the first year of life, socioeconomic status, stability of family, and continuity of the primary caregiver, the last two variables measured over the first two years of life. The predicted or criterion variable, assessed at age 4 years, would be performance on a valid cognitive development measure. The multiple regression analysis would denote which single variable best predicted the outcome variable, as well as how much this prediction improved via a combined weighting of the other predictor variables. A large number of subjects is needed for most multiple regression studies; the recommended ratio of number of subjects to number of predictors is 10:1.

Several advantages of correlational research can be noted. First, since variables are not manipulated, they can examine "nature" as it is, can address topics that would be impractical or even impossible using experimental methods, and can study directly nonmanipulable variables. Second, the relationships between a number of variables can be examined at one time. Third, the correlational method allows for the preliminary identification of a relationship that *may be* cause and effect. Disadvantages, each related to the advantages, can also be noted. First, the absence of variable manipulation often leaves the researcher with findings that are interesting but very difficult to explain and interpret. Second, as the number of variables in correlational research increases, so does the cost of the research, particularly in the search for suitable measures and, often, in the amount of time required of subjects to respond. Third, the temptation to view statistically significant correlational relationships as cause-and-effect linkages is often too strong to resist, with researchers ignoring good practice in their interpretation of correlational research results.

Research Examples in Early Childhood Education

The relationship of physical attractiveness to peer status and social competence of preschoolers was examined by Vaughn and Langlois (1983). The attractiveness of a group of 4- and 5-year-old preschoolers enrolled in a nursery school was judged by college students from photos of the children. The children underwent sociometric exercises wherein they viewed photos of all possible pairs of their classmates and selected which of each pair they liked better; they also identified three of their classmates whom they especially liked. Each child received a sociometric status ranking based on the number of times they were selected as "liked." As a measure of social competence, the researchers used observational ratings of the attention that each child received from his or her classmates. Physical attractiveness turned out to be a significant correlate of sociometric status for all children, and especially so for girls (that is, those judged more attractive were more likely to have been selected as liked). On the other hand, attractiveness was not related to attention, although attention was found to be positively related to sociometric status. The authors concluded that young children's sociometric status may be influenced more by variables like attractiveness than by measures of social competence.

In their predictive correlational study, Maclean, Bryant, and Bradley (1987) first determined 66 British children's knowledge of nursery rhymes (measured in terms of the child's skill at reciting them). The rhymes used were "Baa-baa Black Sheep," "Hickory Dickory Dock," "Humpty Dumpty," "Jack and Jill," and "Twinkle Twinkle Little Star." Each child's vocabulary, intelligence, and parents' socioeconomic status (SES) were also measured; the children were just over 3 years of age at the start of the 15-month study. In several sessions at home across the study period, the children's phonological skills were assessed, especially the detection and production of rhyme and alliteration. A substantial and statistically significant relationship was found between the children's knowledge of nursery rhymes at 3 years and their emerging phonological skills across the next 15 months. This relationship remained even when intelligence and SES were controlled. Generally, knowledge of nursery rhymes at 3 years predicted early reading, but was not related to early arithmetic capabilities.

Family and child variables that might predict young children's television viewing of "Sesame Street" were examined by Pinon, Huston, and Wright (1989). Subjects, initially 3- and 5-year-olds, were studied for 2 years, with families keeping diaries of who watched what television shows. Viewing of "Sesame Street" peaked at about age 4. Variables negatively related to the amount of time "Sesame Street" was viewed were having older siblings, hours per week in child care or school, and amount of maternal employment. Conversely, positive relationships with viewing the show were noted for having younger siblings and amount of parental encouragement to view it, for the younger children only. Amount of "Sesame Street" viewing was not related to parental occupation or education, child's gender, or child's vocabulary level. In all, the authors concluded that children's attributes were less important in predicting educational television viewing than family ecology variables such as maternal employment, age of siblings, and the child's participation in child care and school.

CAUSAL-COMPARATIVE RESEARCH

A third quantitative research method is known as causal-comparative. Descriptive and correlational research, as already discussed, rarely concern causal relationships; however, causal-comparative research, as implied by its name, does. At the same time, the "cause" has already occurred in this third type of research. It sometimes is called *ex post facto* (Latin for "after the fact") research in that the presumed cause has taken place prior to the initiation of the study. Causal-comparative research, then, serves as a bridge with descriptive and correlational designs on one end and the experimental designs yet to be considered on the other.

Basic Design Elements and Primary Uses

The purpose of causal-comparative research is to identify possible cause-and-effect relationships in cases where experimentation is not possible. The method is sometimes confused with both correlational and experimental research. The puzzlement in the former case arises in that neither correlational nor causal-comparative investigators manipulate any variables (e.g., they do not assign subjects to treatment and control conditions). Note, though, that they are dissimilar in that more than one group is involved in causal-comparative research, unlike most correlational research. The confusion between the causal-comparative and experimental methods occurs because both involve more than one group and both seek to establish cause-and-effect relationships. Distinctively, though, the causal-comparative approach involves no manipulation of variables, while experiments do. Further, in causal-comparative studies, the subjects are not assigned to conditions by the researcher as they have already been "grouped by nature" into categories such as male-female, good and poor readers, high-low socioeconomic status, and motivated-uninspired.

The initial step in designing causal-comparative research is to identify a problem area with interesting effects as well as a likely cause. Past research, theory, experience, and intuition help guide problem selection. Suppose a researcher became interested in the wide range of subject-matter mastery shown on standardized achievement tests by children at the end of second grade; this serves as the effect of interest. The investigator might wonder further if having been in preschool laid the foundation for these individual differences in achievement; preschool experience (or lack thereof) becomes the possible cause.

In the next design step, the researcher would attempt to identify rival hypotheses, other than preschool attendance, for the observed differences in second-graders' achievement. For example, one possibility might be that better scoring second-graders had experienced better teachers in K–1–2. Another rival hypothesis might be that children achieving better at the end of second grade had attended K–1–2 in schools with an academic focus or with some other special emphasis. Or, as compared with the lower scoring children, they had appeared to display greater motivation in grades K–1–2. Another rival hypothesis possibly "explaining" the observed achievement differences might be the age of the children, with older children achieving better.

The researcher's next step is to identify representative students finishing second grade, some having had preschool and some not, for comparison purposes. The researcher would strive to have the groups as similar as possible on all other variables, so that the independent variable of interest—preschool or lack of preschool—was the only apparent difference between the groups. The investigator must also keep an eye on the representativeness of the children selected, so as to enhance the study's generalizability.

Data collection and analysis occur next. Often the data already exist and need only to be identified, collected, and put into usable form for analysis. Note that the researcher also must collect data pertinent to the several rival hypotheses identified. The strength of the case that a cause-and-effect relationship has indeed been established often rests on how adequately the rival hypotheses have been ruled out. Data analysis consists of using essentially the same procedures as one would use in experimental studies.

The final element in this type of research concerns the interpretation of the results. Here the researcher has to present the merits of the possible cause initially identified; the case must be made to establish it as *the* cause of the effect of interest. This involves ruling out rival hypotheses or, in some cases, giving them their just due as potential causes if the data did not rule them out. The researcher generally must show considerable restraint insofar as claiming to have identified a cause-and-effect relationship, given the lack of definitiveness inherent in the causal-comparative method.

Advantages of this method are several. First, the causal-comparative method permits an examination of potential causes for outcomes that emerge from the environment as worthy of explanation after the fact. Second, variables that cannot be manipulated, due to ethical or feasibility reasons or both, can still be investigated as possible causes in a formal research undertaking. Third and related, no manipulation of variables is involved and the outcome variable of interest typically is already available. Weaknesses primarily involve the researcher's lack of proactivity in identifying a causal relationship in that no manipulations or interventions occur. Thus, some believe this type of research only flirts with cause-and-effect linkages, and encourage restraint by the researcher in reporting findings, as well as caution by the consumer in considering them.

Research Examples in Early Childhood Education

A cross-cultural study of task persistence in 7-year-olds in the United States and Japan was conducted by Blinco (1992). Subjects came from four schools in each country, two urban public, one urban private, and one rural public. Each child was given stage one of a manipulative, puzzle-like game to solve independently under noncompetitive conditions. Once successful, the child moved to the next stage; stages in the game were of increasing difficulty. What was measured was how long the child persisted in attempting to solve the problem once it was at a level of difficulty where solution was very unlikely. Gender and type of school were included as attribute independent variables; both showed nonsignificant relationships with the dependent variable. Japanese children consistently persisted significantly longer on the problem than did American children. Blinco considered a rival hypothesis–that a larger proportion of Japanese children had attended preschool. Still, she assembled considerable and, for her, compelling evidence that culture was undoubtedly the variable leading to the differences in persistence.

Another illustration of causal-comparative research is provided by Schenk and Grusec (1987). They examined the prosocial behavior and reasoning of children who had attended child care centers and those who had not, the latter primarily spending the preschool years at home. Children's reactions were measured, both to an adult needing help after "accidentally" spilling a box of office supplies and to an adult who had bumped her knee, and so was their willingness to share stickers and crayons with hospitalized sick children. The children's reactions to stories depicting need in others, both children and adults, were also assessed. In general, the children with the home and child care backgrounds were much alike in social reasoning and most prosocial behaviors. The notable exception was that children cared for at home made significantly more prosocial responses to adult needs (that is, helping when the box was spilled and sympathizing when the knee was bumped). The authors believed this finding resulted from mothers at home, as compared with care providers at centers, having more time to instruct their home-bound children in prosocial responses appropriate in interacting with adults. Other rival, alternative explanations for the outcomes were considered; the authors believed additional research was needed on whether interactions in child care centers might lead to strong prosocial behavior toward peers.

A third example of causal-comparative research sought to denote differential effects of early childhood programs (Stipek, Feiler, Daniels, & Milburn, 1995). As over 200 children completed either child-centered preschools and kindergartens or didactic ones, they were compared on a number of variables. The child-centered programs were characterized by teacher warmth, child initiative, and positive control, while the didactic programs stressed basic skills, performance, and evaluation. Children enrolled in didactic settings did significantly better on a test of letters and reading achievement, but not on a numbers achievement test. At the same time, children who had experienced the didactic settings displayed areas of concern motivationally. For example, compared with the children in the child-centered programs, the didactic-program children reported worrying more about school, rated their abilities lower, showed less pride in their accomplishments, expected less success on academic tasks, and revealed more dependency on adults for approval and permission. Children from both low and middle socioeconomic homes showed similar effects.

EXPERIMENTAL RESEARCH

In experimental research, the experimenter manipulates at least one variable (the active independent variable, as described in Chapter 2) in a proactive attempt to establish a cause-and-effect relationship. This manipulation distinguishes this type of research from the types already reviewed. Much attention is given to this research method here so that the reader can become aware of its particular strengths, uses, and limitations. Before we consider pre-, quasi-, and true experimental designs and "threats" to the validity of experiments, a notation system useful in describing experimental designs is detailed.

A Notation System for Experimental Research

Campbell and Stanley (1963) advocated the greater use of experiments in education, set forward a notation scheme useful in depicting representative experimental designs, and examined threats to the validity of such research. Much of what follows builds on their seminal work; in adapted forms, it has become commonplace in describing and evaluating such research.

The symbols used and their definitions are as follows:

R = Random assignment of subjects to experimental conditions.
O = Observations, such as test scores, ratings, or the like; the measurement of the dependent variable.
X = Experimental treatment (the program or unique experiences) received by persons in the experimental group (while the absence of "X" denotes subjects in the control group); if there is more than one experimental group, subscripts by the X are used to differentiate the experimental groups.

There are other conventions used with the symbols and design depiction:

1. Each group "appears" on a single, separate horizontal line.
2. The passage of time is represented by a left-to-right sequence.
3. Dotted lines appear between groups that have not been formed by random assignment (to emphasize their possible nonequivalency prior to the start of the study).

A few examples are offered here to illustrate the use of the notation scheme. Suppose a study was depicted as below:

O X O

The interpretation would be that a single group was involved, an initial observation was obtained (such as a pretest), then the group experienced some defined intervention or treatment (such as a new program), and after that a final observation was secured (such as a posttest).

In contrast, note this study's depiction:

R X O

R O

In this study, two groups were formed using random assignment, one group received the treatment (i.e., the top group, as represented by the X) while the other served as a control group, and the same observation of both groups (such as ratings of behavior) occurred at the conclusion of the study. The active independent variable is receiving the treatment or not receiving the treatment, while the O represents the dependent variable.

Consider yet a third case:

O X_{BP} O

- - - - - - - - - - - - - - -

O X_{WL} O

- - - - - - - - - - - - - - -

O O

Here there are three groups involved, each pre- and post-measured, and the dotted lines remind us of the groups' possible nonequivalency (note, too, the absence of Rs). There are three levels of the active independent variable—one group of children receiving a basal phonics approach to reading (hence the BP subscript), a second group in a whole language (WL) approach, and a third untreated or control group. With this notation scheme in mind, let us proceed to consider pre-experimental designs.

Pre-Experimental Designs

In some ways, we hesitate to include this section. In the past, we have witnessed persons using pre-experimental designs as "legitimate" for their research because of their depiction in books such as this. In fact, we include them to illustrate their inappropriateness, especially in terms of their minimal control of threats to internal and external validity, as subsequently discussed. Possibly a more pejorative label—such as primitive designs—would alleviate this problem. Nonetheless, as displayed in Figure 3.1, three designs are included here: the one-group posttest-only design, the one group pretest-posttest design, and the static group comparison design.

The *one-group posttest-only design* is also known as the one-shot case study. Only a single group is involved. A treatment of some sort is received by the group and then an observation or measurement of the subjects takes place. While the investigator is attempting to establish cause and effect (that is, that X caused what was obtained as O), the control in this design is so minimal that the results are very untrustworthy.

The next pre-experimental design, the *one-group pretest–posttest design*, also involves one group. Now, however, some estimate of where the group started in terms of O is available, such as a pretest. Thus, this design represents an advance over the one-group posttest-only design. Still, many threats to internal and external validity remain, as soon will be noted.

FIGURE 3.1 Experimental Designs

Pre-Experimental Designs	
One-Group Posttest Only:	X O
One-Group Pretest–Posttest:	O X O
Static Group Comparison:	X O ---------------- O
Quasi-Experimental Designs	
Nonequivalent Pretest–Posttest Control Group:	O X O ---------------- O O
Time Series:	O O O O O X O O O O O
True Experimental Designs	
Pretest–Posttest Control Group:	R O X O R O O
Posttest-Only Control Group:	R X O R O
Solomon Four Group:	R O X O R O O R X O R O

The third pre-experimental design of note is the *static group comparison design*, or the posttest-only with nonequivalent groups design. To its credit, this design does involve two groups, one treated and the second included for control or comparison purposes. The dotted line between the groups in the diagram in Figure 3.1 reminds us, however, that the groups may not be equivalent at the study's inception. Overall, this design shares many weaknesses inherent in the other pre-experimental designs, as detailed in a subsequent section on the specific threats to the internal and external validity of experiments.

Quasi-Experimental Designs

The prefix *quasi* taken literally means almost, or in some sense or degree. In Victor Hugo's classic, *The Hunchback of Notre Dame*, the humpback hero of sorts was Quasimodo. Hugo's grotesque and unflattering description of Quasimodo caused us to think of him as "almost-man." Over the years, this has helped us classify quasi-experiments as being almost, or in some sense, like true experiments. Both quasi- and true experiments use systematic experimental procedures to gauge the effects of the independent variable. Their essential difference is that true experiments randomly assign subjects to conditions, but quasi-experiments do not. Special care must be taken in estimating the credibility of the knowledge resulting from quasi-experiments.

Two common quasi-experimental designs are presented in Figure 3.1. The *nonequivalent pretest-posttest control group* (NPPCG) design appears frequently in research journals. Note that the groups are not equivalent (thus, e.g., one set of preschools located in a different city or region than the other set). At the same time, this design improves the pre-experimental static group comparison by adding the same pre-measure for each group. In effect, the investigator now has at least one relevant index on which to examine the equivalence of the two groups prior to the start of the study. Still the fact remains that the groups may not be equivalent in many important ways, and the researcher must exert considerable effort to establish the nature of each group and to examine their comparability.

The *time series* (TS) design is another quasi-experimental method that deserves attention. In effect, this design also constitutes an "improvement" of a pre-experimental design, namely the one-group pretest-posttest. The TS procedure gains its respectability by adding periodic measurement of the same variable both before and after the introduction of the treatment or X. The series of observations made prior to the commencement of the treatment is then compared with the series of measurements made after the introduction of the treatment; discontinuity in the two sets of observations can indicate that the treatment caused the change reflected in the second series. This procedure has been applied especially in situations where records have been systematically kept, say, on an annual or even more frequent basis. For example, imagine an urban child welfare office that has kept an annual record for 20 years of the number of child abuse cases reported in the region. Midway through this period, after 10 years, a massive public announcement campaign on behalf of children was launched aimed at reducing the incidence of child abuse. Using the TS design and associated analysis procedures, the number of child abuse cases in each of the first 10 years can be compared with the number in each of the second 10 years to estimate if the media campaign had an effect. Glass (1988) has detailed the vital need to have many data observation points for the study's baseline, as well as a detective's ability to extract as much meaning as possible from such investigations.

True Experimental Designs

The distinguishing feature of true experiments is the random assignment of available subjects to experimental conditions. That is, chance alone determines, in the simplest case, whether a given subject is assigned to the experimental or to the control group. Random assignment does not guarantee equivalent groups at the start of a study, but the groups should be as equivalent as one would expect via the operation of chance. Particularly as groups get large, random assignment does well in this role.

Three true experimental designs are depicted in Figure 3.1. In the *pretest–posttest control group design*, note that the subjects have been randomly assigned to the two groups—chance alone determined whether they were assigned to the treatment group or to the control group. All the subjects receive the same pre-measure, the experimental group receives the treatment, and then the two groups are post-measured. The active independent variable is represented by the X or its absence (in the control group); the dependent variable is the second O for each group. Recall that the dependent variable is the presumed effect, and thus must be measured at the conclusion of the study.

The second true experimental design is the *posttest-only control group design*. Note that this design is identical to the pretest-posttest control group design except that pre-measures are not involved. Obviously, some simplification results from not having pre-observations. As will be seen, there are both pluses and minuses linked to this no pre-measure feature.

The *Solomon four group design*, also portrayed in Figure 3.1, is simply a merger of the other two true experimental designs. The available subjects are randomly assigned to one of four groups. With this design, the researcher can estimate the effect of having or not having a pre-measure. A shortcoming of the design is the much larger number of subjects required, thus raising the overall costs of the research in time and money. Probably because of this, this design is used less often.

Other Design Elements and Primary Uses

The obvious purpose and primary use of experimental research is establishing cause-and-effect relationships between variables. The researcher introduces the active independent variable as the presumed cause and looks for concomitant variations in the dependent variable, the presumed effect. While using experimental methods does not guarantee that the researcher will identify causes and related effects, the experimental method generally offers the highest probability of identifying such relationships. Several design elements were presented in Figure 3.1 and subsequently discussed. Other matters related to design require elaboration prior to considering the validity of experimental designs, and associated validity threats.

It is important for the researcher to keep in mind some basic, overriding principles required for effective experimentation. Kerlinger (1986) provided a set of three main goals for those designing and conducting a quasi- or true experiment:

1. The researcher should maximize experimental variance by assuring that the levels of the active independent variable are indeed different. Suppose the effects of parents' reading to their preschoolers is of interest. Rather than having one group of parents read to their children 15 minutes per night and a second group 20 minutes per night, it would be better to increase the difference between the levels of the independent variable. Thus, one group might read to their children 20 minutes nightly and the other group not at all during the study.
2. The experimenter should attempt to control systematic extraneous variance. Techniques available to address this goal include using random assignment when possible, building attribute independent variables into the design, and sometimes using subjects homogeneous on a probable relevant extraneous variable. To elaborate these last two techniques, assume that the gender of the child seemed likely to create important, systematic variance in the reading study above. One option available to the researcher would be to bring the variance due to gender under control by including gender in the design as an attribute independent variable. On the other hand, if

available funds did not permit including sufficient numbers of both boys and girls, the researcher might decide to use only girls—in effect, eliminating gender as a variable in the study.
3. The experimenter should minimize error variance. Error variance is variability in outcome data (i.e., on the dependent variable) that the researcher cannot account for or explain. In essence, it is "random noise" in the experimental system. If too pronounced or extensive, error will mask differences due to the treatment. The researcher attempts to attain this third goal by controlling experimental conditions and by using measures with high reliability.

Designing solid, effective experiments is complex. A number of design considerations involve avoiding or minimizing internal and external validity threats in the experiment, as now detailed.

Internal and External Validity, Related Threats, and Experiments

Researchers conducting experiments strive to achieve high internal and high external validity. Validity in this context has to do with the credibility and generalizability of an experiment—it should not be confused with the validity of a measuring instrument as described in Chapter 4. *Internal validity* is defined as the degree to which the experiment results in "truth" in terms of the trustworthiness of the knowledge generated in the experimental situation itself. "Internal validity is the basic minimum without which any experiment is uninterpretable: Did in fact the experimental treatments make a difference in this specific experimental instance?" (Campbell & Stanley, 1963, p. 5). Therefore, an internally valid experiment yields a trustworthy answer to questions such as whether the experimental treatment had an effect or whether one treatment had a different effect than another.

External validity, on the other hand, concerns the generalizability of the knowledge obtained via an experiment. It refers, therefore, to the applicability of a study's findings to other settings, populations, and conditions. Of interest is the fact that, while both high internal and high external validity are the ideal, the experimenter frequently must make decisions in favor of one over the other. Say the experimenter wished to study 3-year-olds' reaction to frustration, and wondered whether to study the phenomenon in the laboratory or in the field. This could be done in the laboratory setting by showing a 3-year-old some attractive toys, but then blocking their use by dropping a see-through gate between the child and the toys. In the laboratory, this same exact scenario then could be repeated independently with a number of 3-year-olds. Conversely, frustration could be studied in a "normal" environmental or field setting, for example by observing a series of 3-year-olds' reactions when, one by one, they were unable to ride the single tricycle available at their child care center (as compared with their behavior when several tricycles were made available). While the laboratory setting with its extensive control might result in high internal validity, it could be artificial to the extent that external validity or the generalizability of the results was compromised. On the other hand, one would expect greater external validity in the study done in the child care center (as it was conducted in "real world" under near-normal conditions). The internal validity of the child care version might be at risk, however, for a number of uncontrolled variables might be impinging on the experimental situation, leaving each child to experience some changes in the experimental scenario.

Some experimental research has been designed to attain at least moderate internal and moderate external validity. A good example is microteaching. In attempts to do research on teaching, many investigators thought it too artificial to study a single teacher with a single child, despite the probable high internal validity that would accrue. At the same time, conducting the research in a classroom with a single teacher and 25 to 30 children seemed to many to lack sufficient control to get solid answers to the research questions, despite the probable high external validity of so doing. Therefore, some investigators opted for a microteaching context for conducting research on teaching. In effect, teaching was simplified by miniaturization—say, a single teacher, five students, a lesson of only 30 minutes—and by some greater control than is usual in the typical classroom (e.g., by eliminating fire drills, interruptions from the office, a reduced number of student-to-student interactions unrelated to the instruction). This scaled-down setting represented a middle ground between the tutorial and the full class situations, and thus one that would achieve at least moderate internal *and* external validity.

Internal Validity Threats. In examining the strength or credibility of an experiment, a good first step is to diagram the study using the notation scheme previously described. Once this is done, the design of the study can be identified. Then a series of potential threats to the validity of the experiment can be considered for their possible applicability. Common threats to both internal and external validity are defined in Table 3.1.

The three true experimental designs depicted earlier in Figure 3.1 generally avoid the internal validity threats (except as noted subsequently), since more than one group is involved and the groups are formed by random assignment. Therefore, we illustrate most of the internal threats in terms of the pre-experimental designs, especially the one-group pretest-posttest design, or O X O.

TABLE 3.1 Threats to Internal and External Validity in Experimental Research

Internal Threat	Definition
History	Events unrelated to the experiment occur between pre- and posttesting, which affect the performance of one group on the posttest.
Maturation	Changes in subjects over time due to physical, biological, and psychological processes that have effects independent of the treatment.
Testing	Effects of taking a pretest on later performance on the same, or a related, test; a type of practice effect.
Instrumentation	Changes in measuring instruments or procedures (tests, questionnaires, observations) from pretest to posttest that cloud true treatment effects.
Statistical Regression	Tendency for persons with extreme scores on an initial test to score closer to the mean when taking the test or a related test a second time.
Selection	Pre-existing differences between groups of subjects (e.g., treatment and control) potentially confounding the experiment's effects.
Experimental Mortality	Differential loss of subjects by groups in an experiment that renders the results less interpretable.
Intra-session History	Unusual events or conditions, unrelated to the experiment, that impact a single group, markedly affecting its performance.
External Threat	**Definition**
Unrepresentative Sample	Subjects in a study are not representative of the larger group to which the experimenter hopes to generalize the results.
Time	All groups in a study are affected by external events or the existing social context; results fail to generalize to later times and contexts.
Pretest Sensitization	The pretest sensitizes experimental subjects in ways such that they experience the treatment differently than they would have if un-pretested.
Hawthorne Effect	Subjects perform differently simply because of their awareness of being in an experiment and, thus, of being observed.
John Henry Effect	Subjects in control or "traditional method" groups who, learning that they are in a study, perform much better than they would ordinarily.
Novelty Effect	Subjects in an experimental group who perform better simply due to the unusualness or newness of the treatment experience.
Experimenter Effect	Biases and expectations of the researcher that influence subjects, assistants, and conditions in ways that lead to less than objective results.
Multiple Treatment Interference	Subjects in an experimental treatment group also receive other treatments or programs, confounding the effect due to the experimental treatment.
Non-generalizable Dependent Variable	Measures used in a study may not represent well other measures of the dependent variable (due, perhaps, to weak psychometric validity and reliability).
Ambiguous Independent Variable	The treatment or active independent variable may be vaguely conceptualized and defined, masking its nature and making replication problematic.

The *history* threat to internal validity occurs when one or more significant "outside" events occur between the pre- and post-measurements. When only a single group is involved, as in the O X O design, the effect of the outside event, if any, becomes fully confounded with the effect of the treatment. That is, it is impossible to determine what changes in the second or post-observation are due to the treatment as distinguished from the historical event. Imagine that the street-crossing behavior of children is measured before and after the initiation of a new program in which the children take turns being street-crossing guards. A marked decrease in unsafe behavior is recorded from the first to the second measurement. However, suppose that as the new program began operating, the city on its own launched an extensive media campaign aimed at pedestrian safety. The city's campaign becomes a potential source of invalidity due to a history threat. If a second group serving as a control group had been involved in the design, on the other hand, then the historical event should have affected both groups equally with the credibility of the final comparison being maintained.

The *maturation* threat occurs due to physical, biological, and psychological processes (e.g., growing older, more fatigued, more coordinated) operating within subjects as a function of the passage of time rather than as a result of particular events. For instance, a researcher using an O X O design might claim that preschoolers increased their coordination dramatically over 12 months by taking part in a special physical education program featuring dance and creative movement. The claims are suspect, however, because preschoolers naturally become more coordinated during this time period due to maturation.

Another threat to the internal validity of an experiment is *testing*. This threat is defined as the effects of taking a test (as a pre-measure) on subsequent performance on the same or a highly related test. In essence, the earlier experience can enhance the later performance, due to a practice effect. For instance, imagine that a basic concepts test was given to kindergartners twice, with a three-week interval between testings. Their scores on the second test could be higher simply because of having taken the test the first time. Again, it is obvious that such a threat would emerge in the single group O X O design, but that having two groups take the pre-measure should keep in balance any effect due to the initial test. Other things being equal, the shorter the time interval between the two testings, the more problematic the testing effect becomes.

The *instrumentation* threat occurs due to changes in instrumentation (tests, observers, raters, questionnaires) that might produce changes in subjects' scores over time independent of any actual effect due to the experimental treatment. For example, observers recording fantasy play on the playground may be more attentive at time 1 than later at time 2. Or the researcher might decide to use a different measure as a posttest from that used as a pretest. This threat certainly could occur in an O X O design. Those using the time series design must carefully inspect the data collected over the numerous measuring points to discern whether changes in the instruments or in the rules concerning their use have occurred over time.

The *statistical regression* threat is the tendency of persons with extreme scores (either high or low) on a first test to have less extreme scores, on average, the second time they take the test. This is due to an artifact—extremely high scores on the first test in part are, on average, due to positive (plus) measurement errors. Very low scores on the initial test in part are due to negative (minus) measurement errors. These errors are random, so they tend to even out and move in the opposite direction on the next test—that is, they regress toward the mean. Regression occurs if the two tests are not perfectly correlated, which is virtually always the case. Thus, in an O X O design, if children are placed in a special reading program due to their very low scores on a reading test, their scores on a subsequent reading test on average will improve regardless of the effect of the reading program itself.

The *selection* threat involves all the elements that make one group of subjects different from another group of subjects at the beginning of an experiment. Random assignment protects true experiments from this threat. All other designs involving two or more groups are subject to it. For instance, an investigator might compare the reading scores of second-graders in School P, which uses a phonics approach, with the reading scores of second-graders in School W, which uses a whole language approach. The scores from School P might differ from those of School W because of a number of initial differences between the two schools' students (e.g., motivation, intelligence, attitudes, socioeconomic status, and so forth) that are unrelated to the experimental treatments.

The *experimental mortality* threat involves the differential loss of subjects from the two groups being compared in an experiment. For example, imagine that a researcher introduces a soccer program for one group of first-graders with the stated purpose of improving their physical endurance; a second group of first-graders serves as a control group. The coach establishes a very rigorous training regime—early morning and late afternoon practices, seemingly endless calisthenics, and long runs *and* wind sprints. A number of less-motivated children quit the soccer team to escape the zealous coach, but the untreated control group remains intact with no dropouts. On the final endurance measures, the soccer group does better but it is not clear how those quitting the team would have done on the measures. Because of this threat, the researcher must document the apparent reasons for subjects' terminating their participation in a study. Note that this is the first of the threats that might concern even a researcher conducting a true experiment.

Two additional points related to internal validity threats bear mention. First, interactions between threats are possible. In a given study, for example, maturation in its own right might not appear to be a threat. However, if selection is established as a threat, then the interaction between selection and maturation looms as a possible threat. Second, another threat often of concern, even in true experimental designs, is *intra-session history*. This threat occurs when, within a given group, something occurs that is unintended and that colors and affects the group independent of the treatment. For example, suppose that a randomly formed group of 4-year-olds in a comparative study is to receive the High/Scope approach. However, the teacher for this group has little enthusiasm for this particular approach and fulfills her role in a low-energy fashion. As a result, the High/Scope approach appears less effective than it would have with a typical teacher implementing it.

External Validity Threats. Recall that true experiments, those in which subjects are randomly assigned to groups, are relatively free of internal validity threats. Thus, they and other experiments with high internal validity have an excellent chance of establishing "truth" or credible knowledge in terms of the experimental situation itself. Random assignment, however, provides no immunity in terms of external validity threats. In ascertaining a study's generalizability, all studies must address several external validity threats.

An external threat that commonly is difficult for studies to elude is *unrepresentative sample*. This threat operates when the subjects participating in the study are not representative of the population to which we want to generalize the findings. It is unusual for researchers to have sufficient resources to draw a random sample from the target population, especially if the population is widespread geographically. This threat typically functions to some extent due to the type of sampling used or the refusal of some selected subjects to participate, or both.

A second external validity threat is *time*, or the interaction of treatment with history. This threat can occur if the historical context or historical events, at the time of the study, impact the results. The context or historical events occur to the subjects in both or all groups; if they occur to just one group, the threat would be the internal validity threat of history. As an example of the external threat, imagine that a true experiment was underway with the treatment focusing on elementary school children's attitudes toward space and space exploration. As the study was being conducted, the U.S. space shuttle *Challenger* exploded. This event could well interact with the treatment and obviously would dramatically impact all the groups in the study.

A series of external validity threats is linked to the interaction of treatment and persons. Collectively known as *reactive effects*, these threats materialize if the conditions of the study (other than the independent variable, of course) cause the subjects to behave or react differently from the way they ordinarily would. The more common reactive effects, which we describe below, are pretest sensitization, the Hawthorne Effect, the John Henry effect, the novelty effect, and the experimenter effect.

Pretest sensitization occurs when the pretest alone modifies the subjects or their expectations in such a way that they react differently to the treatment than would unpretested persons. Thus, subjects in the experimental group might experience the treatment differently simply because they had been pretested. As was noted, the Solomon four group design was advanced as a means to estimate the effects of pretesting in an experiment.

The *Hawthorne Effect* was first identified in a series of studies conducted in the 1930s in Western Electric's Hawthorne plant near Chicago. The purpose of the studies was to examine work conditions so as to improve productivity. Serendipitously, it was learned that the attention given to plant workers as experimental subjects was one variable causing high employee production, regardless of the varying work conditions established (Roethlisberger & Dickson, 1941). Thus, this external threat involves concerns that the experimental subjects are, in part, performing differently (and presumably better) simply because they know they are subjects in a study and are being observed.

A related reactive concern is known as the *John Henry effect*. In folklore, John Henry competed against a new steam machine that threatened to displace manual laborers. While John Henry won the competition by displaying a dramatic and inordinate effort, he then died due to overexertion. Learning that the program they are in is being "competitively" compared with a new approach, control-group subjects sometimes have been observed to perform much better than usual, as if to defend their way of doing things or to respond to the "threat" of another approach. Some experimenters attempt to blunt the John Henry effect by having the control group undergo a "treatment" of their own, one that is unrelated to the dependent variable of interest.

The *novelty effect* occurs when the responses of the subjects are in part a function of the "newness" of the experimental treatment. In general, "new" has a connotation of better, and so it is when the treatment consists of a new method or approach. The exuberance and excitement that can surround the introduction of a new treatment might last for several months. If a study of the new approach's effects is done during this period, part of the "effect" observed may be due to the favorable aura surrounding the new method, rather than to the method itself. The wise experimenter attempts to dampen the novelty threat by conducting the study over a longer period of time or by using follow-up measures to discern if effects observed early on have persisted.

Yet a final reactive external threat is the *experimenter effect.* This threat concerns the subjects' giving responses that partly are a function of the way in which the experimenter administered the treatment, responses different from those that might be obtained by another researcher. Close to what is frequently termed an expectancy effect, this threat can involve the experimenter's expectations coloring the performance of the study's subjects. It has been shown that concerns in this area are far from idle (e.g., Rosenthal, 1966); for example, data collectors or others working for the researcher may be subtly influenced by the experimenter's expectations in ways that lower their objectivity and compromise their credibility.

Several other external validity effects can be noted. The threat due to *multiple-treatment interference* can appear when multiple treatments are being received simultaneously or when multiple treatments are applied sequentially and subjects experience cumulative effects. Outcomes due to the various treatments cannot be sorted out. The threat termed *nongeneralizability of the dependent variable* occurs when the instrument used to measure the dependent variable does not represent well the "population" of such measures that are available. If the study were to be redone using a different measure, the results might not be the same. A final threat to external validity is *ambiguous independent variable.* This threat occurs when the active independent variable is not clearly and operationally defined. Replication of the experiment becomes difficult if not impossible under such conditions.

Research Examples in Early Childhood Education

You may already know of a classic true experiment with important theoretical implications. Harlow (1958, 1959) tested the then popular assumption that infant monkeys become attached emotionally to their mothers because the milk received from the mothers reduced the primary drive of hunger. Primary drives have internal, physiological bases. He used surrogate monkey mothers for the study, one made of wire mesh and one made of terry cloth. The surrogates were identical in terms of warmth (the wire mesh mother was warmed by radiant heat) and in terms of providing postural support for the newborn. Their essential difference was in the greater contact comfort of the terry-cloth mother. Eight baby monkeys were used. Each had access to two surrogate mothers, one of terry cloth and one of wire mesh. Four baby monkeys were randomly assigned to wire-mesh mothers who gave milk and terry-cloth mothers who did not; these conditions were reversed for the other four monkeys. The primary-drive theory would predict that the infant monkeys would become attached to whichever surrogate mother provided milk, but the data suggested otherwise. The infant monkeys spent most of their time with the terry-cloth mother, whether or not she was the lactating mother. Also, when fear-producing stimuli like teddy bears and large mechanical spiders were lowered into the cages, all the infant monkeys found and clung to their terry-cloth mothers.

Another of our favorite true experiments in early childhood education—possibly also approaching "classic" status—examined whether different television programs led to aggressive and prosocial behaviors (Friedrich & Stein, 1973). Nursery school children, 4 and 5 years old, were observed during play time for three weeks and then were randomly assigned to one of three television program groups: (1) prosocial ("Mister Rogers' Neighborhood"); (2) aggressive ("Superman" and "Batman" cartoons); and (3) neutral (programs with minimal prosocial and aggressive content, such as travelogues). Programs were watched daily for four weeks; the children's behavior was also observed during free time then, as well as during the two following weeks. Children who viewed the aggressive programs, especially those above average in aggressiveness during the pre-observation period, displayed the greatest amount of interpersonal aggression (shoving, pushing, breaking toys), as well as less rule obedience and tolerance of delay. Prosocial program viewers from lower socioeconomic status families displayed increased prosocial interpersonal behaviors (helping others, sharing toys), and the entire prosocial group evidenced higher task persistence, rule obedience, and tolerance of delay. The authors concluded that television programming did cause behavior changes in young children in the expected directions, at least in the short run.

Another true experiment examined the effect of being "testwise" on readiness test performance of Hispanic kindergartners (Dreisbach & Keogh, 1982). Over 100 Spanish-speaking children from low socioeconomic status homes were randomly assigned to treatment and control groups. The treatment group received two sessions on how to take tests (e.g., listening, keeping on the right page/item, marking multiple-choice answer sheets), not on the test's content. Children in the control group spent comparable time in an organized coloring book activity. One week later, the children took readiness-like tests in both English and Spanish, with the order of the tests counter-balanced, adapted from Circus (Anderson & Bogatz, 1979), a battery of measures including mathematics, perception, problem solving, prereading, and others. Treatment-group children outperformed the controls on both tests. While girls did better overall, the treatment especially increased the test scores of boys. Children usually did better on the Spanish version, and scores on the English version were higher if the Spanish form was taken first. The authors concluded that testwiseness was an influential factor to consider when testing children from minority backgrounds.

In a true experiment, Newman (1990) investigated the effects of varying instructions on 4- and 5-year-old children's memory; using real toys or pictures of them constituted another variable. Children were randomly assigned to experimental conditions. Some children were given pictures of 16 toys to interact with, while others received the actual toys; these groups were again divided in that half of the children were told "to remember" the toys while the others were told "to play with" the toys. The children's language and behavior were recorded as they interacted with the materials. Surprisingly, children receiving the "play" instructions with the actual toys demonstrated better recall of the toys than those children in the group directed to remember the toys; also, the actual toys prompted better recall than did the pictures. Newman analyzed the children's behaviors and concluded that children in the play condition engaged in more functional play activities, like eating the banana or putting the shoe on the elephant, while those in the remember condition spent considerable time merely naming the objects.

Turning to quasi-experiments, the nonequivalent pretest-posttest control group design was illustrated in a study by Jennings, Jennings, Richey, and Dixon-Krauss (1992). Sixty kindergartners were formed into experimental and control groups. The treatment group received a program that incorporated children's literature into the mathematics curriculum for five months. For example, the modified book *Jim and the Beanstalk* was used to introduce concepts of measurement, money, comparison, and number using a variety of manipulatives. The control group received the traditional mathematics curriculum. Children were pre- and posttested on the Test of Early Mathematics Ability (TEMA) (Ginsburg & Baroody, 1983) and posttested on quantitative parts of the Metropolitan Readiness Test (MRT) (Nurss & McGauvran, 1986). Treatment-group children performed better on both the TEMA and the MRT, and at a statistically significant level on the TEMA. The authors concluded that the treatment was effective, citing both the TEMA results and an enriched mathematical vocabulary of the experimental-group children.

In a study with a similar design, Thomson and his colleagues (1992) noted considerable lack of sophistication in young children's ability to cross roads safely (for example, their selecting brows of hills or positions close to parked cars as good spots to cross). They divided 5-year-olds into small groups for training on road-crossing safety. Children were trained either in the real road environment or via a table-top model; a control group also was utilized. Pre- and post-measures were taken individually at actual road sites where children without prompting were asked to specify how they would cross. Both training methods resulted in safer road-crossing selections than those shown by control-group children, both immediately and after two months.

Turning to quasi-experimental time series designs, the study by Seekins and his colleagues (1988) is illustrative. They examined the seating in automobiles of infants and of young children both before and after the passage of pertinent state laws. In seven states, observers at designated sites looked into temporarily stopped cars to determine if children up to 5 years of age were appropriately restrained (i.e., location, type of restraint, properly connected and hooked). Using time series analysis, safer seating practices were observed overall, although compliance actually regressed in two of the states. Endorsing such experiments that examined public compliance with legislation, the authors noted the implications of their research for public policy.

SINGLE-SUBJECT RESEARCH

The final quantitative research method we consider is single-subject research. Some authors refer to it as single-subject experimental research to distinguish it from the in-depth study of a single case using more qualitative procedures (see Chapter 5). This research method shares with experiments the search for cause-and-effect relationships. However, an essential difference between this type of research and all those examined previously is that it utilizes a single subject, or several subjects treated individually, rather than a group of subjects.

Basic Design Elements and Primary Uses

In essence, this research concerns an individual, focuses on a given behavior of interest that is to be changed (the target behavior and also the dependent variable), and introduces a treatment, often a program or method for delivering positive reinforcement (the independent variable). The target behavior is observed and recorded over a period of time, known as the *baseline*, prior to the introduction of the treatment. The behavior is also measured (most often via observation) during the *treatment* period. Depending on the full design, one of several options is then implemented. One common option, for example, is to chart the same target behavior during a *withdrawal* (or return to baseline) period during which the treatment is stopped but measurement of the target behavior continues.

One common single-subject design is known as the A B A design, where A denotes baseline and B signals treatment. Using our notation scheme, the A B A design would be depicted as below:

Baseline	Treatment	Baseline
	X X X X X	
O O O O O	O O O O O	O O O O O

Of special interest are the five middle observations to discern if the introduction of the treatment is having an effect on the observed target behavior. Of import, too, are the observations recorded in the "second baseline" or withdrawal period when the treatment is suspended. A number of variations of the single-subject design exist. For example, the A B A B design appears often in the research literature.

Sometimes, depending on the target behavior, it is inappropriate, undesirable, or even unethical for the researcher to return to baseline. Imagine a situation in which the target behavior is biting on the part of a 3-year-old. Let's assume that the child is quite an avid biter, and is observed to bite a classmate on average every 10 minutes in class during the baseline period. The treatment, consisting of adult praise for every 5-minute period in class that the child does not bite a neighbor, reduces the frequency of biting others to every 60 minutes, on average. Withdrawing this apparently effective treatment might well be deemed inappropriate. If such is the decision, then the A B A design simply becomes an A B design. What the investigator might do in such a case is to move to a *multiple-baseline* design, whereby a series of A B designs is used across settings, behaviors, or individuals. Thus, here, the researcher might decide to also implement the A B strategy across settings for the same child, by charting the baseline of biting behavior on the playground and then implementing the treatment there too.

The basic purpose of this type of research is to establish cause-and-effect relationships in a case where the unique behavior of a given individual is of great interest. Often a companion purpose is to alter that behavior in a direction prejudged to be more desirable or more appropriate. This type of research is more likely to be utilized in certain contexts, such as individualized instruction and classroom management, as well as in certain fields, such as special education and counseling. Representative instructional situations would be determining means or methods to enhance learning by the individual; classroom management techniques most often take the form of behavior modification. In special education and counseling, the match emanates from the great likelihood that a given child or client is receiving an individualized intervention or treatment.

Several guiding principles for this type of research have been identified (following Best & Kahn, 1993; Borg, Gall, & Gall, 1993; Gay, 1987; and McMillan & Schumacher, 1993):

1. The behavior of interest must occur with considerable frequency and be observable. Tests are rarely used in such designs because of concerns like the practice effect of repeated testings.
2. The measurement of the behavior must be reliable (as defined in Chapter 4) and repeated. With only one subject, the accuracy of the many measurements that must be made takes on great importance.
3. Conditions that make up the treatment and that surround the measuring process must be fully described. For instance, it is important that the measurements of the behavior occur under the same conditions across the entire study.
4. The baseline and treatment periods must continue until a degree of stability is observed in the incidence of the target behavior. It is also recommended that the baseline and treatment phases last about the same amount of time.
5. The single-variable "rule" must be followed. This rule dictates that only a single variable, that is, the treatment, can be varied or else it is impossible to discern the treatment's effect.

Results from this type of research typically are not treated statistically. Rather, the target behavior is plotted during the baseline and treatment periods to determine if the changes across the periods are obvious or not. As you might imagine, this type of research is often vulnerable to external validity threats given that only a single subject may be utilized. Still, if the researcher is able to use a multiple-baseline procedure across several individuals and to show similar results in each of several cases, the external validity of the study is enhanced.

Research Examples in Early Childhood Education

Single-subject procedures were apparent in a study conducted by Levy, Wolfgang, and Koorland (1992). Three kindergartners were observed during the baseline period to determine their language performance (number of words spoken in 15 minutes, average length of utterance, number of specific words, and number of concept words) during impromptu play.

Then, using a multiple-baseline strategy, intervention occurred at separate points in time for the three subjects. The intervention, enriched sociodramatic play, consisted of a shared background of information to provide a theme, sufficient space and time and a supply of props, and facilitation by an adult who helped expand and enrich the play. The authors noted increases in the four language variables during the intervention for all three subjects and concluded that enriched sociodramatic play could enhance language performance.

Two related single-subject studies, also using multiple baseline procedures, were conducted by Stark, Collins, Osnes, and Stokes (1986). In the first study, they used eight preschoolers, initially establishing a baseline for healthy or unhealthy snack food choices. The intervention consisted of an adult's labeling snack foods either green (healthy) or red (unhealthy), and teaching the children to use cueing sentences, in effect praising themselves for a green food choice. All of the preschoolers increased their green food choices at school during and after the intervention; at home such increases occurred for some children but to a lesser degree. In the second study, involving nine new subjects, only nutrition training occurred, and not training in cueing. Choice of healthy snacks took place and was maintained at school, but this generalized to home for only one child. The authors concluded that snack choice at school could be affected, but that generalization of such behavior to other settings required additional and individualized strategies.

A variation of the single-subject design, which might be termed the single-group design, was enacted by Karnes, Johnson, and Beauchamp (1989). Using 10 mildly handicapped preschoolers as subjects, the researchers first established engaged and active as well as off-task behavior of the subjects while doing maze and design replication problems. The intervention consisted of teaching the children how to overtly verbalize problem-solving strategies, cognitive modeling, and task structuring so that they could monitor their own progress. Six of the 10 subjects, 4 of them markedly so, displayed improved task engagement and persistence during intervention. The researchers concluded that additional studies were needed to determine which aspects of the intervention had been most influential in causing these effects.

CRITIQUING QUANTITATIVE RESEARCH

Here we list questions that should enable one to examine the essential features of quantitative research. First, questions that are generally applicable to quantitative research, separated by research phase, are listed.

Second, questions more pertinent to, and organized by, the various types of research are presented. In general, we have tried to detail the more important questions based on our review of a number of sources (e.g., Gay, 1987; Isaac & Michael, 1981; McMillan, 1996; McMillan & Schumacher, 1993; Smith & Glass, 1987; and Symonds, 1956). In many but not all cases, information has been or will be presented in Chapter 4 to guide the answering of the questions.

Questions Applicable to All Quantitative Research

The questions below, relevant to most quantitative studies as they are reported in journal articles, are ordered as they are often considered by the researcher.

Problem

1. Is the problem clearly stated?
2. Is the problem accurately reflected in the article's title?
3. Is the problem significant theoretically? Practically?
4. Are theory and rationale underlying the problem detailed?
5. Are conceptual and other assumptions clear and justifiable?

Related Literature

1. Are links between prior research and the problem made clear?
2. Is the review relevant, significant, and well-organized?
3. Is the review comprehensive and comprehendible?
4. Are important studies—recent and older—in the bibliography?

Questions/Hypotheses

1. Are the questions and hypotheses clear and precise?
2. Are the questions stated so they can be answered?
3. Are the hypotheses stated in a testable form?

Methodology/Procedures

1. Are key variables identified and defined precisely?
2. Are the research method and design adequately described?
3. Does the method match the research problem and questions?
4. Is the study sufficiently described that its strengths and weaknesses can be identified?
5. Are the population and sample fully described?
6. Is the sampling method appropriate? Is the sample biased?
7. Is the sample representative and large enough to permit sound conclusions?

Instrumentation (Measures, Observations, Questionnaires, etc.)

1. Do the measures match the variables central to the study?
2. Are the measures valid for the purposes for which they were used in the study? Are supporting data indicated?
3. Are the measures reliable for the purposes for which they were used in the study? Are supporting data indicated?
4. Is administration of the measures described clearly?
5. Are data collection, interviewing, and recording procedures fully and clearly described?
6. Are clear and distinct scoring and judging categories used?
7. Are the qualifications of scorers and judges described?
8. Is interrater reliability described and adequate?
9. Are potential judgmental biases identified and controlled?

Statistical Analyses

1. Are appropriate analysis methods selected and described?
2. Are the methods applied correctly?
3. Are the analysis results presented and reported clearly?
4. Are data in tables and graphs interpretable?
5. Does the information in the text match the accompanying tables and graphs?

Interpretations/Conclusions

1. Are the interpretations based on the data?
2. Are findings reported for each question asked and each hypothesis tested?
3. Are conclusions logical and confined to the evidence at hand?
4. Are conclusions considered in terms of both statistical significance *and* practical significance?
5. Is the stated generalizability of the conclusions warranted?
6. Are inferences and opinions clearly labeled as such?
7. Are the results related to outcomes from other research?
8. Is any bias on the part of the researcher detectable?
9. Are implications of the findings stated, and is further research suggested?

Final Questions

1. Is the study organized, logical, and interesting?
2. Are limitations of the study and any inconsistencies stated?
3. Are the bibliography, tables, and figures accurate and important additions?

4. Does the article's tone reflect an unbiased attitude?
5. Is the study described clearly enough and in sufficient detail that replication would be possible?
6. Do the study's results add credible knowledge to the field?

Questions Specific to Types of Quantitative Research

We now consider questions germane to specific research methods. The sources reviewed for the general critique questions above were again consulted, as was Jaeger (1988) for descriptive survey research. The questions listed below are representative of important questions that might be asked about each type of research.

Descriptive Research/Survey

1. Is the target population (to which generalization is desired) identified?
2. Are the sampling procedures used, and available sampling frames, fully described?
3. Is the representativeness of the sample drawn noted, as well as its "match" with the target population?
4. Is the importance of the study addressed?
5. Are informed consent and confidentiality procedures for respondents described?
6. Are clear and unambiguous directions provided to respondents?
7. Is the overall response rate reported, and are specific items that frequently were not answered identified?
8. If the response rate appears low, is a follow-up reported?
9. Is a nonrespondent bias check performed (to determine the similarity between respondents and nonrespondents)?
10. Are questionnaires or interview protocols included; if not, are sources noted for obtaining them?
11. Are slanted or leading questions avoided?
12. Are procedures (mailing, fieldwork, and so forth) well described?
13. Are the qualifications and training of interviewers noted, and is their interreliability adequate?
14. Are graphic displays of data accurate and not misleading?
15. Are relationship or causal conclusions avoided?

Descriptive Research/Developmental

1. Are the subjects and the sampling procedures fully described?
2. If cross-sectional, is the study focused on and proactive in minimizing other than age differences between subjects?

3. If the study is longitudinal, is the number of remaining subjects sufficiently high, and how has attrition been minimized?
4. Are the qualifications and training of observers described, and is their resultant interreliability sufficiently high?
5. Are observational systems and other instrumentation included in the study report; if not, are sources noted for them?
6. Are the results logical and generally consistent with developmental data generated by other methods over time?

Correlational Research

1. Are the variables selected carefully, with theoretical and research support bases?
2. Is the sample for the study fully described with an eye toward the generalizability of the study's results?
3. Is the sample likely to be sufficiently varied on the variables under investigation?
4. Are the validity and reliability of the measuring instruments for each variable reported and sufficiently high?
5. Are scatterplots used to detect possible curvilinear relationships between variables?
6. Are restriction of range and attenuation considered when interpreting correlation coefficients?
7. In a prediction study, is a rationale provided for the predictor variables selected?
8. In a prediction study, is the criterion or predicted variable well defined?
9. In a prediction study, is the resultant prediction equation validated with a second group of subjects?
10. Are causal inferences avoided in the study's interpretation?

Causal-Comparative Research

1. Is the research focused on establishing cause and effect?
2. Has the presumed effect (the independent variable) occurred?
3. Is the sample fully described?
4. Are the two groups to be compared fully described, including the nature of each at the time the presumed cause occurred?
5. Are the two groups to be compared similar on all demographic variables except the independent (presumed cause) variable?
6. Are potential threats to internal and external validity recognized and discussed?

7. Are rival hypotheses—other plausible explanations for the outcomes observed—identified and ruled out?
8. Are findings cautiously stated insofar as cause and effect is concerned?
9. Is it possible to have entertained the cause-and-effect question via an experiment?

Quasi-Experimental Research

1. In the nonequivalent pretest-posttest control group (NPPCG) design, is group identification and formation detailed?
2. In the NPPCG design, is the sample fully described with an eye toward the generalizability of the results?
3. In the NPPCG design, is the groups' equivalency examined?
4. In the NPPCG design, are the levels of the active independent variable quite different?
5. In the NPPCG design, is the treatment well implemented?
6. In the NPPCG design, are critical extraneous variables identified and controlled?
7. In a time series (TS) design, is there a sufficient number of pretreatment data points?
8. In a TS design, is the treatment introduced at a single, distinct point in time?
9. In a TS design, are consistent measuring instruments and methods used across time?
10. Are threats to internal validity adequately addressed?
11. Are threats to external validity adequately addressed?
12. Is balanced attention given to, and control established for, both internal and external validity?
13. Is a true experiment a possibility?

True Experimental Research

1. Is the sample fully described with an eye toward the generalizability of the results?
2. Is the process of assigning subjects to groups indeed random?
3. Are the levels of the independent variable quite different?
4. Is the treatment well implemented?
5. Are critical extraneous variables identified and controlled?
6. Are threats to internal validity adequately addressed?
7. Are threats to external validity adequately addressed?
8. Is balanced attention given to, and control established for, internal and external validity?

9. If the study is conducted in the laboratory, is attention given when generalizing to the match between the experimental conditions and the nature of the "real" world?

Single-Subject Research

1. Is the single-subject design more appropriate in this case than a group design would have been?
2. Is the subject for the study fully described?
3. Is the target behavior (the dependent variable) clearly and operationally defined?
4. Is the target behavior measured reliably?
5. Is the target behavior measured to a point of stability in all study phases (e.g., baseline, treatment, etc.)?
6. Is the treatment condition fully described?
7. Are other conditions in which the study is conducted (e.g., setting, participants, time of day) fully described?
8. Is the treatment variable the single element permitted to vary in the treatment phase?
9. Is special attention given to controlling the observer (or experimenter) effect?
10. Is the graph of the results clear, straightforward, and evidence of a practically significant change in the target behavior during the treatment phase?
11. Are replications reported—across settings, behaviors, or individuals?

SUMMARY

Quantitative research is essentially a deductive process, with detailed prespecification of most of its elements and marked use of numerical analyses and reports. In this chapter, common methods of quantitative research were described, and examples were given of their use in early childhood education. Descriptive research—encompassing both surveys and developmental studies—describes "what is," and involves no manipulation of variables. In correlational research, relationships between variables are examined, sometimes for prediction purposes; it likewise involves no manipulation. Causal-comparative or *ex post facto* research seeks to establish cause-and-effect relationships between variables. However, since it is after the fact, the cause has already occurred and neither manipulation nor random assignment is utilized. The experimental research method is characterized by proactive manipulation of a treatment variable by the experimenter in order to establish cause-and-effect relationships. True experiments result when subjects are randomly assigned to treatment and control conditions. Quasi-experiments involve no random assignment; generally, the designs involve comparing two or more groups that experience different treatments or conditions, or a single group is studied in the time series design. Experimenters seek to achieve both high internal validity—that is, establishing true knowledge in the experimental situation—and high external validity, or generalizability; a series of threats to each type of validity must be controlled. Also targeting causal relationships, single-subject research involves highly controlled conditions with just one subject, or with a series of subjects treated individually and independently. Questions useful in critiquing quantitative research were listed. Basic measurement concepts and numerical data-analysis techniques—both central to quantitative research—will be examined in Chapter 4.

Chapter 4

Measurement and Data Analysis in Quantitative Research

The measurement of the variables in any quantitative research study is critically important. The measurement component is full of frustrations, including the difficulties associated with deciding exactly what variables to measure and then locating or developing suitable measuring instruments. Whether we use existing measures or develop new ones, we must be concerned about their psychometric properties and other factors, such as validity, reliability, relevance, and lack of bias. In this chapter, we discuss basic measurement terms and concepts, describe typical types of instruments used in quantitative research, and present considerations important in the selection of instruments for research use.

Another essential activity in quantitative research involves analysis of the data once they have been collected. This component of the research process requires the use of descriptive and inferential statistical techniques. While complete coverage of statistics is beyond the scope of this book, some of the most commonly used techniques are briefly considered.

BASIC MEASUREMENT TERMS, CONCEPTS, AND ISSUES

Measurement is the process by which persons or things are differentiated. It involves testing, observation, interviewing, or other methods, and results in the assignment of numbers, ratings, or labels to the persons or things measured. Although some variables are quite easily defined and observed—height, weight, age, gender, number of siblings, city of residence—many variables of interest are not directly observable—self-esteem, achievement, motivation, playfulness, creativity, and so on. For these abstract variables, the challenge of measurement is particularly great. We must develop measures that allow us to infer, from a sample of indirect indicators, a person's standing or level on the continuum of the abstract variable. And we want some assurance that the inferences we draw from scores on the measure are appropriate and accurate; that is, we need evidence to support the validity of the inferences.

Research in early childhood education utilizes a variety of types of measure. Studies with a heavy quantitative focus typically include measures that yield numerical scores, while qualitative research focuses on the use of observations, interviews, and other nonobtrusive measures that do not necessarily yield numerical results. The basic measurement terms and concepts presented below actually are important for all measures, although historically they have been particularly applied to quantitative measures. In Chapter 6, measures commonly used by qualitative researchers will be discussed, along with some of the different ways that validity and reliability are conceptualized for those types of measure.

Validity

As defined in the most recent edition of the *Standards for Educational and Psychological Testing* (AERA, APA, & NCME, 1985), validity "refers to the appropriateness, meaningfulness, and usefulness of the specific inferences made from test scores. Validation is the process of accumulating evidence to support such inferences" (p. 9). The meaning of validity has evolved over the past 50 years. Guilford's (1946) oft-quoted declaration, "in a very general sense, a test is valid for anything with which it correlates" (p. 429), characterized the earliest thinking about measurement validity. From the 1950s through the 1970s, the meaning of validity was very use-dependent; that is, it was defined as the extent to which a test fulfilled its intended purpose (AERA, APA, & NCME, 1966). In the 1980s and 1990s, measurement theorists such as Cronbach (1980, 1988, 1990) and Messick (1980, 1988, 1989, 1995) have espoused the revised definition that emphasizes the accuracy and appropriateness of the inferences to be drawn from scores. Also recently, they and others (e.g., Linn, 1994; Moss, 1992; Shepard, 1993) have encouraged the consideration of both intended and unintended *consequences* of measurement as part of validation efforts.

Since the publication of a classic article by Cronbach and Meehl (1955), and later the *Standards for Educational and Psychological Tests and Manuals* (AERA, APA, & NCME, 1966), validity has been categorized as three types: content, criterion-related, and construct. With the shift in the definition of validity that occurred in the 1980s, measurement experts began to question the usefulness of the three-part breakdown. The 1985 *Standards*, while retaining this traditional categorization scheme, did note that "the use of the category labels should not be taken to imply that there are distinct types of validity" (p. 9). More and more, construct validity is seen as the unifying theme or "umbrella" under which all types of validity evidence belong; Messick (1989, 1995) opined that all validity evidence is construct validity evidence. Given the historical definition of construct validity, this type of evidence is required if we plan to infer from a person's score on a measure his or her standing on a psychological concept or construct. Since many instruments purport to measure abstract constructs (aptitude, achievement, creativity, etc.), it is not surprising that concerns about this type of validity evidence dominate.

In general, obtaining construct validity evidence involves operationally defining the construct, usually in terms of an underlying theoretical framework; developing hypotheses from this same theoretical basis; and using logical and empirical methods to test the hypotheses. Usually, many different hypotheses can be derived for the validation of a measure, and testing them all calls for a variety of different approaches. The hypotheses can pertain to the content of the measure, to correlations with other variables, to differences between groups, to the measure's factor structure, and to expected consequences of using the measure.

Inferences About the Content of a Measure. Traditionally termed *content validity*, evidence pertaining to this type of inference is commonly sought, especially for achievement measures and certification/licensing examinations. The concern is how well we can infer from the *sample* of items that comprise the measure to a larger domain or universe of items. We plan to use the score an individual earns as an indicator of how much, or what level, of the abstract property that person possesses. Obtaining content validity evidence usually is judgmental rather than empirical. Experts are asked to indicate how well the sample of items represents the defined domain or universe. For achievement measures, both content and process objectives are considered. Since the judgments are necessarily subjective, the dependability of this evidence is enhanced by clear instructions to the judges and by assessing interjudge reliability.

Inferences About Relationships with Other Variables. Validity evidence that examines the relationships between scores on the measure and other variables is traditionally called *criterion-related* validity, often further differentiated into *predictive* and *concurrent* validity. Predictive validity is relevant if we wish to infer from a score to some future criterion, a characteristic or behavior. If the inference is to another behavior or characteristic occurring at the same time the measure is being used, concurrent validity evidence is important. Many of our measures have purposes that are either of a predictive or a substitution nature, so this type of validity evidence is required often.

Sometimes, a hypothesis of interest in validation research states that scores on a measure will *not* correlate with some other variable; this is denoted as *discriminant* validity. Campbell and Fiske (1959) introduced the concept and argued that both concurrent (which they called *convergent)* validity and discriminant validity evidences were needed for measures of abstract concepts. That is, it was important to show that a measure correlated well with other variables that it should relate to, theoretically, and did not correlate with variables from which it was theoretically distinct.

A frequent dilemma in criterion-related validity research is the "criterion problem." The measures of the criteria in these studies must have adequate evidence of validity, reliability, relevance, and lack of bias. Locating existing measures to serve as criteria that have such qualities is very difficult, and sometimes impossible. It is a "Catch 22" of sorts, especially for new measures needing evidence of concurrent validity: If a criterion measure with good validity, reliability, relevance, and unbiasedness is already available, why are we developing a new measure of this construct? Although there is no "quick fix" to this criterion problem, suggestions that help address it are using multiple criterion measures (since each will have different strengths and limitations) and looking for evidence of both concurrent and discriminant validity.

Most criterion-related validity studies report results as correlation coefficients (discussed in the last major section of this chapter). During the last decade, there has been a growing interest in "validity generalization," which involves the use of statistical summarization techniques to determine the extent to which criterion-related validity coefficients generalize across different settings and institutions (Schmidt, 1988). The results of some of this work are challenging a long-held assumption that validity is situational. However, Mehrens and Lehman (1991) warned local users of measures not to put too much faith in this notion, and to continue the collection of local validation data.

Inferences About Differences Between Groups. Hypotheses driving validity studies often state that there will be differences in mean scores on the measure for members of already constituted groups, such as males and females, older and younger subjects, or members of different ethnic groups. This is referred to as a "known-groups" or "contrasted-groups" design (Crocker & Algina, 1986). An experimental counterpart design occurs when the hypothesis states that subjects who receive an experimental treatment, designed to change their scores on the measure, will have a significantly different mean score from that of subjects not exposed to the treatment. If hypothesized differences are not found, possible explanations include failure of the treatment, failure of the theory underlying the measure, or failure of the instrument to accurately measure the construct.

Inferences About the Structure of the Measure. A statistical technique known as factor analysis can be used to help determine the internal structure of a measure (Child, 1970; Crocker & Algina, 1986; Hair, Anderson, Tatham, & Black, 1992; Kachigan, 1991). This approach to obtaining validity evidence is most appropriate if hypotheses are posed a priori about the number and type of factors that will emerge. The factor analysis, based on correlations among items, is then employed to test the hypotheses. As some have noted (e.g., Goodwin & Goodwin, 1991a), the use of factor analysis alone is insufficient for validating a measure.

Inferences About the Consequences of Using the Measure. As noted earlier, studying the positive and negative consequences of using a measure—as a part of overall validation efforts—is a relatively new notion (Messick, 1989). Linn and Gronlund (1995) gave an example of positive and negative effects of standardized achievement assessments that could be investigated; the possible positive effects included increased student learning, while possible negative effects included a narrowing of instruction and an increase in the student dropout rate. Certainly, there are many potential negative effects of measuring young children, especially with standardized tests, which have been well-articulated (e.g., Meisels, 1987; Shepard, 1994). Considering such matters as a part of the validation of a measure is definitely warranted.

Reliability

Reliability is consistency. As with validity, it is not a measure per se that is reliable or not reliable; rather, the scores or observations have a certain degree of stability or consistency (Sax, 1980; Thompson, 1992). Reliability traditionally has been classified into several different types. Each type defines "consistency" variably, viewing different factors as "error." Another way of thinking about reliability, in fact, is that it is the absence of measurement error. The higher the reliability coefficient (which is a correlation coefficient), the less the amount of measurement error in the scores. Reliability coefficients vary between 0 and 1.

Errors of measurement can be either positive or negative; that is, they result in a person's *obtained score* being higher or lower than that person's *true score*. The true score is the score the person would receive if there were no error. If all persons' scores were error-free, the reliability of the measure would be perfect. While perfect reliability is virtually impossible, very high reliability coefficients—in the .90s—can be achieved.

What are the common sources of measurement error? One grouping considers errors due to several factors:

- *Administrative factors* include poor instructions, failure of the administrator to follow directions, and too little time available to elicit respondents' maximum performance or complete responses.
- *Environmental factors* include such problems as noise, inadequate lighting, uncomfortable room temperature, crowded conditions, and so on.
- *Scoring errors* are particularly problematic with measures that use a subjective scoring scheme—essays, observations, unstructured interviews, portfolios, and performance assessments. They can occur with objective measures (those with preset scoring guides, such as multiple-choice tests), but are not nearly as common.
- *Characteristics of the measure* itself that can contribute to measurement error include length or number of items. Other things being equal, longer measures are more reliable than shorter ones; with young children, however, this "maxim" has to be carefully weighed against such consequences of longer measurements as increased inattention, boredom, or neighbor-poking (Goodwin & Goodwin, 1993). Other features of measures that lower reliability are ambiguity in the questions and lack of homogeneity among the subparts or items.
- *Intra-individual factors* are sources of error in the scores individuals receive. Among the most difficult sources of measurement error to control, they include factors like fatigue, hunger, poor health, boredom, low motivation, and anxiety—all of the many different feelings and conditions that individuals bring to test-taking and other measurement situations.

A basic notion from classical test theory is that reliability is necessary, but not sufficient, for validity. To illustrate this notion, consider a bathroom scale. Further, suppose that your weight has not changed during the past four weeks. Your scale might be consistent—informing you, for example, that you weigh 140 pounds each week—but not valid. You learn of its invalidity when you visit your physician, whose scale reads 152 pounds. Another way of conceptualizing the relationship between reliability and validity is that a measure cannot correlate with something else (the "criterion" in criterion-related validity) if it does not first correlate with itself (reliability). This long-held assumption continues to be reasonable for most measures, but it recently was challenged by Moss (1994) for performance assessments.

Types of Reliability Coefficient. There are five distinct types of reliability coefficient. The *coefficient of stability* or test-retest reliability coefficient indicates the degree of consistency in scores over time. To obtain such a coefficient, the same group of persons takes exactly the same measure twice, with an "arbitrary but meaningful" time interval between administrations. The correlation between the two sets of scores is the stability reliability coefficient. Usually, the longer the time interval between the two administrations, the lower the coefficient. Important sources of measurement error for this type of reliability include nonsystematic shifts over time in respondents' attitudes, levels of achievement, or whatever is being tapped by the measure.

A second type of reliability is the *coefficient of equivalence*. This is relevant only for measures that have "parallel" or "alternate" forms intentionally developed to be as similar to each other as possible, in terms of content coverage and difficulty level. This coefficient is obtained by administering both forms to the same group of subjects at essentially the same time, and then calculating the correlation between the two sets of scores.

The third type of reliability, the *coefficient of stability and equivalence*, is a combination of the first two types. The two alternate forms of the measure are given to the same group of persons, but with some appropriate amount of time intervening; again, the two sets of data are correlated. Other things being equal, we would expect the coefficient of stability and equivalence to be lower than other types of reliability. Sources of error that occur with both the stability coefficient, due to changes over time, and the equivalence coefficient, due to lack of perfect parallelism between the two forms, will occur with the stability and equivalence coefficient.

The most commonly estimated type of reliability is the *coefficient of internal consistency*. Its popularity is largely due to convenience factors–it can be calculated with scores obtained from just one form of a measure, given just one time to one group of persons. This reliability coefficient indicates the degree of homogeneity in the items; a high coefficient tells us that the items tend to be measuring the same characteristic of the respondents, while a low coefficient means that the items are disparate in what they are measuring. A high coefficient does *not* inform us that the instrument measures what it purports to measure (validity), but just that the components of the measure all tend to measure the same thing. A number of different equations are available to calculate internal consistency, including Cronbach's alpha, KR_{20}, KR_{21}, and Hoyt's formula. A general way to view the result obtained with these and other formulae is that it is the average interitem correlation.

The fifth type of reliability is usually termed *interrater* reliability; other names for it include interscorer, interjudge, or interobserver reliability. This kind of reliability is essential if the scores obtained depend on subjective judgments made by scorers (e.g., essay examinations), judges (e.g., evaluations of portfolios or performances), or observers (e.g., using structured or unstructured observation instruments). A number of different techniques can be used to obtain interrater reliability (Goodwin & Goodwin, 1991b). A simple study would involve just two raters, judges, or observers; each one would independently rate or judge each subject's performance or behavior, and reliability would then be calculated as the correlation or percentage of agreement in the two sets of ratings. More sophisticated designs that lead to estimates of interrater reliability also are available; particularly useful (although computationally complex) is generalizability theory (Cronbach, Gleser, Nanda, & Rajaratnam, 1972; Goodwin & Goodwin, 1991b; Shavelson, Webb, & Rowley, 1989).

Closely related to the reliability coefficient is the *standard error of measurement* (SEM). This is particularly helpful in situations where we are interpreting and using an individual's scores to make important decisions about that individual—selection, placement, certification, and so on. Generally, the SEM is inversely related to the reliability coefficient; if the reliability is high, the SEM is low, and vice versa. Since understanding this statistic depends on knowing the meaning of two other statistics, the standard deviation and the reliability coefficient (which is a correlation), we will return briefly to the SEM in the last section of this chapter.

Usability

The primary consideration in choosing or developing a measure is that there be strong evidence supporting the validity of scores derived from the measure, with reliability being second in importance. Also important, but less so, are a number of *usability* characteristics, which include technical quality data, test format, cost, administration features, scoring provisions, measure interpretation, and sources of irrelevant difficulty (Goodwin & Goodwin, 1993).

Technical quality data are the information about validity and reliability. The extant evidence, including details about the groups studied to produce the evidence, should be clearly presented in the measure's manual. The number of published measures that fail to provide these data, or do so incompletely, is amazing. If such information is not in the manual, the wise consumer must question if it exists.

The *test format* must be appropriate for the subjects. This usability concern is very important when measuring young children.

> Obvious features are the suitability of instructions (their clarity, brevity, and vocabulary level), and the number and quality of available practice items, the clarity and visual appeal of the actual items, the organization of the content, and the type of response demanded. (Goodwin & Goodwin, 1993, p. 446)

Elements helpful with young children using paper-and-pencil measures are numerous practice items; well-spaced items; distinct pictures and large, clear print; and, for achievement measures, the ordering of items by difficulty level, with easiest items appearing first.

Although the *cost* of a measure cannot be ignored, one hopes that it is not a major determinant in the selection process. Cost includes the purchase price of the test materials, as well as training and scoring expenses.

Administration features also encompass administrator training requirements, time requirements, and whether the measure was developed for group or individual administration. Individually administered measures, such as many intelligence tests and some personality measures, as well as observation tools, can be costly in terms of training and administration time requirements. Also potentially increasing training costs and time is the "developmentally sensitive" requirement for test administrators (National Association for the Education of Young Children, 1988). Keeping group size small is helpful, but also increases the number of groups and, therefore, the administration time and cost. Finally, testing time is an important consideration, especially with young children. Items on measures should be easily understood, interesting, and enjoyable so that maximum performance can occur (Meisels, 1989a).

Scoring provisions, including the objectivity of the scoring, affect reliability and also constitute a usability concern. Objective scoring schemes are those in which the same score results regardless of who does the marking, assuming that instructions are followed and careless errors do not occur. Clear scoring instructions and prepared keys or masks promote quick and accurate scoring. Some published measures offer computerized scoring; while saving time, using such services will increase the cost. As mentioned in terms of reliability, the accurate and reliable scoring of subjective measures is more difficult. Since many measures used with young children do have a subjective element, taking steps to increase interrater, or interscorer, reliability is critical. The steps include carefully preparing clear scoring guidelines and examples of behaviors or responses that should receive certain scores; training of scorers, including calculation of interscorer reliability; and periodic "spot checks" on reliability during the scoring process.

Another usability consideration is the measure's *interpretation.* Extensive training and time sometimes are needed for skilled interpretation of some measures, such as using children's drawings as an indicator of their feelings or beliefs. Numerical scores from many quantitative measures, such as standard scores, percentiles, and stanines, require some knowledge of basic statistics for proper interpretation. While many measures continue to report age- or grade-equivalent scores, these have serious statistical shortcomings; the problems are of such grave concern to psychometricians and others that several professional organizations have called for a ban on their use (Bennett, 1982).

The final category of usability features is broad in scope. *Sources of irrelevant difficulty* are characteristics of the measure that are unrelated to the behaviors, abilities, and traits that we are trying to measure—but that affect the children's responses and reduce the accuracy of scores obtained. These problems often relate to usability concerns discussed above, such as time constraints, unclear instructions, and less than optimal testing conditions. They can affect individual children differently, such as problems due to anxiety and test-wiseness. Or, they can be systematic in the sense that all children are similarly affected, such as taking a test in a noisy, hot room. If a measure's content unfairly favors members of one ethnic or cultural group over others, or one gender over another, there is *bias* in the measure. Detecting and reducing measure bias is very important, and has been the subject of much work over the past two decades; in fact, studying the type and extent of bias is increasingly being included as a key component of overall validation efforts (Geisinger, 1992). Several strategies for detecting bias exist (Cole & Moss, 1989).

TYPES OF MEASURE

There are several different ways to categorize or sort measures: by the type or nature of the variables measured (cognitive, affective, psychomotor); by purpose (individual assessment, program evaluation, other research); by format (paper-and-pencil, observation, interview, nonreactive); by degree of reactivity; and by degree of standardization. This list of possibilities is not exhaustive; other categorization schemes, or combinations of those given above, could be developed.

Since our focus is on the use of measures in early childhood education research, we chose to present the following description of measures according to a type-of-variable breakdown—cognitive, affective, and psychomotor. At the same time, we acknowledge that this tripartite scheme is somewhat arbitrary, since human behavior does not neatly partition itself into three separate domains. We begin this section with a differentiation of norm-referenced and criterion-referenced measurement, and conclude it with other types of measure, such as quantitatively oriented questionnaires and observation schedules. Note that this chapter focuses on measures that are considered more or less quantitative rather than qualitative. The latter—typically including participant observation, interviews, collection of information via field notes and other ethnographic techniques, and nonreactive measures—will be presented in Chapter 6.

Norm-Referenced and Criterion-Referenced Measurement

For the past three decades, measurement experts have discussed and debated the difference between norm-referenced and criterion-referenced measurement. Glaser (1963) was credited with drawing the distinction between the two approaches and with promoting criterion-referenced measures as an alternative to the more traditional norm-referenced ones.

Norm-referenced measures have norms, sets of scores obtained from one or more samples of respondents. Norms are not standards or goals, although they can be inappropriately used this way; an example is declaring that "all of our third-graders will be at or above the 50th percentile on this test next year." The purpose of a norm-referenced measure is to compare a person's score with the scores of others, that is, the norms. Typical types of score reported for norm-referenced measures include percentiles, standard scores (z-scores, T-scores, etc.), and (unfortunately) age- or grade-equivalent scores. A major concern in the selection and use of a norm-referenced measure is the adequacy of the norms. Important questions include the composition of the norming sample and how recently the data were collected. Many norm-referenced measures are intelligence, aptitude, or achievement tests. They are not restricted to the cognitive domain, however. Affective measures, including personality tests, often include norms to guide the interpretation of individuals' scores. Measures for young children that are norm-referenced include the Wechsler Preschool and Primary Scale of Intelligence-Revised (WPPSI-R) (Wechsler, 1989) and the Peabody Picture Vocabulary Test, Revised (PPVT-R) (Dunn & Dunn, 1981).

By purpose and design, norm-referenced measures are often global in content coverage. Recognizing the inappropriateness of such types of measure in helping educators make day-to-day instructional decisions, Glaser (1963) introduced the notion of *criterion-referenced measures*. These measures

> are used to ascertain an individual's status with respect to some criterion, i.e., performance standard. It is because the individual is compared with some established criterion, rather than other individuals, that these measures are described as criterion-referenced. The meaningfulness of an individual score is not dependent on comparison with other testees. We want to know what the individual can do, not how he stands in comparison with others. (Popham & Husek, 1969, p. 2)

Sometimes termed "domain-referenced" or "objectives-referenced," criterion-referenced measures do not yield comparison scores like percentiles. Rather, typical types of score are percentage of items correct and diagnostic "flags" indicating areas of particular strength or weakness. Many of these types of measure result in pass/fail decisions—for example, those used for certification or licensing purposes. If so, a cutoff score, also called the "standard," must be determined. Many problems are associated with determining the cutoff score fairly and validly, and different approaches to doing so have been suggested. "The standards problem is the biggest liability of the criterion-referenced testing movement. Although some may argue that cutoff scores can be set wisely . . . all agree that they rely on human judgment and thus are fallible" (Shepard, 1979, p. 28). Some of the comprehensive reviews on the topic of standard-setting include Glass (1978), Jaeger (1989), Kane (1994), Livingston and Zieky (1982), and Shepard (1984). Examples of criterion-referenced tests designed for young children include the Learning Accomplishment Profile or LAP (Sanford, 1974); in part, the Denver Developmental Screening Test (DDST) (Frankenburg, Dodds, Fandal, Kazuk, & Cohrs, 1975); and the Early Screening Inventory (ESI) (Meisels & Wiske, 1983).

Cognitive Measures

"Cognition is the intellectual process by which knowledge is gained and utilized; important cognitive processes include perceiving, knowing, learning, thinking, assigning meaning, and intellectualizing" (Goodwin & Goodwin, 1993, p. 452). As compared with the affective and psychomotor domains, there are more measures available for use with young children in the cognitive domain. Further, the psychometric respectability (reliability, validity) of cognitive measures tends to be stronger than that of psychomotor or affective ones.

There are a number of subtypes of measure that can be placed in this category, including intelligence, aptitude, achievement, creativity, readiness, screening, and diagnostic measures. Many of the specific measures are *standardized*, meaning that they have carefully defined content, explicit administration instructions, fixed scoring procedures, and usually norms (Hopkins, Stanley, & Hopkins, 1990).

Intelligence (IQ) tests measure general mental aptitude. Designed to assess a person's mental capacity, they usually include several different types of item and produce a single IQ score and/or subtest scores (e.g., verbal, quantitative, performance). About a century old, IQ tests have had a volatile history and complaints of misuse are common, particularly when they are used with young children (Shepard, 1994). Examples of IQ tests for young children include the WPPSI-R (Wechsler, 1989) and the Stanford Binet Intelligence Scale: Fourth Edition (Binet IV) (Thorndike, Hagen, & Sattler, 1986). Other *aptitude* tests are similar in purpose to intelligence tests, except more narrow in focus. They are intended to predict later performance in specific areas, such as music. Their development/use with young children is rare.

Achievement measures are intended to determine a student's current level of knowledge or skill. While standardized achievement tests are not typically used with young children, some of the well-known ones do have forms available for kindergartners, such as the California Achievement Test (CTB/McGraw-Hill, 1985) and the Iowa Tests of Basic Skills (Hieronymus, Hoover, & Lindquist, 1986). As with intelligence tests, the use of standardized achievement tests with young children has been criticized, particularly for "high-stakes" purposes and if not balanced with information from other sources. Some achievement measures, of course, are teacher-constructed and are designed to match instructional activities and focuses.

During the past half-century, there has been much interest in defining and measuring *creativity*. While early childhood educators have great interest in young children's creative behaviors–inventiveness, original thinking, independence, artistic displays–they tend to question the feasibility or even the possibility of formal measures of this multifaceted and challenging construct. Assessment of creativity in very young children is complex (Torrance & Caropreso, 1991), and the validity and reliability evidence of creativity measures–generally speaking–is not very strong. The best-known battery for kindergarten and primary grade children, the Torrance Tests of Creative Thinking (Torrance, 1974), has been used in many research studies since the late 1950s. The Torrance measures purport to gauge potential for creative thinking, and yield scores for such characteristics as fluency, flexibility, elaboration, and originality. A different approach possibly more developmentally appropriate for preschoolers, Thinking Creatively with Action and Movement (Torrance, 1981), assesses movement and related verbalizations. Other measures seeking to determine creativity in young children include the S.O.I. Learning Abilities Test (Meeker & Meeker, 1979) and Make-A-Tree, a Circus test (Anderson & Bogatz, 1979).

Readiness tests are used to determine if a child is ready for instruction. They combine features of achievement tests, by focusing on current performance and achievement levels rather than on developmental potential, and aptitude tests, by their predictive purpose. Their use has been controversial (Bredekamp & Shepard, 1989; Kagan, 1990; Meisels, 1989b). Criticism has centered on the lack of validity evidence to support the consequences for some children–delayed school entrance, placement in 2-year or at-risk kindergarten programs, and referral for special education programs (Shepard & Graue, 1993). Examples of readiness tests are the Metropolitan Readiness Test (Nurss & McGauvran, 1986), the Boehm Test of Basic Concepts-Revised (Boehm, 1986b) for children in kindergarten through grade two, and a simpler preschool version (Boehm, 1986a) for children ages 3–5 years.

Screening measures are used to identify children who may have a problem or a delay that could affect their learning. A *diagnostic* measure is more specific, may be used as a follow-up to a screening test, and is intended to determine specific strengths and weaknesses. Developmental screening measures often include items in three areas: language and cognition; visual-motor/adaptive; and gross motor/body awareness. Meisels (1989a) noted four screening measures considered, with some reservations, to yield fairly valid scores: the DDST (Frankenburg et al., 1975); the ESI (Meisels & Wiske, 1983); the Minneapolis Preschool Screening Instrument (Lichtenstein, 1982); and the McCarthy Screening Test (McCarthy, 1978). Measures used for diagnostic purposes include the McCarthy Scales of Children's Abilities (MSCA) (McCarthy, 1972) and the Kaufman Assessment Battery for Children (K-ABC) (Kaufman & Kaufman, 1983).

Affective Measures

The affective domain includes the social and emotional aspects of behavior; thus, measures of personality, self-concept or self-esteem, attitudes, and social skills and competencies belong in this category. In addition (or sometimes subsumed under the general rubric of "personality" and "attitude") are measures of such constructs as interests, preferences, beliefs, values, intuitions, and emotions. Affective behaviors and characteristics of young children have long been important to both researchers and early childhood educators (e.g., Zigler, 1970). Martin (1991) noted two recent phenomena that have accelerated pressure for affective assessment of very young children: the "continuing explosion" of information about social and emotional development, and the increase in out-of-home experiences for children and concomitant accountability demands on child care centers and related settings.

Measurement in the affective domain is difficult and challenging, and doubly so with young children. Some time ago, Ball (1971) noted problems of social desirability and susceptibility to response sets (such as answering yes, regardless of the question asked). More recently, Martin (1991) lamented the lack of measurement choices with young children; self-report measures, projective devices, and interviews are especially difficult, so that parent and teacher rating scales become the most common choice. In general, the evidence for the validity of affective measures is weak or nonexistent; often, the only information relates to content validity. The norms for norm-referenced affective measures frequently are problematic as well—based on small, nonrepresentative samples, and out of date.

Personality usually refers to a wide and diverse set of characteristics and traits. Self-report inventories and projective techniques (e.g., asking respondents to interpret pictures or inkblots) are typically used in personality measurement. Interpreting results, especially with projective measures, requires special training. For very young children, personality and socioemotional characteristics are often measured by rating scales completed by parents or teachers. Personality measures designed for young children include Animal Crackers: A Test of Motivation to Achieve (Adkins & Ballif, 1973), the Personality Inventory for Children (Wirt, Lachar, Klinedinst, & Seat, 1984), and the Martin Temperament Assessment Battery (Martin, 1988). Examples of *self-concept* scales are the Behavior Academic Self-Esteem scale (Coopersmith & Gilberts, 1982) and the Preschool Self-Concepts Picture Test (Woolner, 1966/1968).

Attitudes are generally considered to be less stable than personality characteristics. Most attitude measures are paper-and-pencil, self-report rating scales. While easy to administer and score, they are also easily susceptible to faking and social desirability. Many of the attitude measures used in research are developed for a particular study. One commercially available example is Circus, which includes two subtests on reactions to school activities (Anderson & Bogatz, 1979). Measuring *social skills and competencies* in young children has been of more interest than some of the other affective areas during the past 10 years. Examples of available instruments in this area include the Scale of Social Development (Venn, Serwatka, & Anthony, 1987), the Social Skills Rating System (Gresham & Elliott, 1990), and the Vineland Adaptive Behavior Scales (Sparrow, Balla, & Cicchetti, 1985).

Psychomotor Measures

The psychomotor domain has played a major role in early childhood programs, curricula, and research. Categorization of psychomotor behaviors can occur in a number of different ways. Probably the most common approach is to classify behaviors as either fine motor or gross motor; although this system seems quite simplistic to some, it is common to find fine and gross motor sections in developmental screening measures. In light of the prominence of psychomotor tasks and behaviors in practice, there are relatively few commercially available measures. Representative measures include the Bruininks-Oseretsky Test of Motor Proficiency (Bruininks, 1978), the Developmental Test of Visual-Motor Integration (Beery, 1989), and the Southern California Sensory Integration Tests (Ayres, 1980). Some developmental screening measures give substantial attention to motor areas (e.g., the Miller Assessment for Preschoolers, Miller, 1982), and there are many informal psychomotor measures (Wortham, 1995).

Other Types of Measure

While the prior sections list a number of existing standardized measures in the cognitive, affective, and psychomotor domains, often the researcher must develop instruments. At times, questionnaires and observation schedules are developed that cross the three domains and also ask questions quite unrelated to the domains per se.

The nature of questionnaires, interviews, and observation schedules can vary dramatically. In general, but certainly not in every case, questionnaires designed for use in quantitative studies are quite structured, with respondents choosing from a set of possible responses. This closed format permits easier scoring and quantification. In descriptive survey research, questionnaires are in common use, and many books exist on questionnaire design. If quantitative researchers interview subjects, they most likely will do so using a predetermined set of questions, often with the subject selecting a response from several suggested by the interviewer. In general, the interview questions and format are fixed, and vary little from subject to subject. Likewise, quantitative research that makes use of observation schedules more frequently utilizes moderately or highly structured category systems. The instruments are built prior to the start of the study, observers are trained to make category judgments reliably, and usually the observer assumes a psychologically distant, objective stance when using the instrument during the research study.

As will be noted in Chapter 6, qualitative research investigations make extensive use of interviews and observation; on a very rare basis, questionnaires might also be used. In general, however, the qualitative instruments bear only limited resemblance to the interview and observation strategies in quantitative research. Qualitative interviews tend to be much more open-ended with both questions and responses less predictable; in fact, some conceptualize qualitative interviewing more as informal discussion. Similarly, observation in qualitative research can and often does involve much more participation on the part of the observer. Observations are less structured and preplanned; rather, meaning and constructs are inductively derived from field notes and other recordings made. These quite varied approaches to using interviews and observation will be elaborated in Chapters 5 and (especially) 6.

CONSIDERATIONS IN THE SELECTION OF INSTRUMENTS

In this section, we briefly offer some suggestions for researchers who are faced with the problem of selecting instruments for use in quantitative research studies. For "consumers" of published research articles and reports, these points should also help in critiquing the measures used.

1. *Be clear about purpose.* Before embarking on a search for an existing instrument, one must identify and operationally define the dependent variables. The characteristics of the subjects (age, language, and so forth) also should be known, as well as any possible time or setting constraints.
2. *Be systematic in the search.* It is wise to start by pursuing compendia of existing measures. The *Mental Measurements Yearbooks* have been published since the mid-1930s, and are available in the reference sections of most academic libraries. The most recent (Conoley & Impara, 1995) includes descriptions and reviews of over 400 published measures in many different areas. Also helpful is the *Test Critiques* series (Keyser & Sweetland, 1994). The *ETS Test Collection* includes five volumes (e.g., Volume 5, *Attitude Tests,* 1991) of information on thousands of available instruments. Other sources of information about measures for use with young children include Axtman (1992), Aylward (1991), Boehm (1992), and Langhorst (1989). If a search through such sourcebooks does not produce instruments deemed suitable, calling other researchers working in the same or related areas might be helpful. If all else fails, the researcher may have to develop measures specifically for use in a given study. Albeit difficult and time-consuming, such a step can be assisted by adapting parts of existing instruments, and may lead to greater relevance and sensitivity.
3. *Locate and study the psychometric evidence.* Existing information about reliability and validity should be clearly presented in the manual of the measure. Some measures have separate administration and technical manuals; if this is the case, the psychometric data usually are in the technical one. It is critical that there be validity evidence that supports the inferences to be drawn from scores collected in the research study. The "consumer" should look for descriptions of the psychometric integrity of measures used in research studies, within the research article or report.
4. *Consider other usability features.* If one is satisfied with the psychometric evidence, other usability characteristics should be considered. These include norms, relevance, cost, administration and scoring requirements, and so on.

Using this four-step sequence, the researcher can directly address the instrumentation needs for a given investigation. The sequence does not assure that high-quality measures will result. However, it should allow the identification of the best available measures or dictate the adaptation of existing, or the development of new, measures. For the research consumer, the sequence focuses attention on how crucial measures are in judging a study's merit.

DATA-ANALYSIS TECHNIQUES

In this section, an overview of the four scales of measurement and some of the most commonly used descriptive and inferential statistical techniques is provided. Complete coverage of statistics is beyond the scope of this book. For those interested, there are many basic statistics textbooks available (e.g., Gravetter & Wallnau, 1988; Hopkins & Glass, 1986; Spatz, 1993; Sprinthall, 1990). This introduction should serve to acquaint you with statistical methods often used in research articles and reports, so that your understanding of the results will be enhanced.

Scales of Measurement

Some variables are easily expressed in numerical units (e.g., weight), but others do not have intrinsic numerical equivalents (e.g., hair color). Four scales of measurement—nominal, ordinal, interval, and ratio—exist to convert variables to numbers. A *nominal measurement scale* assigns numbers arbitrarily to values of a variable; the size of the number does not equate to relative amounts of the characteristic. Examples of nominal scale variables are gender, nationality, religion, predominant language, and occupation. Persons are first grouped according to their different features of the characteristic. Then all persons displaying the same feature are assigned the same number. For example, if gender were the variable, males might be assigned the number 1, while females are assigned the number 2. The number "names" the category, but does little more than that. For such variables, frequency counts and the calculation of the mode are permitted; that is, they are among the few statistical operations legitimate for nominal scales.

An *ordinal measurement scale* involves rank-ordering objects or persons with respect to amounts of a variable; then numbers are assigned in corresponding order. For example, assume that 15 children in a group are ordered by height, and then are rank-ordered. If rank 1 is assigned to the tallest child and so forth, we also know that the child ranked 15 is the shortest. But only the order on the variable is known rather than the exact differences between each pair of ranks; thus, the ranks cannot be meaningfully added, subtracted, multiplied, or divided. Ordinal numbers, though, express more or less of a characteristic and thus convey more meaning than nominal numbers. Examples of ordinal variables are professorial rank, military rank, and rank in graduating class. Permissible statistics with ordinal numbers include medians.

An *interval measurement scale* is more sophisticated in that differences between the assigned numbers are meaningful. The Fahrenheit and centigrade temperature scales represent interval scales. The difference between 40°F and 20°F is the same—20 degrees—as between 80°F and 60°F. The zero points on these scales are arbitrary, however. For example, 0°F does not indicate the absence of temperature. Thus, if the temperature was 35°F yesterday and 70°F today, we cannot say that it is twice as warm today, but we can say it is 35° warmer. Numbers on an interval scale can be added and subtracted, but not multiplied and divided. Many measures used in research are interval-scale measures. Additional statistics permissible with the interval scale are the mean and the standard deviation.

A *ratio measurement scale* has a true zero point—that is, zero on the scale represents the absence of the property being measured. Examples of this scale include age, weight, distance, length, width, the Kelvin temperature scale, and number of children. With ratio scales, numbers can be meaningfully added, subtracted, multiplied, and divided. A child weighing 80 pounds weighs twice as much as a child weighing 40 pounds—and this ratio has the same psychological meaning as the ratio of two other children weighing 100 and 50 pounds.

Descriptive Statistics

Descriptive statistical techniques are used to summarize characteristics of sample data. (Recall in Chapter 2 that we introduced the concepts of sample and population.) In most research studies (especially quantitative ones), data from one or more sample groups are collected; however, the goal is to generalize from the sample to a larger population. While the calculation of the descriptive statistics is the starting point, researchers then frequently have to use one or more *inferential* statistical techniques in order to generalize to the population. If generalization to a population is not desired or relevant (which is unusual), inferential statistics are unnecessary; the researcher would just calculate and report the appropriate descriptive statistics.

There are many different descriptive statistics. In the following sections, we present some of those most frequently used. They include measures of central tendency (mode, median, and mean), measures of variability (range and standard deviation), and measures of relationship (correlation coefficients). Before considering inferential statistics, we will connect this discussion to the psychometric concepts already covered: validity and reliability coefficients and the standard error of measurement.

In Table 4.1, hypothetical data for 20 4-year-olds are presented. We will refer to these data to illustrate the statistics. Three *variables* are listed in the table: gender (female or male), scores on the Boehm Test of Basic Concepts-Preschool Version, or Boehm-PV (Boehm, 1986a), and scores on a measure of "verbal fluency" or VF. The Boehm-PV yields scores that can range from 0 to 52. This individually administered instrument was designed for children ages 3 to 5, and measures their mastery of relational concepts of size, direction, quantity, and position in space. For the VF measure, we

TABLE 4.1 Hypothetical Data for 20 Four-Year-Old Children

Name	Gender	Boehm PV Scores[a]	Verbal Fluency Scores[b]
Annabelle	F	37	68
Bianca	F	38	75
Charlene	F	38	73
Diana	F	44	79
Ellen	F	45	88
Frances	F	42	62
Greta	F	36	40
Heather	F	34	51
Irene	F	37	50
Jane	F	46	91
Kirk	M	38	20
Luther	M	44	73
Matthew	M	47	90
Nathan	M	42	43
Oliver	M	34	28
Peter	M	38	48
Reggie	M	36	65
Sam	M	43	50
Tim	M	36	35
Victor	M	45	39

[a] Boehm Test of Basic Concepts—Preschool Version (Boehm 1986a); scores can range from 0 to 52.

[b] Verbal Fluency Scores obtained by counting the number of words in a story that each child told.

will assume that the scores were obtained by showing each child a picture and saying "Please tell me a story about this picture." Prior to the actual administration, two "practice" stories were elicited, using different pictures, so that the children would feel comfortable with the procedure. Each child's story was recorded verbatim, and then the number of words it contained was tabulated as the VF score.

Measures of Central Tendency. The measures of central tendency provide summary numbers that inform us about the "typical" score in a set of data. The three most common measures of central tendency are mode, median, and mean. They differ among themselves in the way that "typical" is defined.

The *mode* defines "typical" as the most frequently occurring score. To obtain the mode for a set of data, the number of times each score occurs is first counted. The score that occurs more often than any other score is the mode. If two scores tie for most frequently occurring, we say that the distribution is bimodal. For the data in Table 4.1, note that there is no mode for "gender," since the number of males and females is exactly equal (10). The mode for Boehm-PV is 38; there are four children with scores of 38, and no other score occurs more often than four times. The VF variable is bimodal at 50 and 73, since two children have each of those scores and every other score occurs just once. Compared with the median and the mean, the mode is not a very precise or powerful statistic. Besides the fact that some distributions do not have a mode, it can easily change. For example, if just one of the Boehm-PV scores of 38 were changed to a 36, the mode for those data would also become 36. On the other hand, an advantage of the mode is that it is a permissible statistic for any of the four measurement scales.

The *median* defines "typical" as the 50th percentile. Percentiles are points on the distribution below which a certain percentage of scores fall; in all, it is possible to find the score equivalents for 99 percentile points. To determine the 50th percentile or median, the scores must first be ordered (from high to low, or low to high). Then, the exact midpoint is found. Since there are 20 scores in our hypothetical data set, the exact midpoint is the 10.5th place in the ordered set of data. For Boehm-PV, that place is between two of the scores of 38, so the median is 38. The median VF score is 56.5 (the average of the two middle-most scores, 51 and 62). Note that it is not permissible or meaningful to calculate a median for gender, since it is an example of a nominal measurement scale variable.

The *mean* is the arithmetic average. It is found by summing all scores, and then dividing by the number of subjects. The symbol for a sample mean is $\bar{X}$. For a population mean, the Greek lower-case letter mu, μ, is used as the symbol. Of the three measures of central tendency, the mean is considered the most powerful or precise, because it uses all the information in the data; that is, every score is used in its calculation. The means of the Boehm-PV and VF scores are 40 and 58.4, respectively. Again, we would not report a mean for gender since it is not a variable measured on an interval measurement scale.

For the Boehm-PV as well as the VF scores in Table 4.1, the values of the three measures of central tendency are not the same. That is because both distributions are slightly skewed rather than symmetrical. If a distribution is symmetrical, the mean and median will be equal to each other. And, if the distribution is a special symmetrical one known as the *normal* distribution (the familiar bell-shaped curve), the values of all three of the measures of central tendency—mode, median, and mean—will be equal. In highly skewed distributions, the values of the three statistics can be dramatically different and, if only one is reported, the interpretation can be misleading. Consider, for example, a variable such as "teacher's salary." For a representative sample of teachers in a district or state, yearly salary is positively skewed—there are relatively few teachers with very high salaries, compared with those with moderate-sized ones. In a certain year, the median salary might be $30,000, while the mean is $39,000. In a negatively skewed distribution, the reverse will occur—the mean will have a smaller value than the median. With data that are very skewed, it is best and fairest to report the values of at least two, if not all three, of the measures of central tendency.

Measures of Variability. While the measures of central tendency are important because they summarize the "typical" score, we also desire a statistic that informs us about the amount or dispersion or variability in the data set. As with the measures of central tendency, there is more than one available measure of variability. The two most commonly reported are the range and the standard deviation. As will be seen, another measure of variability that is obtained en route to the standard deviation is the variance. Although the variance is not as informative as the range and standard deviation as a descriptive statistic, the standard deviation cannot be calculated without it. Further, the variance is involved in many inferential statistical techniques.

To illustrate the importance of the concept of variability, consider two distributions of scores obtained with the same measure (such as the Boehm-PV). Assume that both distributions have the same mean. However, one distribution has a large amount of variability around the mean, while in the other the children's scores are clustered tightly around the mean. Practical consequences of this difference are important. Designing activities for the children in the first group will be a greater challenge (in terms of finding suitable concept-related activities for all children) because of the greater heterogeneity in their mastery of the concepts measured by the Boehm-PV. In contrast, determining activities for children in the second group should be easier, as the children are more similar to each other.

The *range* is a relatively crude measure of variability in that it takes very little information into account; in its relative imprecision, it is rather like the mode in comparison to the median and the mean. Also, like the mode, the range is quick and easy to calculate. The *exclusive range* is simply the difference between the highest and lowest scores in the data set: 13 for the Boehm-PV scores and 71 for the VF scores. The *inclusive range* adds 1 to the exclusive range, and is "inclusive" in the sense that both end points are included. Thus, the value of this statistic is 14 points for Boehm-PV and 72 points for VF. One can see quickly in either case that the children's VF scores are much more variable than their Boehm-PV scores.

The *standard deviation* is a much more precise measure of variability, and also is more complex to calculate and to understand. We illustrate its calculation for the Boehm-PV scores in Table 4.2. As will be seen, the steps in the calculation will also produce the variance.

Basically, the standard deviation is the average amount of difference between individuals' scores and the mean. If everyone has the same score (which is equal to the mean), then the value of the standard deviation will be zero—that is, the average amount of difference between scores and the mean is zero. So a larger standard deviation indicates that, on average, there is more dispersion around the mean, while a smaller standard deviation conveys a relatively smaller amount of spread in the scores. The symbol s represents the standard deviation for a sample, while the symbol σ (lowercase Greek letter sigma) represents a population's standard deviation. The variance is the square of the standard deviation, and the symbols s^2 and σ^2 represent the variance of a sample and a population, respectively.

When we examine the calculation of the standard deviation in Table 4.2, the role of the variance becomes apparent. Remember, what we want is the average amount of difference between individuals' scores and the mean. For any one child, that difference can be represented by the equation $X - \bar{X}$, where X is the individual's score and $\bar{X}$ is the mean. For example, Annabelle's difference, also called her *deviation score,* is 37 – 40, or –3; her score is 3 points below the mean of 40. Note that the sum of the column of differences is zero. A Σ is the "summation sign." $\Sigma(X - \bar{X})$ means "Sum the values of $(X - \bar{X})$ for all subjects." Since the mean is the "balancing point" in any distribution, the sum of differences around it always equals zero. Thus, we cannot just average those differences as the average, too, equals zero.

TABLE 4.2 Calculation of Variance and Standard Deviation for Boehm-PV Scores

Name	Boehm-PV Score (X)	Deviation Score $(X-\overline{X})$	Deviation Score Squared $(X-\overline{X})^2$
Annabelle	37	37−40 = −3	9
Bianca	38	38−40 = −2	4
Charlene	38	38−40 = −2	4
Diana	44	44−40 = 4	16
Ellen	45	45−40 = 5	25
Frances	42	42−40 = 2	4
Greta	36	36−40 = −4	16
Heather	34	34−40 = −6	36
Irene	37	37−40 = −3	9
Jane	46	46−40 = 6	36
Kirk	38	38−40 = −2	4
Luther	44	44−40 = 4	16
Matthew	47	47−40 = 7	49
Nathan	42	42−40 = 2	4
Oliver	34	34−40 = −6	36
Peter	38	38−40 = −2	4
Reggie	36	36−40 = −4	16
Sam	43	43−40 = 3	9
Tim	36	36−40 = −4	16
Victor	45	45−40 = 5	25
		$\Sigma(X-\overline{X})=0$	$\Sigma(X-\overline{X})^2=338$

Equations and calculations:

$$s^2=\frac{\Sigma(X-\overline{X})^2}{n-1}=\frac{338}{19}=17.79 \qquad s=\sqrt{s^2}=\sqrt{17.79}=4.22$$

The *variance* helps us overcome this problem. To calculate it, we first square each person's deviation score, that is, $(X - \bar{X})^2$. Next, the squared deviations are summed, which equals 338 in our example. To obtain the average, we divide by n - 1. (Although we ordinarily divide by n to arrive at an average, we need n - 1 in this case; the reasons are complicated, and relate to the role of the variance in inferential statistics.) As can be seen in Table 4.2, the value of s^2 for the Boehm-PV data is 17.79. As a descriptive statistic, the variance is not particularly useful since it indicates the average amount of squared dispersion from the mean. By taking the square root of it, however, we obtain a standard deviation of 4.22 for the Boehm-PV data. For the VF scores, the standard deviation is 21.04 points (refer to Table 4.1). On average, then, the children's scores vary around the Boehm-PV mean of 40 by about 4 points, while the average amount of difference from the VF mean of 58.4 is much larger, about 21 points.

In the special case of the normal distribution, the meaning of our definition of the standard deviation ("the average amount of difference from the mean") is particularly apparent. The normal distribution has several known properties. These include the percentages of scores falling in intervals measured in standard deviation units away from the mean. Thirty-four percent of the scores are in the interval that extends from the mean to one standard deviation above the mean. Since the normal distribution is symmetrical, the same percentage of scores—34%—is in the interval that extends from the mean to one standard deviation below the mean. Together, then, about two-thirds of all scores, the middle 68%, surround the mean. This is where the "typical" or "average" person's score is found.

Measures of Relationship There are a number of different statistics available to describe the type and extent of the *relationship* between two variables. Since many quantitative research questions concern relationships among variables, these statistics are used frequently. They are needed, too, in measurement studies, particularly for the estimation of validity and reliability. In this section, we will discuss one frequently used measure of relationship, the Pearson product-moment correlation, and refer to it as simply the "correlation." Basic statistics textbooks cover this statistic in more detail, as well as other measures of relationship.

The Pearson correlation indicates the strength and direction of the relationship between two interval- or ratio-level variables. It can range in size from 0, which indicates that there is no systematic relationship between the two variables, to either +1.00 (a perfect positive relationship) or –1.00 (a perfect negative relationship). While we do not show the calculation of the correlation (it can be found in most basic statistics textbooks), we present a picture of the relationship between the Boehm-PV and VF scores for our 20 hypothetical children. This is called a *scattergram* or *scatterplot*, and appears in Figure 4.1. As can be seen, there is a positive relationship between the two variables. There is a tendency for children with the higher Boehm-PV scores to have the higher VF scores, and children with lower scores on one measure to have lower scores on the other. The relationship is far from perfect, however; a child like Victor, with a relatively high Boehm-PV score (45) but relatively low VF score (39), illustrates a deviation from the tendency for the higher scores on one variable to be associated with the higher scores on the other variable. Cases like Victor's result in a less-than-perfect correlation. The value of the correlation, shown in the figure, is moderate: .57.

The symbol r or r_{xy} represents a sample correlation (while the Greek lower-case letter rho, ρ or ρ_{xy} represents a population correlation). The Pearson correlation is a measure of the size of the *linear* relationship

FIGURE 4.1 Scattergram and Correlation Between Boehm-PV Scores and Verbal Fluency Scores for 20 Four-Year-Old Children

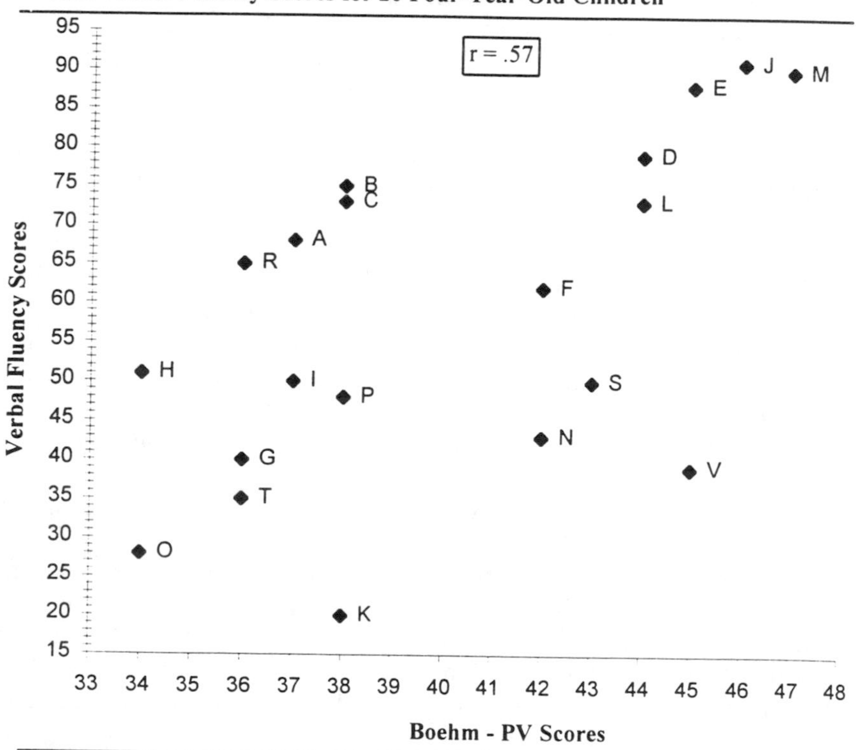

between the two variables. It is possible for there to be meaningful relationships among variables that are nonlinear or curvilinear; a scattergram usually helps spot such a relationship, and then other statistical techniques are employed to describe it.

There are other characteristics of the correlation that are helpful to know about when interpreting results. One is that this statistic informs us about the noncausal relationship between two variables; it is not appropriate to interpret correlations as causation (see the discussion in Chapter 3 about correlational vs. experimental research). Another consideration involves the amount of variability in both variables, X and Y. The correlation depends on variability. In the extreme case of no variability in scores on a variable (i.e., everyone has the same score and the standard deviation is zero), the correlation between it and any other variable will be zero. Finally, the square of the correlation coefficient (r^2) is called the *coefficient of determination* and is a useful statistic, especially in prediction studies. It indicates the proportion of variability in one variable (usually Y) that can be predicted from the other variable (X). In our example, the value of r^2 is .32. If we were to develop a prediction equation (also called a "regression" equation) with these results, for the prediction of VF from Boehm PV (or Boehm-PV from VF) for a future group of children, we would be able to account for only about 32% of the variability in the predicted variable. Another way to think about this is that, if we made predictions for a large group of children in the future, our predictions would be accurate for only about 32% of the children.

There are many extensions of the simple bivariate correlation. For example, when more than one predictor variable is used to predict an outcome or dependent variable, a statistical technique known as *multiple regression* is used. Statistics textbooks designed for intermediate-level statistics students (e.g., Glass & Hopkins, 1984; Hair et al., 1992; Lomax, 1992) present coverage of these and other multivariate statistical techniques.

Two final topics involving correlation deserve mention—psychometric studies and the standard error of measurement. As we mentioned earlier in this chapter, the correlation is frequently calculated in studies of the validity and reliability of measures. Most estimations of criterion-related validity (concurrent or predictive) are given as the correlation between the measure and one or more "external criterion" measures. Factor analysis (and related techniques), which can reveal the internal structure of a measure and is sometimes employed as part of the study of the construct validity, is based on the correlation. Nearly all estimations of reliability are correlations. The symbol used for reliability is r_{xx}. Note the subscript; the symbol means "the correlation of the measure (X) with itself." Of course, exactly what data are correlated will differ, depending on the type of reliability being estimated. A stability reliability coefficient, for example, is produced by correlating two sets of scores, obtained from the same persons at two different times. If the reliability estimate is one of internal consistency, the calculation of r_{xx} involves an averaging of all of the inter-item correlations.

We introduced the standard error of measurement (SEM) concept earlier, and noted its utility when interpreting an individual's score on a measure. Its calculation uses the standard deviation and the reliability coefficient:

$$\text{SEM} = s\sqrt{1 - r_{xx}}$$

Many uses of the SEM involve setting an interval around a person's obtained score. A 68% confidence interval is obtained by finding the interval that extends from one SEM below the person's score to one SEM above it; a rough interpretation of this interval is that there is a 68% chance that the person's "true score" lies in the interval. Even more common is the determination of a 95% confidence interval. This is approximately equal to the interval found by adding and subtracting two SEMs from the person's obtained score. Thus, we would say that there is about a 95% chance that the person's "true score" lies in the interval. (For more about use of the SEM, see Crocker & Algina, 1986, or Hopkins et al., 1990.)

Inferential Statistics

As we mentioned in the introduction of this data analysis section, most quantitative research studies rely on both descriptive and inferential statistical techniques. The inferential statistics are needed in order to generalize from the sample to a population. There are many different inferential statistical techniques. An overview of inferential statistics is presented here, with descriptions of a few common techniques.

Null and Alternative Hypotheses. Inferential statistics result in an acceptance or rejection of the "null hypothesis," symbolized by H_0. For every inferential statistical test, there is an appropriate way to state H_0. If we have calculated a correlation from sample data, and we wish to generalize to a population, the null hypothesis is:

$$H_0\colon \rho = 0$$

In words, this says, "The population correlation is zero." This example illustrates well why H_0 is called the "null" hypothesis; it is a statement of no relationship between the variables in the population. Many inferential statistical techniques involve means. A simple case is a two-group experiment, in which the mean of one group is compared to that of the other group. The null hypothesis for this significance test is:

$$H_0: \mu_1 = \mu_2$$

In words, this H_0 says, "In the population, there is no difference between the two means." Again, this example illustrates well why H_0 is called the null hypothesis.

When the inferential technique results in the researcher's rejecting H_0, we say that the findings are *statistically significant*. In the population, there most likely is a non-zero correlation, or a difference in means. If H_0 is rejected, the alternative hypothesis is accepted—that is, is considered plausible. The symbol for the alternative hypothesis is H_1. Alternative hypotheses can be directional or nondirectional. If the researcher believes that a population correlation is positive, the appropriate alternative hypothesis is:

$$H_1: \rho > 0$$

If the researcher believes that the population correlation is negative, the alternative hypothesis is:

$$H_1: \rho < 0$$

If the researcher has no presupposition about the direction of the relationship, the alternative hypothesis is nondirectional:

$$H_1: \rho \neq 0$$

In the two-group study in which means are compared, the possible directional alternative hypotheses are:

$$H_1: \mu_1 > \mu_2 \quad \text{or} \quad H_1: \mu_2 > \mu_1$$

A nondirectional alternative hypothesis is:

$$H_1: \mu_1 \neq \mu_2$$

Level of Significance. Another integral concept in inferential statistics is the *level of significance*, often referred to as "alpha" because of its symbol (α). This is the probability of making a *Type I error*, which is rejecting

H_0 when it is really true. The researcher, by setting alpha, has direct control over this probability. Typical values for it are .01, .05, and .10. If the researcher sets alpha at .05 (which is the most common level), it means that he or she is willing to take a 5% chance of making a Type I error. Of course, there also is the possibility of a *Type II error*—accepting a false H_0. While the probability of Type II error can be determined, it is not under the direct control of the researcher; it relies on a number of factors and its estimation can be complex.

Once the steps in the inferential statistical technique are finished, H_0 is accepted (deemed most likely true) or rejected (deemed most likely false). The researcher usually hopes that H_0 will be rejected, since that will support the research hypothesis—that there is some relationship between the variables, or some difference in means for the different treatment groups. If H_0 is rejected, the "p-value" of the result will be reported (and may be reported when H_0 is not rejected, too). The *p*-value is "alpha after-the-fact," or the probability of a Type I error once all calculations have been completed and a decision has been made to reject H_0, or not. As an example, consider the correlation we obtained between Boehm-PV and VF scores, .57. We ran a test of the null hypothesis,

$$H_0: \rho = 0$$

against the alternative hypothesis,

$$H_1: \rho \neq 0$$

The results of the test showed a *p*-value of .009. Assuming that alpha had been set at .05, we reject H_0 since .009 is smaller than .05. We conclude that there most likely is a non-zero relationship between the two variables in the population to which we are generalizing. There is only a .9% chance that this conclusion is incorrect—and that there really is no relationship between the two variables in the population.

The t-test and Analysis of Variance. To explore statistical significance tests a bit further, we discuss two commonly used tests on sample means. The independent-groups *t*-test is used to compare two sample means, obtained from two different groups of persons. (A dependent-groups *t*-test is used if the two means came from the same group or persons, or groups related to each other. Examples of designs in which this test is appropriate are a pretest-posttest study involving just one group of persons, and a study comparing the means of mothers and their daughters.) Analysis of variance (ANOVA) is a more general technique, used to compare means of two or more groups.

The calculations required in the *t*-test produce a result known as the obtained *t*-statistic. This value is the difference between the two sample means, divided by a measure of variability. By referencing the appropriate sampling distribution of the *t*-statistic, the *p*-value of the obtained *t*-statistic is determined. This is compared to alpha; as in the example we gave above with the test of the significance of the correlation, if the *p*-value equals or is less than alpha, we reject H_0. We conclude that the difference we found between the two sample means probably did not occur by chance.

We ran two *t*-tests on the data in Table 4.1. In each, the independent (grouping) variable was gender. The dependent variables were Boehm-PV scores and VF scores. Alpha was set at .05 for both tests. The test on Boehm-PV scores compared the girls' mean (39.7) with the boys' mean (40.3). Given how similar these means are to each other, it is not surprising that the *t*-test did not yield a statistically significant result. The value of the obtained *t*-statistic was –.31, which has a *p*-value of .76; if we rejected H_0, we would be taking a 76% chance of a Type I error. The test on VF scores compared means that appeared to differ substantially: 67.7 for girls, and 49.1 for boys. The obtained *t*-statistic was 2.16, which has a *p*-value of .05 and thus was statistically significant. H_0 was rejected as it seemed likely that the girls did exhibit higher VF scores than boys.

A simple one-way ANOVA is an extension of the independent-groups *t*-test, allowing for the comparison of means obtained from two or more groups. Since many quantitative studies involve more than two groups, ANOVA is frequently employed. The underlying assumptions are the same as for the *t*-test, although the calculations differ. Instead of an obtained *t*-statistic, ANOVA yields an *F-statistic*. Like the *t*-test, this will have a *p*-value that is compared to alpha; if the *p*-value of the F-statistic equals or is less than alpha, the H_0 (stating that there are no differences among the means in the population) is rejected.

There are many extensions of ANOVA, and also there are many other inferential statistical techniques available to quantitative researchers. For example, it is not uncommon for more than one independent variable to be built into the design; if so, factorial ANOVA might be used to analyze mean differences for each independent variable (called "factors") and to detect interactions among the factors.

Cautions About Inferential Statistical Tests. There are many good reasons to conduct inferential statistical tests, and the results are informative. However, it is important to note that *statistical* significance is not the same as *practical* significance. Inferential tests are based on probability theory, and whether statistical significance emerges depends on a number of factors: the size of the descriptive statistic(s), the size of the sample, the amount of variability within groups (for tests on means), alpha, and the amount of measurement error. Some well designed and conducted quantitative research studies fail to produce statistically significant results due primarily to a very small sample; conversely, some studies with large samples can yield statistically significant results, but the practical significance of the findings is small and therefore questionable. The calculation and reporting of the "effect size" (Glass, McGaw, & Smith, 1981), which is not directly influenced by sample size, can be helpful—especially in studies that include comparisons of means. In correlational studies, reporting the actual size of r (and r^2), in addition to the results of the statistical tests, is necessary. "Wise consumers" of statistical information put the inferential test results in perspective with details about the design, the measures and their psychometric properties, and the descriptive statistics.

SUMMARY

Measurement is a process integral to research that involves testing, observation, interviewing, and other methods, and results in the assignment of numbers or ratings to the persons or things measured. To have high psychometric quality, measures must be reliable and valid. Reliability generally refers to the consistency of a measure, and is a necessary but not sufficient condition for validity. Validity concerns the appropriateness and meaningfulness of inferences made on the basis of scores from the measure. Usability features of a measure (e.g., cost, ease of administering) are important, but less crucial. Measures can be classified by how their resultant scores are referenced—either to norms (involving comparisons with others) or to a criterion such as a preset standard or level of performance. Classification can also be by domain assessed: cognitive (e.g., intelligence, achievement, or readiness); affective (e.g., personality, attitudes); or psychomotor. Among common types of measure used in quantitative research are standardized tests, objective measures developed specifically for a study, and structured questionnaires and interviews.

Data analysis in quantitative research must be sensitive to whether the number scale in use is nominal, ordinal, interval, or ratio. Descriptive statistics are utilized to describe a set of data, by calculating and displaying measures of central tendency (e.g., mode, median, mean), variability (e.g., range, standard deviation, variance), and relationship (e.g., correlation coefficient). Inferential statistics permit estimating population parameters based on sample statistics, and testing hypotheses at set probability levels. Two common inferential procedures for comparing group means are the *t*-test and the analysis of variance or ANOVA. In Part III, emphasis shifts from quantitative to qualitative research with methods and early childhood education examples of the latter presented in Chapter 5.

PART III

QUALITATIVE RESEARCH

Chapter 5

Types of Qualitative Research

Here, we turn our attention to qualitative research. In Part II, we examined types of quantitative research as well as measurement and analysis with quantitative data. Now, we address analogous topics in terms of qualitative research.

In Chapter 5, two principal types of qualitative research are considered. Ethnography is presented in some detail, especially in terms of the themes or principles that underlie that qualitative orientation, and the steps typically taken when doing such research. Then analytic research is described, especially historical, with some limited mention of the related areas of legal and policy studies. Examples of these types of research, drawn from early childhood education, also are described in this chapter.

In Chapter 6, data in qualitative research are presented in terms of types and their collection and analysis. Elements to be examined in critiquing qualitative research are discussed in Chapter 6 (rather than in Chapter 5, at the conclusion of the "opening" chapter on such research, as was the pattern for quantitative research) for two reasons. First, analysis begins quite early in, and as an integral part of, the qualitative research process; second, the overall quality of such research is heavily dependent on the analyses used.

ETHNOGRAPHIC RESEARCH

Other candidate terms for *ethnographic research* include *naturalistic, interpretive, case study, participant observation,* and *phenomenological*. While there are some differences among these terms, they have a great deal in common (Erickson, 1986). Although we have opted to look in detail at ethnographic research, the choice of terms should not mask the fact that there are a number of closely related qualitative research methods. Further, our painting of the ethnographic research picture will in general suffice to illustrate this entire category of research, especially in its numerous variations from quantitative research methods. Space limitations preclude us from describing the case study method in detail. At the same time, however, it should be noted that most of the themes, features, and issues subsequently presented in this chapter on ethnographic research also apply to case studies. The unique characteristic of case studies is that a single case or event is researched. Most other considerations in case study research match well those we present for ethnographic research. For a more comprehensive discussion of the case study method, see McMillan and Schumacher (1993).

Some special mention should be made of *interpretive research*, as comprehensively described and endorsed by Walsh, Tobin, and Graue (1993), because of its potential "match" with early childhood education. They followed Erickson's (1986) lead and defined interpretive research as inclusive, not anti-quantitative in its connotations, and particularly centered on elucidating human meaning in social life. They were concerned that elements of the ordinary conduct of life had not been examined fully by researchers, especially aspects as perceived by young children, their teachers, and their care providers. For them, qualitative interpretive research via case studies and ethnographies offered promise for meeting this shortcoming by its focus on how participants construct meaning out of actions in their daily lives. They noted two other advantages for interpretive research. First, it was seen as potentially powerful in giving meaning to research findings. Second, they opined that interpretive research was readily interpretable by practitioners, a characteristic often absent in much quantitative research. While we endorse the line of argument advanced by Walsh, Tobin, and Graue, we have opted to use ethnography as the principal form of qualitative research examined in this chapter, given its status and frequent use in qualitative undertakings.

Both quantitative research and qualitative research strive to generate knowledge. Yet recall from Table 2.1 that quantitative and qualitative research vary substantively on a number of features. For example, we noted there that quantitative approaches draw ideas and nurturance primarily from academic disciplines such as psychology and economics, while qualitative schemes owe more to linkages with history and, especially, anthropology. Such distinctions are important in conceptualizing how the approaches differ. Possibly the central distinction is the differing views of what constitutes reality. Quantitative methods assume that a single, objective reality exists. Ascertaining that reality is accomplished by using linear, detached, structured, and generally impersonal means to obtain data from subjects. On the other hand, qualitative orientations hold that multiple realities exist. Determining those realities and their associated meanings requires flexible and evolving strategies, with a key part being personal and focused attention on the unguarded views of participants themselves.

"Ethnography is the art and science of describing a group or culture" (Fetterman, 1989, p. 11). This definition also applies to specific subgroups, and to all the elements making up a given group's environment. Ethnography has been viewed as interactive research (McMillan & Schumacher, 1993), that is, it includes considerable interaction between the subjects and the researcher. Ethnography can be conceptualized as descriptive anthropology, in which the researcher has an in-depth involvement in a culture for the purpose of fully portraying it; certainly most of its methods emanate from anthropology. The use of ethnographic research in education is relatively recent—about the past three decades. While quantitative research continues to be far more common in education even today, the attention given to ethnography and similar research forms has steadily increased.

Central Themes or Features

A number of themes and conceptual features that collectively constitute ethnographic research are considered in this section. At times overlapping, they have been drawn particularly from the work of Patton (1990), with some amplification by Creswell (1994), McMillan (1996), and Sherman and Webb (1988). Taken together, they both help define ethnography and differentiate it from the various methods of quantitative research examined in Chapter 3.

- *Holistic perspective*. The culture, group, phenomenon, or situation under study is considered in its entirety. While this may result in examining a complex nonlinear network of features, ideas, and even persons, the capability of ethnography to encompass the whole system is seen as a strength. The matter being researched is greater than the sum of its parts, and its full significance emerges by maintaining a broad encompassing perspective.
- *Naturalistic orientation*. Whatever is being researched is studied in its "natural" state. Fieldwork occurs whereby the researcher studies the culture or phenomenon as it exists and evolves; the researcher, in a sense, "takes up residence" on site in order to accomplish a fully elaborate study. This real-world orientation also includes an openness to whatever emerges from the inquiry. An excellent resource in terms of procedures and ideas related to "real-world" research, whether in ethnographic or other contexts, is Robson (1993). As will be seen, the degree to which the researcher observes *and* participates in the process can become a matter impacting this desired naturalism.
- *Nonintervention, nonmanipulation*. This distinctive feature of ethnographic research sets it well apart from experimental research meth-

ods, and stands as a corollary to the naturalistic orientation just discussed. Whatever is under study should speak for itself. The noninterventionist tone should extend to the methods used by the ethnographer—that is, the methods should not alter that which is being researched.

- *Context sensitivity*. Ethnography, as it seeks a holistic perspective, is sensitive to the contextual features of the phenomenon being studied. Considerable attention is given to analyzing social settings. Context is crucial for fully understanding behavior and social events. One concern about much quantitative research is its "context-stripping," undermining the meaning of any data obtained (Mischler, 1979). For us, this is a particularly vivid term, as it links in our minds to the practice of "strip-mining," which in turn conjures up images of landscapes left nearly unrecognizable after the mining. Analogously, context-stripping could render the phenomenon or culture studied devoid of crucial identifying features.
- *Importance of participants' perspectives*. This characteristic emphasizes the perspectives of the participants in understanding a culture, subculture, or phenomenon. Said differently, the ethnographic researcher seeks out and considers in depth the points of view of insiders, those actually experiencing the culture or phenomenon. Prior to starting fieldwork, ethnographers avoid assuming how participants behave, believe, and perceive; rather, these elements—both external behavior and statements and internal attitudes and values—become important data to observe, consider, and understand. Sometimes referred to as an *emic perspective*, this is a central feature of most ethnographic research for it highlights the acceptance of multiple realities and a phenomenological orientation overall. Fetterman (1989) noted that while ethnographers invariably seek an emic perspective, they need to use an *etic perspective* (an external, social scientific view of reality) in order to fully analyze their data and understand the phenomenon being studied.
- *Process and change orientation*. The dynamics of change are matters of great interest to ethnographers. Change is expected and important to chronicle, especially as it accompanies new or altered cultural or personal phenomenon. While outcomes are important here as they are in quantitative research, so too are the processes that led up to the outcomes. In the case of a program being studied, this emphasis on process could take the form of documenting the developmental changes made over time in the program, and the reasons for them. Patton (1990) phrased it well:

> Naturalistic inquiry assumes an ever-changing world. This perspective is nicely captured by the observation in the ancient Chinese proverb that one never steps into the same river twice. Change is a natural, expected, and inevitable part of the human experience. Rather than trying to control, limit, or direct change, naturalistic inquiry expects change, anticipates the likelihood of the unanticipated, and is prepared to go with the flow of change. (p. 53)

- *Direct collection of data.* In ethnographic research, emphasis is placed on direct and personal means of collecting data. Thus, the researcher acquires considerable data from personal observation during fieldwork and from the copious notes then recorded. Or, the researcher will interview directly and in depth a number of participants to generate relevant data. There are few "go-betweens" in ethnographic research, and "subcontracting out" portions of the research process is rare. Data collection is a direct and very personal process.
- *Rich, descriptive data.* Emphasis is placed on full and elaborate descriptions of the culture or phenomenon being researched. Nothing is prejudged to be trivial, mundane, or unimportant. Data are most frequently recorded in narrative, rather than numerical, form. Embellished, in-depth recording is the rule. Direct quotations are used to capture the substance and nuances of participants' perspectives and beliefs; diagrams of rooms or settings are sketched in detail. A full portrayal and record are sought through rich, elaborated data collection.
- *Researcher as the primary instrument.* While possibly overstated, an important feature of ethnographic research is that most data are collected by the researcher. This highly personal role extends to making frequent decisions about what to record, how, when, and in what depth. Once recorded, data are put through the analytic process, possibly several times over, again with the researcher serving as the prime filter and interpreter. The researcher's own experiences and insights in the field also constitute important data sources. This pivotal and continuing role for the ethnographer has resulted in many envisioning the researcher as *the* instrument in a qualitative study. Regardless of whether claiming such a vaulted position is warranted or wise, clearly the ethnographer's role in research instrumentation is pervasive, continuing, and expansive.
- *Personal contact with empathic neutrality.* Ethnographers relish personal contact with those whom they study. Fieldwork—being out in the field directly observing, interviewing, and interacting with the study's participants—is the sine qua non of ethnographic research; that is, such direct human contact is absolutely essential. At the same

time, the researcher must display empathic neutrality (Patton, 1990), entering the field with no theory to prove and no predetermined outcomes to verify. Rather, the ethnographer is committed to understanding the phenomenon as it emerges, and to capturing its complexities by balanced reporting of all the data encountered. A thin and taut tightrope must be walked at times, that is, seeking extensive personal contact and yet simultaneously adopting an empathic yet neutral position among varying viewpoints and constituencies.

- *Design flexibility*. This theme highlights the emergent, evolving nature of an ethnographic study. As will become quite obvious in the following section describing the basic steps in ethnographic research design, flexibility is a hallmark of such activity. Prior to the commencement of fieldwork, it would be inappropriate for the researcher to list undergirding theory, hypotheses to be tested, or detailed procedures to be followed on a precise timetable. Rather, the specifics of the design take shape as the fieldwork in fact unfolds. It is also true that the ethnographer is quite ready to make unsignaled, abrupt turns and to change direction to pursue emergent leads as she or he proceeds along the road of investigation. This flexibility in design requires great tolerance for both uncertainty and ambiguity on the researcher's part.
- *Inductive analysis*. The general research process followed by the ethnographer, including analysis, is inductive. This means that the researcher avoids fixed preconceptions, and rather starts with data details from fieldwork observations and interviews, and assembles possible concepts, meanings, and relationships. Eventually, generalizable understandings or even elements of grounded theory (that is, theory "grounded" in actual observations—theory constructed from the ground up) might emerge. Analysis in quantitative research typically commences once all the data have been collected, toward the end of a generally deductive investigation. In ethnography and related qualitative approaches, on the other hand, analysis begins soon after the first data are recorded. The process then is continuous, with the ethnographer active in attempting to induce important elements and understandings from the data. In a very real sense, the inductive process is internal to the researcher with new data elements entering into the "data mix" and analysis process, on some level, virtually as they are received.
- *Discovery of meaning and understanding*. Consistent with the inductive orientation that pervades qualitative research efforts and the reluctance to "rush to judgment," discovery of relationships or matters that lead to new insights constitutes an important feature of ethnog-

raphy. Simultaneously, the discoveries frequently come as a natural by-product of the ethnographer's quest for understanding and meaning of the culture or phenomenon. Beginning without firm preconceptions now becomes a "blessing" for the ethnographer, as this condition better allows being open-minded and truly surprised by the messages emanating from the inductive analysis of the data.
- *Prolonged period of activity in the field.* A final ethnographic theme of note concerns the length of time over which the study is conducted. Some years ago, Rist (1980) sarcastically identified "blitzkrieg ethnography."

> Whereas the classical approach was one of spending considerable time in the field learning the nuances and "deep meanings" of the system, we now find "hit and run" forays into the field being termed "ethnography." The view is that rapport, familiarity, trust, and insight can all be manufactured instantaneously. It was in all seriousness that an educational researcher recently told me he had perfected a new form of ethnography: "blitzkrieg ethnography." That there was a fundamental contradiction between the two terms was lost on him. Not accepting the domain and underlying assumptions that have heretofore guided the method has essentially left him free to improvise and relabel a community survey as a new form of ethnography. (p. 9)

This theme is emphasized to counter the blitzkrieg mentality. True to their anthropological roots, serious ethnographers are adamant that a long period of time is required to conduct a research study properly. The in-depth understandings of a culture, site, or phenomenon that are sought by the ethnographer simply cannot be generated quickly. Wolcott (1988) noted the ethnographic tradition that a minimum of 12 months would often be required to observe a full cycle of activity.

Basic Steps in the Research Design

Qualitative research, including ethnography, is basically inductive. Therefore, the steps involved in designing ethnographic research can be specified to a certain degree. At the same time, the plans must be thought of as emergent or tentative because much evolution and greater specification occurs over the course of actually conducting the study. Said differently, the early plans serve as starting points rather than as fixed goals to be achieved.

In Chapter 2, we listed eight steps involved in research, including qualitative methods such as ethnography. Here we expand on these steps, particularly the first and third, which focus on problem selection and preliminary design. Steps 4 to 8, involving data collection, analysis, and interpretation, as well as reporting and reproducing results, are considered in less detail here as they are integral to Chapter 6.

1. ***Conceptualizing a topic to research.*** In *Argonauts of the Western Pacific* (1922), the famed anthropologist Bronislaw Malinowski described the culture of the natives on the Trobriand Islands off the eastern end of New Guinea; his classic observations were based on several years of life with the natives. In his book, the first of several, he also commented on certain methodological issues for ethnographers. Germane to this first step, he warned against the researcher's entering the field with preconceived ideas. At the same time, he considered it crucial for the ethnographer to have a sense of "foreshadowed problems," a sketchy notion of a topic or related topics along with some substantive related background information and ideas.

Creswell (1994) provided a number of specifications for the qualitative researcher's problem statement. He advised defining the central idea or concept being explored in the study, using words such as *intent, purpose,* and *objective* to clearly highlight it. Further, he suggested the use of words that would convey the emergent and inductive nature of the design, like *develop, understand, describe,* and *discover.* Simultaneously, he called for the elimination of words in the problem statement that conveyed a directional orientation to the effort; for example, including words such as *comparison* or *relationship* was deemed unwise as they typically were used in quantitative research undertakings such as correlational studies and experiments. Rather, Creswell considered it important to use words clearly oriented toward the qualitative methods—words such as *ethnographic, phenomenological,* and *grounded theory.*

Several practical suggestions related to determining a research topic area were offered by Bogdan and Biklen (1992). They opined that the researcher should select a topic about which she or he had feelings that involved at least "a touch of passion" (p. 60); that is, the topic should hold considerable interest for the ethnographer. Further, the general topic conceptualized should be reasonable in size, complexity, and manageability, with "reasonableness" in part determined in light of the ethnographer's prior experience as a researcher. They also believed that the ethnographer should keep the significance of the potential problem area in mind.

Thus, in all, the researcher should identify a working topic or problem area as the first step in conducting an ethnographic study. The topic selected should be stated in general terms that both identify the study as clearly qualitative and promise greater specificity via an emergent process over time. Also, the topic should hold considerable interest for the researcher and be feasible in terms of overall size and ethnographer competence.

2. ***Reviewing the extant literature on the topic.*** This step is problematic in the sense of how much literature review is appropriate before the ethnographer enters the field. The general impression one gets after reading the work of a large number of ethnographers is that some review is warranted, for it allows the researcher to get better oriented and prepared. At the same time, an exhaustive review rarely occurs early on for fear that the ethnographer's analysis of it would become a set of blinders that unduly restrict and channel subsequent insights and discoveries during fieldwork.

Thus, the wise ethnographer starts a literature review at this point in time, but is careful to maintain a delicate balance between the work that has been done and the ideas that will soon emerge. Fetterman (1989) stated it well:

> Ethnographers are noted for their ability to keep an open mind about the group or culture they are studying. However, this quality does not imply any lack of rigor. The ethnographer enters the field with an open mind, not an empty head. Before asking the first question in the field, the ethnographer begins with a problem, a theory or model, a research design, specific data collection techniques, tools for analysis, and a specific writing style. (p. 11)

Since ethnographers strategically hope that discoveries will result from their research, they are to be reminded of Bruner's (1961) admonition that discovery favors the prepared mind.

3. ***Designing the procedures of the study.*** In this third step, the planned study's procedures begin to take shape in greater detail. Again, though, given ethnographers' commitment to the attractiveness of the unknown that is to follow, it is best to consider the details specified as a working or emergent design. Bogdan and Biklen (1992) considered the design phase important for establishing preferences, but not single-mindedness. They used the analogy of a funnel for the design, with the wide end utilized early in the study and with greater design focus and specificity (the narrow end of the funnel) emerging out of actual work in the field.

The researcher early on must consider the sampling plan that will be used and, most often simultaneously, the site or sites. In general, adding more sites and subjects increases the complexity of the research undertaking. From Chapter 2, recall that qualitative researchers usually implement a purposeful sampling plan, that is, they select persons or a site that will yield important data on the topic of interest. They likely will avoid probabilistic sampling procedures, like random selection, because representativeness often is not one of their primary objectives. There are a large number of variations of purposive sampling strategies, nicely outlined by Patton (1990). Rather than detail all 16 strategies, we have selected several examples to illustrate their general nature. Two mentioned by Patton were identified in Chapter 2, namely *convenience sampling* and *snowball or chain sampling*. Selecting readily available subjects via a convenience strategy is efficient, saving time and money, but it also lacks credibility and may often result in low-yield or information-poor cases. The snowball or chain technique, whereby the present subjects nominate additional persons for the researcher to use as subjects, can lead to the inclusion of a number of viable subjects, although they may be more like the nominator than different.

Additional strategies of the 16 presented by Patton (1990) varied in their purpose. In *extreme or deviant case sampling*, the ethnographer selects subjects representing great variability on a dimension of interest. Thus, a few very high achievers in the early grades might be purposely selected and studied, and a similar procedure followed for a few very low achievers. In the *homogeneous sampling* strategy, the researcher picks subjects who are generally alike, and this focus and reduced variability facilitates group interviews and simplifies analysis. Via *criterion sampling*, all persons meeting a certain criterion are included in the sample. For example, the criterion for selection as subjects might be all children in the site between the ages of 48 and 60 months who weighed between 2 and 4 pounds at birth. Patton also identified an *opportunistic sampling* strategy, whereby the researcher would be flexible and aggressively pursue new subjects as leads to them arose during fieldwork.

A special element related to sampling in ethnographic research is the identification and use of *key informants*. These individuals, within the site under study, are especially knowledgeable, articulate, and perceptive, and they are willing to interact frequently with the ethnographer. Goetz and LeCompte (1984) pointed out that key informants often have access to observations involving the culture or phenomenon under study that would otherwise be denied to the ethnographer. They might be particularly astute about cultural mores and issues, involved in central community institutions, or long-time residents of the site. Some researchers use key informants extensively, certainly more than other subjects, because of their reflective and insightful capabilities. This utilization can even extend to trying out preliminary ideas and "findings" with key informants to get their reactions. These individuals can help unravel the complexities of the processes under investigation. Still, balance is important here too—the ethnographer does not want to over-rely on the input of a small set of informants in the quest for reliable knowledge on the topic being studied.

Under the general topic of sampling and site selection, Bogdan and Biklen (1992) presented a number of pertinent ideas. They indicated that, at times, the researcher might narrow the focus sufficiently so that all persons in a site can be studied in some depth—and, thus, sampling subjects would not be a major concern. They noted that, while it was crucial to identify a site in which the phenomenon or topic of the study was clearly present, some practical concerns also had to be kept in mind. For example, the distance to the site was important because a great number of trips to it would probably be in the offing. An additional factor of importance was the ease of access or of gaining entry to do research in the site. Time-of-day and time-of-year issues often arise in qualitative studies involving education. Bogdan and Biklen also opined that using one's own workplace as the site for a study would undoubtedly present many difficulties. One principal concern would be attempting to adopt the role of researcher in contradistinction to one's prior role and interrelationships at the site. Note, though, that their view concerns the role of an ethnographic researcher and site selection—it does not contradict the current trend toward teachers' conducting research locally as noted in Chapter 2. There teachers were seen as continuing their primary role and, simultaneously, blending into it several features typical of researchers in order to study the instructional process in their classrooms.

Using a somewhat different framework, Lofland and Lofland (1984) visualized three main concerns in site selection. First, the *appropriateness* of the site had to be determined in the light of the foreshadowed problem of interest. They promoted the use of investigator logic to increase the probability of identifying an appropriate site likely to yield relevant and rich data. Second, *access* issues must be evaluated. To matters already mentioned like the researcher's relationship to the setting, the Loflands added the importance of ascriptive categories of the researcher and the subjects, like age, ethnicity, and gender. These were seen as important differences between people in some settings that might influence the interactions between the subjects and the ethnographer. Another access issue described by the Loflands concerned settings difficult to research. Their examples included prisons and settings experiencing political strife and armed conflict. In terms of early childhood, difficult sites to gain access to for the purpose of research might include centers or families under investigation for child abuse and intervention programs receiving scrutiny because of alleged ineffectiveness. Third, the Loflands emphasized *ethics* in evaluating a potential site for selection with two central questions involved. First, should a particular site or group be studied by anyone? If yes, then should this particular researcher conduct the study? In general, the Loflands gave serious and continuing attention to ethical issues in qualitative research.

An ethical issue of special note should be mentioned here. In general—in both qualitative *and* quantitative studies—research subjects must be aware that they are in a study and that their participation is voluntary. Termed *informed consent,* this procedure involves describing the study to the potential subjects along with any known risks and explaining their right to terminate their participation if they choose; usually, anonymity and confidentiality are also promised to subjects. Willing subjects sign informed-consent forms for the researcher whereby they agree to participate. Additionally, if a qualitative ethnographic study involves extensive interviewing of subjects or collections of their "products," such as drawings or compositions, it has become increasingly important for the researcher to obtain signed releases from the subjects (or their parents if the subjects are minors). The signed releases permit the researcher to publish portions of the interviews or selected drawings or whatever is deemed relevant to illustrate the study's findings. Tracking down subjects "after the fact" to obtain such permissions is very difficult and, at times, impossible.

An additional matter that the ethnographer must address in this third step is determining her or his role in the field study. Will it be complete observer or complete participant or somewhere in between? This matter is of long-standing importance in ethnography, and we give considerable attention to it in Chapter 6.

Another element to be determined in this step is the ethnographer's plan of how to begin. That is, once in the field, how will the researcher initiate the study? There are countless options. The researcher might decide to initially take a low-profile position, and to establish some foundational understandings of the phenomenon under study. Or the plan might be to take part in some important events for the knowledge they might yield. One idea we particularly liked was planning to enter the field by first asking a *grand tour question,* or observing with such a question centrally in mind. This involves a question related to the topic area, but one stated in its most general form (Creswell, 1994). Posed in this general form, and used first in the study, the grand tour question is endorsed because it should not set preset limits on the inquiry. In addition, the researcher often will have another set of follow-on subquestions, say a half dozen or so. Thus, in a study of curriculum change in preschools, the grand tour question might be: What are the major processes through which curriculum changes occur in preschools? Or, alternatively, what factors appear to stimulate or depress preschool curriculum change?

When a design emerges to a sufficient point, the ethnographer is ready to enter the field. Once there, the researcher evolves the design further via daily interactions and reflective insights. That is, the study continues to move through the design funnel, mentioned earlier, toward its narrower end. Remember, though, the ethnographer enters the field with flexibility as a companion, and expects this greater detailing in the specifics of the study to occur quite smoothly over time.

4. ***Collecting data.***

5. ***Analyzing data.***

6. ***Interpreting the data analyses.*** These three steps are considered together because they in fact occur simultaneously for the most part, with step 6 possibly following steps 4 and 5 by half a step. We provide limited attention to them here, as they constitute much of Chapter 6.

The Loflands (1984) designated the main objective of the ethnographer as collecting the richest possible data. By rich data, they meant a broad and diverse range of information collected across a relatively long period of time. For them, the most valuable strategy in this regard was naturalistic, involving prolonged immersion of the researcher and numerous face-to-face interactions with subjects. They considered the mainstay types of data collection to be participant observation and intense interviewing.

Indeed, most sourcebooks on qualitative research list three principal sources of data. First, and sometimes singled out as most important, *participant observation* and resultant *field notes* made by the researcher are noted. (We discuss issues surrounding participant observation in Chapter 6.) Field notes, as elaborated in the next chapter, can deal with description (e.g., of subjects or events) or reflection (e.g., about analysis or the observer's perceived next steps). Second, *interviews* are typically presented as a data source. While interviews take several forms, material presented in Chapter 6 makes it apparent that ethnographic studies most often use unstructured, free-flowing formats. Thus a grand tour question and a set of subquestions might serve as interview starting points, with each interview soon taking on its own character. Further, some subjects might be interviewed in depth several times, especially key informants. The third data source frequently mentioned is *documents*. This is a fairly broad category, including both personal and official documents, artifacts, photographs, official statistics, and the like.

Two pivotal questions come up during these steps. The first is how much to record in one's field notes, based on observations, and how much of interviews to record, either by notes or via mechanical recorders. Comprehensiveness is urged at first until no new ideas are being generated; in Chapter 6, we discuss this further under the topic of saturation. The second question concerns how much of the recorded observational and interview data to actually transcribe—that is, to put into written form for further analysis. Transcription is a costly process in terms of time and money. Strauss and Corbin (1990) offered the guidance that only as much as is needed should be transcribed, but admitted that such a determination was difficult. They suggested full transcription of early observations and interviews, with increased selectivity over time in terms of exactly what warrants transcription. They also cautioned that it was generally better to transcribe more rather than less.

In terms of interpreting the various qualitative data analyses conducted, recall that the ethnographer principally follows an inductive process. Via extensive data coding, described in Chapter 6, the researcher identifies topics and categories and synthesizes them to form patterns of concepts, subjects, or themes. Based on these patterns, the investigator's ultimate objective is to reach understandings about the phenomenon or culture and, if appropriate, to establish grounded theory. As defined by Strauss and Corbin (1990):

> A grounded theory is one that is inductively derived from the study of the phenomenon it represents. That is, it is discovered, developed, and provisionally verified through systematic data collection and analysis of data pertaining to that phenomenon. Therefore, data collection, analysis, and theory stand in reciprocal relationship with each other. One does not begin with a theory, then prove it. Rather, one begins with an area of study and what is relevant to that area is allowed to emerge. (p. 23)

Other aspects of steps 4 to 6 are presented in an integrated fashion in Chapter 6.

7. ***Reporting results.*** The process of reporting results from a qualitative study, and how such result formats typically vary from quantitative investigations, is fully described in Chapter 6. Suffice it here to note that reports of qualitative research, such as ethnographies and case studies, are most often characterized by long, substantive narratives. As such, they are comfortable for most persons to read, describing in great detail derived understandings about the phenomenon that was studied, generating grounded theory if appropriate, and linking the investigation to the work of others.

8. ***Reproducing the outcomes of the study.*** One commonly mentioned concern about qualitative research is its degree of generalizability. Would another researcher studying the same topic or phenomenon in a similar group generate the same findings? Said differently, to what extent are the study's outcomes reproducible? Some degree of reproducibility probably can be claimed through the use of "arm-chair techniques," whereby ethnographers detail logical connections and consistencies between their results and the outcomes reached by other scientists. Even more impressive would be additional studies by the researcher in similar sites that yield compatible findings. Engaging in this step—essentially redoing the initial study—is, of course, quite expensive in time and resource costs, and, therefore, frequently is foregone. One should not criticize qualitative researchers alone for not reproducing study outcomes; quantitative researchers very often do not replicate their studies, either.

Research Examples in Early Childhood Education

A delightful qualitative ethnographic study focusing on kindergartners' construction of play during snack time has been conducted by Holmes (1992). One day per week throughout a school year, she served as a participant observer in a morning kindergarten class of 21 children. Over time, her focus became the play that evolved from the children's interactions during mid-morning snack. She joined the children for snack, kept notes on the children's conversations, and at times asked probing or other questions intended to elaborate and clarify the children's views. Deliberately seeking an emic (that is, the children's) perspective, Holmes recorded nearly 400 episodes of play activities during snack time. A content analysis identified five categories of episodes. In the kindergartners' terms, the categories and their percentages of the total were

1. Playing with your drink, 40% (e.g., blowing bubbles in your milk, shooting the paper wrapper from the straw).
2. Pretending, 25% (e.g., transforming food into play objects).
3. Telling a joke, 20% (e.g., joking, telling knock-knock jokes).
4. Fooling around, 10% (e.g., taboo humor).
5. Goofing, 5% (e.g., removing the chair as someone was about to sit down, hiding someone's milk).

Other observations made by Holmes were that only boys exhibited behaviors in the fooling around and goofing categories, and that different children appeared to have individual and consistent preferences for a given category of play activity. She observed that children also convert other areas of the school—such as spaces designated for academic tasks only—into places where they could engage in play.

In an earlier related study, Holmes (1991) used similar procedures in two classrooms to determine kindergartners' views of play. Using participant observation and recording extensive field notes, she spent over 300 hours in the classrooms. From an emic perspective, the children constructed four categories of play: (1) games, which were further subdivided into games of chase where everybody plays with you and board games where you move something; (2) not a game, comprised of activities like pretend play and sociodramatic play (e.g., house, cops and robbers), which children insisted were not games; (3) making and building things; and (4) action figures and dolls (e.g., Barbie, G.I. Joe). The children likewise, over time, constructed categories of toys: riding toys, house props, puppets, stuffed animals, and puzzles; function of the toy appeared to be an important element in the children's classification thinking.

A provocative ethnographic study by Dyson (1987) served to challenge the typical value placed on "time on task" in classrooms. Spending two years in an elementary school's primary classrooms, that is, kindergarten through third grade, the researcher (and sometimes assistants) served as participant observer recording field notes and collecting audiotapes of the children's talk and samples of their written and drawn products. Focusing on a set of eight focal children and especially their interactions in unintentional encounters, Dyson examined their verbal interchanges as they constructed, reflected on, and analyzed their respective imaginary worlds. She showed how the children collaborated with one another, critiqued the logic of each other's work, and in general accomplished mutual intellectual development via this spontaneous talk. The latter was characterized by teasing, social chatting, correcting, and laughing. To the casual observer, the children's behavior would be characterized as "off-task," but Dyson concluded that it fulfilled a crucial role in the children's development as writers and thinkers.

A final example is a qualitative case study of an Australian first-grade teacher who taught mathematics in an exemplary fashion (Ciupryk, Fraser, Malone, & Tobin, 1989). The teacher was observed across several months, while other data sources included material from and interviews with the teacher, her principal, colleagues, and students. The central characteristic that highlighted the teacher's actions was her consistent ability to actively integrate all aspects of the curriculum, including mathematics. This meant that aspects of mathematics kept reappearing throughout the school day, such as using poetry for classification practice, turning attendance roll call into a counting game, interweaving rhyme and number, meshing literature and dramatic play with number, and designing a lunch-time mathematics game using tokens for children's lunch orders. Many of the integrated experiences were planned, while others were spontaneous. The authors queried whether the teacher's mastery at subject integration was a characteristic that could be taught to teachers-to-be.

The reader interested in reviewing a number of other qualitative studies in one collection may want to obtain the book edited by Hatch (1995b).

ANALYTICAL RESEARCH

In this relatively short section, we consider qualitative research that is analytical—that is, it analyzes the nature of some entity. While ethnographic research places the researcher in an active, interacting role in the field, analytical research primarily is the noninteractive study of documents. At the same time, ethnographic and analytical research share a number of features, such as using an emergent design, taking a holistic perspective, following a naturalistic orientation, employing nonintervention and nonmanipulation strategies, striving for context sensitivity, seeking full understanding of participants' perspectives, and using inductive analysis (Edson, 1988; Sherman & Webb, 1988).

Our focus in this section is historical research in education. We also give passing attention to legal and policy studies, which have some features in common with historical research. In assembling this section, we are indebted to Gay (1987) and to McMillan and Schumacher (1993) for several pertinent ideas and insights.

Historical Research

The purpose of historical research is to generate new knowledge about past events, or to modify existing knowledge via correction, clarification, or elaboration. It is concerned with description, explanation, and, sometimes, prediction. Historical researchers, then, are often concerned with problems or questions involving precisely how an event occurred (what, who, when, and where) and why. The steps typically involved in such research are described as follows:

1. *Defining the problem.* As is true for most research, historical research commences with the specification of a problem or topic area. This step can include the specification of hypotheses to be tested or questions to be answered. Interestingly, the researcher must select a problem for which there is likely to be sufficient data to allow

hypothesis testing or question answering. That is, this nonmanipulative search through the past does not permit the generation of new data; the researcher is limited to existent data. Best and Kahn (1993) recommended delimiting the problem so that a penetrating analysis of a limited problem would result; they likened the historical researcher to one who hunts for knowledge with a target pistol rather than with a shotgun.

2. *Initiating data collection.* In historical research, much of the "data" exist in the form of documents or extant collections of written materials or "literature." McMillan and Schumacher (1993) classified these data sources as documents, oral history or testimonies, and relics. Records of past events are known as *documents* and can include books, autobiographies, journals, magazines, newspapers, catalogs, bulletins, letters, diaries, personal records, audio and video recordings, films, institutional records, official minutes of meetings, laws, court decisions, policy manuals, and the like. On the other hand, *oral histories* or *oral testimonies* involve the spoken word. For example, they can be eyewitness accounts of an event, taped and subsequently transcribed. Or they might take the form of testimony at a legal or policy hearing. The third data source, *relics*, includes such objects as early textbooks and curriculum materials, equipment, charts and maps, furniture, early student work samples, early student examinations, physical evidence presented in legal proceedings, diagrams and charts integral to policy hearings, and so forth. In a very real sense, if one adopts a broad definition of literature, then literature review and data collection are inextricably intertwined in historical research.

   Two important features of data compilation in historical research require special attention. The first is determining whether the data source is primary or secondary. A *primary source* is an original document, report, or record (e.g., audio, video, or photographic) of the event or series of events under study made by an actual participant. Eyewitness accounts of the event would thus constitute primary sources. A *secondary source,* on the other hand, is an account or record of an event made by someone who was neither a participant in, nor an eyewitness to, the event of interest. While primary sources are preferred, difficulties can be encountered in obtaining them. If the event occurred some time ago, the records could be lost, in poor condition, or centralized at a site (such as a specialized collection in a library) not readily available or easily accessible; participants in, and eyewitnesses to, the event, could all be dead. Thus, depending on the "age" of the event or topic of interest, secondary sources may make up most of what is available to the historical researcher.

The second important feature inherent in historical research data collection involves the rigorous application of external and internal criticism to all data being considered for inclusion in the study. The process of *external criticism* requires a determination of the authenticity of the data source. If, for example, a document purports to be an original record of proceedings made at the event of interest, its authenticity might be checked by attempting to ascertain its age using chemical and physical tests. Similarly, if an eyewitness account appears to have been written by a specific individual, external criticism would be applied to attempt to verify that the named individual in fact wrote the account. While external criticism concerns authenticity, *internal criticism* scrutinizes the data source for its accuracy and trustworthiness. At issue are the proximity of the document's author to the event of interest, his or her attention to the event, to what extent a time delay occurred between the event and the document's creation, biases or motives related to the event that the author may have had, and the competence of the author to analyze and report the event. The skilled application of external and internal criticism requires the researcher to be generally skeptical and to be knowledgeable about the people, behaviors, and customs common during the period of time under study. The logical, thorough application of external and internal criticism sorts through historical data to identify components worthy of being considered trustworthy evidence (Best & Kahn, 1993).

3. *Analyzing data, interpreting the analyses, and determining findings.* This step is examined in Chapter 6.
4. *Reporting results.* As in all research, the process is not over until one shares the knowledge generated with a larger audience of professionals. This step is important for historical researchers, and a number of journals exist to publish study outcomes. The nature of historical research is such that the final published product must be able to withstand rather focused criticism, and potentially varying interpretations, from one's colleagues.

It should be obvious from these several procedural steps that doing effective historical research is neither simple nor quick. It also is appropriate at this juncture to note that some hard-to-classify work involving elements of historical research has appeared. Two excellent examples that combine elements of historical and descriptive developmental research (noted in Chapter 3) have been provided by Aries (1962) and Elder, Modell, and Parke (1993).

Some mention of legal studies and policy studies in education is warranted at this juncture. *Legal studies* essentially constitute a category of historical research that focuses on law and its meaning. Considerable and valuable knowledge can result from legal research that can aid the understanding of past events and provide guidance for the future. *Policy studies* generally are of two types: analysis of the use of power and influence in educational systems, and the specific content of policy and its impact on education. Thus, exemplar studies might be of the differing views and power bases of parents, administrators, and legislators in their varying support of public early childhood education, or of the impact of new policies requiring the provision of services to very young exceptional children and their families. There undoubtedly could be an increase in early childhood education policy research, given the stronger advocacy role being espoused—and training in advocacy being conducted—by organizations such as the National Association for the Education of Young Children on numerous issues (e.g., program quality and funding, adequate compensation for teachers, affordability of child care).

Legal studies and policy studies share many elements with historical research. Problem definition is an important and logical first step in each type of study. Typical data sources for them vary somewhat from historical research, although some overlap is present. Legal studies use data of three types: documents, such as previous cases, court decisions, and laws; oral history and testimony, such as transcripts from a court trial or hearing; and relics, such as physical evidence used in court proceedings. Policy studies also utilize documents, such as government records, legislative publications, and committee minutes; oral testimony and history, such as reports from persons serving on various policymaking groups; and relics, such as graphic presentations and objects forthcoming during the policymaking process. In terms of data analysis and interpretation, note that all three—historical, legal, and policy studies—are analytical and inductive. All three have analogous reporting responsibilities and techniques.

Research Examples in Early Childhood Education

Historical research by Varga (1991) examined influences in the 1920s and 1930s that helped establish play as important for young children's development. Without engaging in overt external and internal criticism, the author stated directly her reliance on the opinions of child development experts as expressed in articles and texts of the time period. Her examination resulted in identifying the scientific child study movement spearheaded by Arnold Gesell as crucial in establishing play as a developmental task. Given a central role in Gesell's (1925/1928) published developmental schedules were normative play behaviors for children ages 2 to 5. In the curriculum of nursery schools, play became both a means for achieving development and a setting in which children's developmental progress could be observed. Varga used writings of the period to establish that play took on a commanding presence as a base for observation, as a consideration in organizing spaces for children, and as a determiner of appropriate materials to provide. Varga concluded that while the role of play in early childhood education has changed somewhat over time (e.g., now being more closely linked to cognitive development than previously), it continued to maintain the central importance ascribed to it some 70 years earlier.

Winterer (1992) explored the question of why infant schools failed to thrive in this country in the early 1800s, while philosophically closely linked kindergartens were considerably more successful later in the century, around the 1860s. Infant schools, primarily located in urbanized population centers, enrolled children from 18 months to 4 years of age, and were designed for underprivileged children to counter the "corrupting" influences of poverty by emphasizing correct morals and early reading and writing skills. However, infant schools failed to thrive and eventually disappeared. While kindergartens also were set up to work with children outside of the home, they differed from infant schools in several ways. Because kindergartens did not enroll children until 4 years of age, the fear of early education's undermining family responsibilities and values was mitigated. Additionally, the orientation of the early kindergarten was a better match with the emerging conception that children should not be pushed into academic learning at too early an age, a change from the orientation of the 1820s infant school. The American public seemed more ready for early education institutions in the 1860s. Winterer went on to detail the convergence of a number of societal elements and influential persons' opinions that buttressed the base of support for kindergartens. An interesting precursor to Winterer's work was provided by Hills (1987); she traced the policy implications of many parents' demands for increased formal academic instruction for their children.

The question of what experts advised parents to do with regard to stimulating their children's intellectual development was the focus of a historical study by Wrigley (1989). She covered the period from 1900 to 1985 by examining over 1,000 popular press articles. For each decade, these were categorized in terms of their central topic: intellectual development, medical issues, nutrition, fresh air (i.e., the need for it), and socioemotional development. The first decades were characterized by heavy emphasis on medical and nutrition topics; only about 15% of the articles concerned intellectual development in each of the first three decades of the century. From 1900 to 1930, almost 40% of the articles that did address intellectual development argued that early stimulation harmed babies. The move toward the endorsement of intellectual stimulation began to change in the 1930s, in part due to the child study movement. Over each of the most recent decades, more than 40% of the articles have addressed intellectual issues. Wrigley pointed out that children's intellectual development moved onto center stage in the 1960s; stimulation is generally endorsed now although some disagreement persists about how structured and formal early learning efforts should be. Wrigley concluded by noting experts' continuing lack of confidence in some untutored parents and raising provocative questions involving parents, their children, and their social class.

Although we have not included full examples of policy and legal research, note that such analytic work often relates to early childhood education. For example, various researchers have examined the efficacy of early childhood programs to inform policymakers (Haskins, 1989), the reigning educational policies in kindergarten (Meisels, 1992; Siegel & Hanson, 1991), the economic aspects of preschool education policy (Barnett, 1990), issues attending a national policy on child care (Lubeck, 1995; Zigler & Finn-Stevenson, 1989), linkages between the law and policies on families (Melton, 1987), and the evolution of legislation and policies affecting young exceptional children (Meisels, 1985). Such research and journals such as *Educational Evaluation and Policy Analysis* and *Educational Policy* serve to generate knowledge in crucial policy and legal areas.

SUMMARY

Qualitative research primarily is an inductive process, commencing with less specified dimensions and becoming more detailed as the actual study unfolds. Types of qualitative research include ethnographic and analytical research; examples of each in early childhood education are presented. Ethnography is a rich description of a specified group, culture, or phenomenon, with the researcher in classical anthropological tradition observing intently and participating to some degree in the matter studied. Among the characteristic themes of ethnography are a holistic approach, a naturalistic viewpoint, sensitivity to participants and their perspectives, a process-and-change orientation, the researcher as the primary instrument, design flexibility, and extensive time in the field. The procedural steps in an ethnographic study are detailed, especially conceptualizing a topic area and setting a preliminary design, including the selection of a purposeful sample. Analytical qualitative methods include historical, legal, and policy research. In historical research, primary sources are preferred over secondary ones; both external criticism (to assess the data source's authenticity) and internal criticism (to gauge the data source's accuracy and trustworthiness) are rigorously applied. Unlike ethnographers, who typically assume an active, interacting role, analytical researchers most often engage in the noninteractive study of documents. Like ethnography, however, historical, legal, and policy studies are inductive and context-sensitive processes, and use similar data analysis procedures, as described in Chapter 6.

Chapter 6

Data Collection and Data Analysis in Qualitative Research

In this chapter, we discuss the commonly used strategies for data collection and data analysis in qualitative research studies. We consider three general areas, noting several important differences between qualitative and quantitative research in the process. First, the typical data-collection strategies used in qualitative research—participant observation, interviewing, and document collection—are reviewed. Unlike quantitative studies, where the researcher is an independent observer with a set of instruments, the qualitative researcher becomes an integral part of the measurement and data-collection experience. Second, we detail the definitions and estimations of reliability and validity in qualitative research, again noting differences from quantitative investigations. Third, qualitative data analysis is examined, highlighting its close connections and interactions with data collection. In all, data analysis is shown to be an inductive rather than a deductive process, usually aimed at developing rather than testing theories. This chapter concludes with some criteria useful for judging qualitative research.

TYPICAL DATA-COLLECTION STRATEGIES

There are a few general guiding principles important to qualitative researchers in the area of data collection. One is the need for multiple methods within a study, so as to corroborate the data collected with a single strategy with data from at least one other strategy, thereby enhancing the trustworthiness of the information. The practice of using multiple methods is called *triangulation* (Denzin, 1988). Different methods (such as observation and interviewing), different data sources, and even multiple investigators with varying theoretical perspectives can be utilized (Patton, 1990).

A second general notion about data collection in qualitative research is that it is flexible and developmental. Throughout the study, there is a continual process of choosing data-collection strategies and "informants." This is quite different from the procedures used in primarily quantitative studies, in which the subjects and instrumentation are planned before data collection begins. Finally, data collection continues until *saturation* occurs (Glaser & Strauss, 1967). This is the point at which the data, information, and findings currently being assembled replicate earlier ones. Saturation helps the qualitative researcher achieve the criteria of adequacy and appropriateness: "Adequacy is attained when sufficient data have been collected that saturation occurs and variation is both accounted for and understood" (Morse, 1994, p. 230). Appropriateness involves selecting information to match the study's needs and emerging theoretical model; purposeful sampling continues until repetition from multiple sources occurs.

Data-collection strategies in qualitative research can be grouped in a number of different ways. One general category scheme that others have used (e.g., Goetz & LeCompte, 1984; McMillan & Schumacher, 1993) distinguishes between "interactive methods," such as participant observation and interviewing, and "noninteractive methods," like artifact and document collection and nonparticipant observation. We have chosen to group the strategies according to the type of activity that the researcher engages in; this scheme, also used by others (e.g., Glesne & Peshkin, 1992), has three major categories: observation, interviewing, and document collection.

Observation

Observational techniques are used in many types of research. As Adler and Adler (1994) said, "For as long as people have been interested in studying the social and natural world around them, observation has served as the bedrock source of human knowledge" (p. 377). In early childhood research—whether the research is primarily quantitative or primarily qualitative—observation is often an appropriate and helpful technique. One major difference in the observational techniques used in the two general types of research pertains to the degree of structure. As noted in Chapter 4, quantitative measurements often rely on fairly structured observation instruments, with preset categories of behavior to record systematically. In this section, we focus on the more naturalistic observation techniques employed by qualitative researchers, especially participant observation.

Participant observation as a data-collection strategy is rooted in ethnography, as discussed in Chapter 5. By taking part in the activities of the individuals being studied, the researcher learns of their perceptions of reality—termed "constructed realities"—as expressed by their actions and in their thoughts, beliefs, and feelings. It is critical that the researcher be familiar with the language of the participants, and that the researcher have excellent listening skills. The data take the form of field notes, which are descriptive accounts of the who, what, where, why, and how of the phenomena under investigation. While the focus of the field notes is descriptive, they also typically include interpretive comments based on the researcher's perceptions. It is common, too, for the researcher to request reactions from participants to drafts of analyses and summaries developed from the field notes.

As Glesne and Peshkin (1992) noted, "Participant observation ranges across a continuum from mostly observation to mostly participation" (p. 40). At the complete "observer" end of the continuum, the data-collection activity is one sometimes used by quantitative researchers; an example is observing behaviors of subjects through one-way mirrors in laboratory settings and tallying behaviors using preset categories. At the other end of the continuum the "full-participant" researcher is a fully functioning member of the group being studied. In between these two extremes are the "observer as participant" and the "participant as observer." With the former approach, the researcher has some interaction with participants but is primarily an observer from the outside. As the amount of participation increases, the researcher moves toward the "participant as observer" position.

Gold (1969) denoted several trade-offs as the ethnographer moved along the continuum from complete observer to complete participant. Thus, the researcher in the complete-observer role has the advantages of detachment, considerable objectivity, and little personal risk. At the same time, limitations present include the dangers of ethnocentrism, few meaningful interactions with informants, and potential misunderstanding of the observed events or people. Conversely, the researcher in the complete-participant role may experience benefits such as becoming privy to information that otherwise would be inaccessible, and having meaningful and significant interactions with informants as the researcher gains "insider" status and is trusted. Dangers here include the researcher's "going native" (of course, this often seems an effective strategy for ethnographers), losing his or her sensitivity, which renders judgments suspect and, possibly, indistinguishable from those of the persons being studied. Relatedly, Davis (1973) generated a nice analogy about these two orientations, describing "Martians" and "Converts." The Martian researcher deliberately seeks psychological distance from subjects as the means to producing credible knowledge, while the Convert investigator hopes to be immersed deeply within the culture or phenomenon to learn its intricacies.

Wolcott (1988) encouraged ethnographers to be active participants rather than passive observers; he also endorsed becoming a privileged observer in a particular site, as contrasted with a limited observer. Most ethnographers select a role somewhere between the complete-observer/complete-participant ends of the continuum. Their choice depends on factors such as the nature of the research question, the researcher's theoretical perspective, and the content and setting of the study.

The procedures used by observers evolve through a series of activities (Adler & Adler, 1994; Glesne & Peshkin, 1992). After selecting a site and gaining entry (see Chapter 5), the researcher (or team of researchers) begins the process of observation. Some field notes follow a free-association form, while others are more structured. Typically, the observation and notes change as the research progresses. Initially, they are very general, descriptive, and broad in scope; as time goes by, they become increasingly focused, narrow, and deep. The descriptions taken during actual observations are supplemented by observer analysis in the form of comments or reflections, which are made concurrently or after the researcher leaves the site each day. Bogdan and Biklen (1992) suggested that the descriptive part of field notes might include portraits of subjects, actual comments of subjects, descriptions of physical settings, accounts of events or activities, and accounts of the observer's own behavior. They viewed the analytic or comment part of field notes as reflections on method, analysis, ethical conflicts or dilemmas, the observer's frame of mind, and clarifying statements. The comments and reflections could also include the researcher's syntheses of the day's activities, plans for the next day, early interpretations of the data, and so on.

Participant observers can supplement their field notes with sketches, photographs, and videotapes. Goetz and LeCompte (1984) described the use of sketches by Goetz (1976) in an ethnographic study of a third-grade classroom. The floor-plan of the classroom was drawn in detail, including furniture and names of children as they occupied particular chairs. Since the teacher and children rearranged the furniture frequently, the study included a number of different sketches, which enhanced the field notes and overall richness of the descriptive data.

Walsh, Tobin, and Graue (1993) described a number of qualitative research studies—both cross-cultural and within-cultural—in early childhood education. Not surprisingly, many of these relied heavily on observation. Examples included a 1985 study by Lubeck, in which a white, middle-class preschool was compared with a working-class African-American Head Start classroom, and Genishi's (1988) study of the use of computers in a kindergarten classroom. Walsh, Tobin, and Graue also discussed some of the special problems that qualitative researchers encounter in conducting "interpretive" studies in early childhood education:

> Both interviewing and observation are much more difficult with young children than with older children or adults because of the distance between the researcher and the subject. Physical, social, cognitive, and political distances between the adult and child make their relationship very different from the relationship between adults. In doing participant observation with children, one can never become a child. One remains a very definite and readily identifiable "other." (p. 470)

Other realistic problems with such young subjects included being willing to let children hang on you, sketch in your notebook, and type on your laptop computer, as well as showing tolerance for runny noses, grimy hands, and the universal presence of ketchup and mashed potatoes when observing in the school's lunchroom (Walsh, Tobin, & Graue, 1993).

Interviewing

A second major type of data collection used by qualitative researchers is interviewing. Interviewing allows the researcher to gain insights into others' perspectives about the phenomena under study; it is particularly useful for ascertaining respondents' thoughts, perceptions, feelings, and retrospective accounts of events. Glesne and Peshkin (1992) colorfully described interviewing when they said:

> We conceptualize interviewing as the process of getting words to fly. To be sure, they do not fly with the regularity and predictability of balls emerging from batting-practice machines that baseball teams use. Interviewing is a human interaction with all of its attendant uncertainties. As an interviewer, you are not a research machine, but you do "pitch" questions at your respondents with the intent of making words fly. Unlike a human baseball pitcher whose joy derives from throwing balls that batters never touch, you toss questions which you want your respondents to "hit" and hit well in every corner of your data park, if not clear out of it—a swatted home run of words. As a researcher, you want your "pitches"—your questions—to stimulate verbal flights from the important others who know what you do not. From these flights come the information you transmute into data. (p. 63)

Interviews can be categorized into a number of specific types. Fetterman (1989) described four general types: structured, semistructured, informal, and retrospective. Patton (1990) also categorized interviews into four types: closed field response interview, standardized open-ended interview, interview guide approach, and informal conversational interview. Fontana and Frey (1994) wrote about structured interviewing, group interviews, and unstructured interviewing. As Seidman (1991) noted,

> the word *interviewing* covers a wide range of practices. There are tightly structured, survey instruments with preset, standardized, normally closed questions. At the other end of the continuum are open-ended, apparently unstructured, anthropological interviews that might be seen . . . as friendly conversations. (p. 9)

Most proposed categorization schemes include basically two approaches: structured and unstructured. With either general approach, a number of different kinds of questions can be asked; Patton (1990) described six kinds of questions: experience/behavior questions, opinion/values questions, feeling questions, knowledge questions, sensory questions, and background/demographic questions.

Structured interviews are those with preset questions. If an interview schedule includes rating scales, ranking questions, or other questions that can be numerically summarized, the structured interview probably fits more easily into a predominantly quantitative rather than a qualitative study. A structured interview in a qualitative study probably emphasizes open-ended questions, or at least a set of response categories that are more complex than simply worded rating scales (such as Likert scales with 5 points, "strongly agree" to "strongly disagree"). Nevertheless, structured interviewing ordinarily means that each respondent is asked the same set of pre-established questions, in the same order, by an interviewer who has been trained to follow the interview schedule almost as if it were a script. Interviewers are instructed *not* to improvise, suggest an answer, deviate from the set sequencing of questions, give lengthy explanations about the study (beyond those provided), or let others interrupt (Fontana & Frey, 1994). Early childhood researchers may find the use of structured interviews with parent, teachers, and other adults facilitative; formal interviews of young children, however, can be quite difficult (Seidman, 1991; Walsh, Tobin, & Graue, 1993).

Unstructured or *informal* interviews are widely used for data gathering in qualitative research studies. Within this interview category, variations can occur in the "naturalness" of the questions and question-asking behaviors. Some researchers will prepare a general interview guide that outlines the topics for questioning, so as to ensure that important areas are covered and that there is some uniformity from one interview to another. In other situations, particularly ethnographic studies, the interview is like an informal conversation and is very open-ended. Questions flow freely and, especially after some opening similarities such as a grand tour question and a small set of subquestions, may differ remarkably from one interview to another. Also, any one informant might be interviewed a number of times during the study's duration. The interviewer might record the interview by tape recorder, by notes taken during the interview, or by notes made as soon after the conclusion of the interview as possible. Informal interviewing appears easy to conduct due to the lack of preset questions, opportunity for free-flowing and unconstrained conversations, and so on. As Fetterman (1989) and others have noted, however, conducting such interviews ethically and productively can be difficult. Characteristics of successful interviewers include the ability to establish good rapport with informants, to engage in natural conversations that will answer the research's key questions, to probe in nonthreatening ways, to know how to follow unexpected leads that appear during the interview, and to listen well.

With young children, informal interviewing in pairs or group settings may be more fruitful than conducting individual interviews. Children may feel more relaxed in the company of peers, and the discussions that ensue are richer because of their interactions. In addition, "interviewing children in pairs may well give children the opportunity to indirectly let researchers know what questions they should be asking" (Walsh, Tobin, & Graue, 1993, p. 471). Other strategies to aid in interviewing young children—like using props or playing a game—were reviewed by Browning and Hatch (1995) and McGee-Brown (1995).

As soon as possible after an interview has been conducted, the qualitative researcher transcribes the tapes or completes the handwritten notes. To the typed account of the interview, the researcher adds comments—such as statements about nonverbal communications that occurred—and early insights. These notes and comments have been called "interview elaborations," defined by McMillan and Schumacher (1993) as "self-reflections on his or her role and rapport, interviewee's reactions, additional information, and extensions of interview meanings" (p. 433).

Document Collection

Compared with observation and interview, this third approach to data collection in qualitative research is not interactive. It involves gathering information from a variety of different kinds of extant material. Lincoln and Guba (1985) differentiated between documents and records: Whereas documents are generally personal (diaries, letters, wills, etc.), records are prepared to attest to a formal event (birth certificates, driving licenses, bank statements, marriage certificates, etc.). Although the distinction is an interesting one, we group all such materials and records into one category in this section.

Strauss and Corbin (1990) wrote about the importance of these materials in qualitative research:

> The nontechnical literature is comprised of letters, biographies, diaries, reports, videotapes, newspapers, and a variety of other materials. Though these are usually not used as sources of data in quantitative studies, they play an essential role in grounded theory studies. They can be used as primary data, especially in historical or biographical studies. In most studies they are important sources of data, supplementing the more usual interviews and observations. For example, much can be learned about an organization, its structure, and how it functions (that may not immediately be visible in observations or interviews) by studying its reports, correspondence, and memos. (p. 55)

In some ways, qualitative researchers particularly utilize their historical and anthropological backgrounds when they collect information from documents, records, and other artifacts. They are seeking information about the behaviors, experiences, beliefs, knowledge, values, and perceptions of the subjects whose materials they study—in order to more fully describe and understand the culture, institution, or other focus of the qualitative research.

A difficulty often encountered in the collection and use of documents is that of determining authenticity and accuracy (via external and internal criticism, respectively, as reviewed in Chapter 5). The concern for accuracy is one reason for the emphasis within qualitative methodology on the use of multiple data-collection techniques. Data obtained through the study of documents must be verified, if possible, by data collected via observations and interviews. If that is not feasible, the careful investigation of other records and artifacts is required. For example, a researcher conducting a life-history study might examine a large number of biographies, letters, newspaper accounts, official records, and other materials before beginning to make interpretations and draw conclusions.

Another type of data that can be collected, and that belongs in this general category, is often referred to as "erosion measures." As with other types of data grouped here, these are nonreactive measures (Goodwin & Goodwin, 1989; Webb, Campbell, Schwartz, Sechrest, & Grove, 1981). They indicate the extent of wear on some parts of buildings, land, or other materials used by persons in the past. For instance, a study of the relative popularity of different sections of a children's museum might include the amount of wear on the vinyl tiles in various areas, the number of times different exhibits have to be repaired or replaced, or a measure of the "grubbiness" of physical objects included in the hands-on displays. Other types of nonreactive measure also could qualify as documents, especially items from archival records, such as portfolios of children's work samples, logs of staff turnover, attendance records, and so on (Goodwin & Goodwin, 1989). Again, it is important to stress the need to supplement such data with information from other sources, especially if the researcher intends to offer causal conclusions from the study.

RELIABILITY AND VALIDITY

As is the case with all research, *reliability* and *validity* are key concerns in qualitative research. However, there are some general differences, between the quantitative and qualitative research traditions, in the theoretical and operational definitions of these properties. In qualitative research, data collection is an integral part of the design and analysis components—more so than in quantitative research studies, in which the measurement of the major variables is done with instruments of independent standing. Because of this, the discussion of validity and reliability in qualitative research is not focused on "measures" per se. Rather, concerns about the reliability and validity of data collection are interwoven with concerns about the reliability and validity of the design—or, actually, of the entire study.

Reliability

The reliability of a qualitative research study pertains, generally, to its reproducibility; more specifically, reliability is the extent to which independent researchers would discover the same phenomena, describe the findings similarly, and agree with participants about their meanings. Goetz and LeCompte (1984) differentiated between two types of reliability:

> *External reliability* addresses the issue of whether independent researchers would discover the same phenomena or generate the same constructs in the same or similar settings. *Internal reliability* refers to the degree to which other researchers, given a set of previously generated constructs, would match them with data in the same way as did the original researcher. (p. 210)

These two types of reliability correspond roughly to reliability in design and reliability in data collection, respectively (McMillan & Schumacher, 1993). Goetz and LeCompte (1984) noted, too, the "Herculean" problem of demonstrating reliability in qualitative research, made difficult by such factors as the nature of the research process or design, the type of data collected, and the fact that traditional ways of conceptualizing, estimating, and presenting evidence of reliability do not apply.

External or design reliability faces threats due to such factors as

- the role of the researcher, including the researcher's relationship with study participants
- the sampling strategy and choice of informants
- the particular social, physical, and interpersonal context and settings studied
- the definitions of key concepts or constructs guiding the study
- the data collection and analysis approaches used

A qualitative study's reliability is enhanced by careful and thorough descriptions of each of these aspects. Although no study (qualitative or quantitative) can be exactly replicated, the opportunity for independent, separate researchers to discover the same phenomena is impossible without full, complete descriptions of how the original research was developed and conducted.

Internal or data-collection reliability is the extent to which multiple data collectors (observers, interviewers, etc.) agree. This type of reliability bears close conceptual similarity to interobserver, interjudge, or interrater reliability of open-ended measurement techniques used in quantitative research studies. The focus here, however, is on agreement between independent researchers, and between researchers and participants, on the *meaning* or interpretation of what is observed, described during interviews, or detected via scrutiny and analysis of various documents. Further, given the kind of data obtained in qualitative research, traditional methods of estimating interrater reliability (presented in Chapter 4) are inappropriate and not usable. In fact, rarely would qualitative researchers actually estimate this or any other type of reliability.

Instead of actually estimating psychometric reliability, qualitative researchers rely on a number of different strategies to reduce threats to internal or data-collection reliability. These include the incorporation of multiple researchers (data collectors) within a study and the use of mechanical devices—such as tape recorders, cameras, and videocameras. Another strategy pertains to the researcher's field notes and interview comments; good qualitative researchers strive to obtain verbatim accounts of events and conversations, and they use "low-inference descriptors" in their field notes and in subsequent longer written descriptions. Silverman (1993) called for the use of "standardized" methods of writing field notes and preparing transcripts. Finally, several strategies are used to check perceptions and interpretations with others: informally checking notes and observations with participants during and after data collection, asking interviewees to review and comment on transcribed interviews, comparing analyses of the same data collected by more than one researcher, and determining the extent of corroboration of findings with other researchers working in the same general area of investigation.

Validity

Validity is the extent of the *accuracy* of findings. It is closely connected to reliability. As is true with the measurement reliability and validity of quantitative instruments, reliability in qualitative research is a necessary precondition for validity—and threats to reliability also threaten validity.

Like reliability in qualitative research, validity is concerned with design and data-collection matters interconnectedly. Goetz and LeCompte (1984) separated validity into two types, *internal validity* and *external validity*. The first type is the extent to which "researchers actually observe or measure what they think they are observing or measuring," and the second type pertains to generalizability of findings: "To what extent are the abstract constructs and postulates generated, refined, or tested by scientific researchers applicable across groups?" (p. 221).

In general, the *internal-validity* issue for the qualitative researcher involves increasing the congruence of the researcher's explanations with those of the participants studied. Typical threats to the internal validity of qualitative research studies are expressed in terms originally used in describing threats to the internal validity of quantitative research (Campbell & Stanley, 1963; Cook & Campbell, 1979). Operationally, the terms have different meanings for qualitative and quantitative research, however, and ways to minimize the problems also differ across the two general types of research. Threats to both the internal and external validity of qualitative research are defined briefly in Table 6.1.

History and *maturation* are two possible threats to internal validity in qualitative research; they can be minimized by the careful recording of baseline data about events, individuals, situations, and contexts. Qualitative researchers recognize that change is a natural part of the phenomena they study, so they do not attempt to control it—just to document it well. Possible *observer* effects—frailties in instrumentation, concerns about the researcher's personal subjectivity, or dangers inherent in going native—are minimized in ways similar to the way reliability is enhanced: by extensive data collection, use of multiple data-collection methods, and use of multiple researchers for corroboration purposes. *Selection* is a potential problem if purposeful sampling has been used; the concern is that findings are representative of just those persons, subgroups, or agencies or institutions

TABLE 6.1 Threats to Internal and External Validity in Qualitative Research

Internal Threat	**Definition**
History	Natural changes occurring in the phenomenon being studied due to historical and other events; requires detailed recording of baseline conditions and data to determine which elements change and which remain stable over time.
Maturation	Failing to fully understand participants' definitions of appropriate or normative behavior for a given context, age, or developmental stage.
Observer	Misinterpreting or going beyond what is actually observed due to researcher/observer subjectivity, limited time in the field, limited data collection, or using single rather than multiple methods.
Selection	Purposeful sampling can be inadequately described, especially when the phenomenon studied is complex and there are many subgroups that cannot all be studied; the sampling decisions made, and the rationale for them, require full explication.
Attrition or Mortality	Loss of sample participants during the study, while normal, can be problematic; full accounts are needed of who is initially involved, who subsequently becomes unavailable, and why.
Spurious Conclusions	Inappropriate, incomplete, or faulty conclusions can occur if the researcher fails to examine alternative explanations of the results and the varying and multiple perspectives of participants, as well as his/her own personal subjectivity.
External Threat	**Definition**
Selection	Subjects and sites selected must be fully described, often even quantitatively (e.g., socioeconomic status, racial composition) to enhance comparability to other studies.
Setting	Settings being studied may become different simply due to the study process, a type of Hawthorne Effect affecting the research context and the nature of any concepts derived.
History	Unique historical experiences of groups or cultures can reduce comparability of results.
Construct	Explanatory meanings of constructs and generalizations may change across times and settings; comparability requires examining current findings along with prior research.

Note: Adapted from Goetz & LeCompte, 1984; McMillan & Schumacher, 1993.

included. Again, careful and detailed description of the sampling procedures and the subjects themselves helps minimize the seriousness of this threat. *Attrition* or *mortality*—loss of subjects during the study's duration—is another possible threat. As with the threats of history and maturation, qualitative researchers generally do not view these as unnatural or unwanted events; careful collection of baseline data and complete recording of events as they unfold aid with their minimization. Finally, the possibility of drawing *spurious conclusions* is a threat to internal validity. Strategies used to combat this problem include comprehensively collecting all sorts of data, spending a lot of time in the field, searching for negative or discrepant cases during data collection and analysis, and seeking an independent review of the entire research process at its conclusion. This latter idea is much like the "audit trail" proposed by Lincoln & Guba (1985).

The issue of *external validity* is somewhat controversial among qualitative methodologists. When conceptualized in the usual sense (which has its origins in traditional quantitative methods), external validity focuses on the extent to which findings can be generalized to other persons, settings, times, and so on. The essential purposes and characteristics of qualitative research lead to very limited generalizations of this sort—and, according to some methodologists (e.g., Guba & Lincoln, 1981), should not be of much concern to qualitative researchers. In fact, Goetz and LeCompte (1984) stated that, of the four types of reliability and validity enumerated (internal and external reliability, and internal and external validity), ethnographers tend to ignore problems of external validity. However, Goetz and LeCompte and other methodologists (e.g., Silverman, 1993) have usefully extended the definition of external validity so that it is meaningful to discuss and try to maximize it in qualitative research studies.

Conditions or effects that limit a study's *comparability* and *translatability* are considered to be threats to external validity. Comparability is the extent to which the components of a study are adequately described, so that the study can be compared with other studies investigating similar phenomena. Translatability is the extent to which the researcher uses theories, definitions, and data-collection techniques in ways that are easily understood and usable by other researchers. Problems that can attenuate comparability or translatability constitute external threats (Table 6.1) and include selection, setting, history, and construct or theoretical effects (Goetz & LeCompte, 1984; McMillan & Schumacher, 1993). Complete descriptions, corroborating observers' records with accounts by participants, and contrasting theoretical findings with prior research outcomes are some strategies used to overcome these threats, thereby improving the study's external validity.

DATA ANALYSIS

As noted earlier, data analysis in qualitative research is closely tied to data collection, and occurs throughout data collection as well as afterward.

It is an essential component of the research process, with the aims of determining key findings and—often—generating theories. Unlike data analysis in quantitative research, here it is an inductive process. While we present a brief overview to the procedures qualitative researchers often use, the topic is multifaceted, with many possible variations on the key elements. Interested readers are referred to more detailed treatments of qualitative data analysis (Bogdan & Biklen, 1992; Denzin, 1989; Fetterman, 1989; Glesne & Peshkin, 1992; Goetz & LeCompte, 1984; Lincoln & Guba, 1985; Lofland & Lofland, 1984; McMillan & Schumacher, 1993; Miles & Huberman, 1994; Silverman, 1993; Tesch, 1990; Wolcott, 1994).

The "heart" of data analysis in qualitative research is *coding*, a process that results in the data being organized into various categories. The data-analysis tasks that can be accomplished during data collection differ somewhat from those undertaken after all of the data have been obtained. Most of the actual data coding is conducted in the latter phase.

Data Analysis During Data Collection

Bogdan and Biklen (1992) offered some good suggestions to qualitative researchers about data-analysis activities during data collection in the field. Several suggestions involved the use of early data analysis as an aid in conceptualizing the study's purpose, setting boundaries, and developing analytic questions. The process of reviewing and reflecting on data as they are collected can help the researcher make decisions that focus the study and clarify its purpose. An early childhood researcher might begin, for example, by "scoping out" an entire child care center, observing and interviewing broadly; after considering the early data, the researcher might decide to explore more deeply the activities and issues surrounding just the youngest children and the adults who work with them.

Data analysis during data collection often entails the researcher's writing "observer's comments" or "interviewer's comments" immediately after a session is complete. These are the researcher's thoughts, feelings, and ideas for the next phase of data collection, early notions about themes and relationships, and so on. Relatedly, qualitative researchers use the technique of writing memos to themselves during data collection; in fact, this is a technique sometimes referred to as "memoing." These memos are brief summaries of collected data and important points that are emerging; they tend to be free-flowing, informal, and increasingly analytic as the study progresses.

Another in-the-field data-analysis strategy is to ask participants for their reactions to emerging interpretations, themes, and relationships. Such informal conversations with key informants and other participants can help the researcher clarify his or her thinking, identify areas for further exploration, and fill in missing information.

Data Analysis After Data Collection

The major data-analysis activity that occurs after data collection is complete is *coding*. "Coding represents the operations by which data are broken down, conceptualized, and put back together in new ways. It is the central process by which theories are built from data" (Strauss & Corbin, 1990, p. 57). Coding can be a time-consuming and difficult task, particularly considering the massive amount of data that can be collected in a qualitative study—including field notes, tapes, documents, and other artifacts. In general, coding requires the researcher to organize the information—all of the words, phrases, behaviors observed, and events recorded—into meaningful categories. There are numerous possible ways to develop the coding categories, and many different ways to conceptualize the types of category that may emerge. As an example, Bogdan and Biklen (1992) offered the following "coding families": setting/context codes; definition of the situation codes; perspectives held by subjects; subjects' ways of thinking about people and objects; process codes; activity codes; event codes; strategy codes; relationship and social structure codes; and methods codes. Once the categories are identified, the analysis proceeds by looking for patterns or relationships and then deciding what is important and how it will be conveyed to different audiences.

Strauss and Corbin (1990) wrote about data analysis in qualitative research as being comprised of three major types of coding: open, axial, and selective; while describing each type in detail, they also noted that there are no firm lines or boundaries among the three types. *Open coding* involves breaking down data, examining them carefully, comparing, and then categorizing. Making comparisons among data segments, in order to identify similarities and differences, is an integral part of qualitative data analysis—one that Glaser and Strauss (1967) referred to as "constant comparison." *Axial coding* generally follows open coding; it involves putting data together in meaningful, new ways, by looking for connections among the categories. During this phase, the researcher is concerned about such features of the categories as their causal conditions, contexts, intervening conditions, and consequences. Subcategories may be identified at this time, too. Finally, *selective coding* is "the process of selecting the core category, systematically relating it to other categories, validating those relationships, and filling in categories that need further refinement and development" (Strauss & Corbin, 1990, p. 116). This stage usually results in an "analytic story line" or explication of a theory "grounded" in the data.

An Example of Data Analysis in Early Childhood Education

At this juncture, some of the analysis procedures described above are illustrated, generally, highlighting again that qualitative data analysis is complex, difficult, and time-consuming. As Miles and Huberman (1994) noted, "A chronic problem of qualitative research is that it is done chiefly with words, not with numbers. Words are fatter than numbers and usually have multiple meanings" (p. 56). In the example presented below, we denote several analytic procedures based on a study of early childhood teachers (Wien, 1991, 1995).

Wien's research focused on the practical knowledge of five teachers each in a different child care center, and on the dynamic interplay between their beliefs and actions. This interplay tended to illustrate either a teacher dominion or a developmentally appropriate framework of action for practice. The two frameworks differed in their conception of the location of power—that is, of having control, taking action, and being an active agent in a given setting. In the teacher-dominion framework, power and authority resided within the teacher unless explicitly surrendered by the teacher; typically, teachers were in charge of everything, such as selecting, implementing, and evaluating activities for children. In the developmentally appropriate framework, children were given considerable agency and were able to self-select a number of activities according to their interests; further, the adults present were skilled at deducing and supporting each child's developmental status.

Methodologically, Wien (1991, 1995) visited each teacher five or six times across several months, observing them from one to three hours and taking field notes. She also interviewed each teacher after each session for about an hour, usually as they viewed a 20- to 30-minute videotape of that day's activities. Interviews focused on the teacher's expectations about what would happen, and comparing these with what actually happened.

Over five months, Wien collected 750 pages of interview transcripts, journal entries, and field notes. Synthesizing and reducing this mass of data constituted her analysis task. The first phase of analysis—her data management plan—included maintaining a separate binder of materials generated with each teacher, as well as a binder that recorded the overall research process itself. These binders were arranged chronologically. She also developed a filing procedure for data generated that concerned each teacher's managing resources, correcting child behavior, and implementing instructional processes; over time, she deemed this procedure inadequate as it was restricted to teacher actions. Accordingly, she replaced it with a second set of interview transcripts that could be partitioned and then sorted in various ways.

Wien's second phase of data analysis had as an early goal the development of a feedback paper for each teacher. A complete set of data was partitioned. Then the elements of the data set for each teacher were coded and sorted into bins, at first not labeled, on the basis of what seemed to belong together. Bins containing related constructs were placed in close physical proximity to each other. Eventually, after an extended iterative process—sorting, examining, re-coding, and sorting again—resultant bins were named as categories. Some categories were evidenced in the case of only a single teacher, but others were common. Each feedback paper synthesized Wien's view of that teacher's practical knowledge and its observed use. These papers were shared with each teacher individually via an in-depth interview. Each teacher first responded to the paper in writing, and these reactions were discussed. Each teacher was also asked questions concerning which criteria of practice represented developmental appropriateness. The interviews resulted in teacher confirmation of many of Wien's interpretations as well as new data for consideration—two new binders of data resulted that documented and chronicled these final interviews. This complex analytic activity involved numerous acts of interpreting and sorting data (several computer programs now exist to facilitate the sorting of qualitative data).

Elements of Wien's work of special interest included examples of teacher dominion and developmentally appropriate practice. For instance, the teacher Sonia illustrated teacher dominion as she focused on content during circle time: "I first wanted to introduce them to shapes, to think about what things are made of certain shapes. . . . I thought it was going to be a lot of trying to get to know these shapes; I hadn't expected them to know them very well" (Wien, 1995, p. 39). Liz, another teacher, demonstrated attitudes consistent with the developmentally appropriate framework when she spoke of the children in her care: "So they're making a lot of decisions on their own, which I feel is really important for them to do at an early age, and they're really in control of their own play" (p. 77). As Wien extracted, grouped, and coded these and hundreds of other examples, she subtly modified her conception of each framework and her ideas about teacher practice as related to the frameworks.

Interestingly, the results showed each of the five teachers operating at a different place on the continuum between teacher dominion and developmentally appropriate practice, and often using a framework different from what they intended. Inductively, Wien generated four explanations of why implementing developmentally appropriate practice was often problematic for early childhood educators. First, she believed teachers might simultaneously have allegiance to several frameworks, shifting between them as they interacted with children. Second, she thought teachers had inherited as well as planned scripts for action using the teacher-dominion framework, and that they exhibited these scripts almost without conscious intent. Third, contextual constraints (e.g., adult-child ratios, physical facilities, scheduling) at times blocked teachers from exhibiting developmentally appropriate practice. Fourth, teachers sometimes were unfamiliar with certain developmentally appropriate concepts and how to operationalize them. Six such concepts Wien noted in the data included observing the individual child to secure data for curriculum decisions; focusing on processes used by the child during activities; understanding a child's play and ways to support and extend it; valuing and generating opportunities for children to make choices; realizing the importance of child-initiated activities; and supporting a child's problem solving.

The relative simplicity with which we described Wien's analysis should not mask its inherent complexity. In general, analysis of qualitative data—including coding; generating categories; using inductive reasoning to identify ideas, constructs, and even theories; drawing conclusions; and reporting the results—is challenging and difficult. While Wien reported her results fully in narrative style, other reporting vehicles could have been used. Miles and Huberman (1994), for example, illustrated the use of matrix displays, context charts, event-state networks, causal networks, time as well as conceptually ordered displays, activity records, and other data analysis and presentation techniques. These procedures convey, again, the complexity of this enterprise; still, Miles and Huberman defended the importance of retaining actual words in the analysis:

> We argue that although words may be more unwieldy than numbers, they render more meaning than numbers alone and should be hung on to throughout data analysis. Converting words into numbers and then tossing away the words gets a researcher into all kinds of mischief. (p. 56)

Data Analysis in Historical Research

As noted in Chapter 5, two key matters must be addressed after collecting historical documents. First, the documents must be classified as primary or secondary sources, with the researcher having a preference for primary or original documents. Second, external criticism is applied to the documents to ascertain their authenticity, and internal criticism is used to ascertain the document's accuracy. These steps accomplished, the historical researcher turns to data analysis per se.

Following Gay (1987), the historical researcher often begins by coding the contents of the documents, sometimes organized into groups relating to the study's hypotheses. Along with the coding of each document, the researcher notes questions about the information, pertinent quotations, and summary comments. At this stage, the researcher must be careful to treat each document in a balanced manner, not attending only to those that support one's biases or are easy to understand while discarding those contrary to one's beliefs or difficult to integrate. Via an inductive and analytical process, the historical investigator then synthesizes the data assembled to frame the study's principal findings.

McMillan and Schumacher (1993) noted that historical researchers essentially engage in a search for facts. Then they must analyze the facts in several ways to determine generalizations and explanations that differ from statistical and commonsense explanations. Analytical explanations and generalizations summarize facts that assert that an event occurred and that suggest multiple causes for any given event. The explanations and generalizations are deemed valid if supported by the facts assembled, especially when considered from different points of view. McMillan and Schumacher also described four predominant analytical schemes available to the historical (or legal or policy) researcher. Via *descriptive narrative*, an event is described chronologically and generalizations are confined to it alone (e.g., the founding of the Montessori method). Using *interpretive analysis*, an event is interpreted also in terms of simultaneous events (e.g., relating the founding of the Montessori method to the political, social, and economic events taking place in Italy at the same time). With *comparative analysis*, a given event is compared with other events occurring simultaneously or at some other period of time (e.g., examining the similarities and differences of founding the Montessori method with the founding of Head Start). Finally, *universal analysis* conveys historical research analyzed in terms of philosophy or theory such as parallels in history or regularities of past trends (e.g., looking at early education movements in society, including the Montessori method, as attempts at improving the "educational odds" for young at-risk children). Analysis in legal and policy research can proceed along similar lines.

The Role of Computers in Qualitative Data Analysis

The rapid development of computers during the past decade or so has influenced qualitative researchers in a number of ways. Certainly the availability of laptop computers has changed the way some researchers collect and record data in the field. Observation and interview notes can be recorded during or immediately after the field experience, with easy retrieval for editing afterward.

Also in recent years, a number of different software programs have been developed to aid qualitative researchers with data storage, retrieval, and analysis (Glesne & Peshkin, 1992; McMillan & Schumacher, 1993; Miles & Huberman, 1994; Tesch, 1990). Miles and Huberman described six types of software program: word processors, word retrievers, text-base managers, code-and-retrieve programs, theory builders, and conceptual network builders. Such programs facilitate the work of the qualitative researcher in many ways, performing a myriad of functions: coding, memoing, data linking, search and retrieval, concept or theory development, data displays, and editing.

Organizing and Presenting Data and Results

Unlike quantitative researchers with their commonly used statistical techniques and standard ways of displaying results, qualitative researchers face more difficult challenges in determining how best to organize and present data from their studies. Miles and Huberman (1984, 1994) wrote two thorough books on the topic of qualitative data analysis, with emphasis on ways to display the data and results. Tables can be used to succinctly provide details of important study characteristics or summaries of key descriptive findings; the tables can include both words and numbers. Bar, line, and other graphs can usefully display relationships or patterns. Matrices also are employed to illustrate patterns or differences; these might include, for example, symbols such as + and – to convey the presence or absence of certain conditions. Other visual displays include diagrams with arrows showing the direction of possible causal links among the key constructs or variables identified. Fetterman (1989) described other useful tools for presentation of findings, including maps, flowcharts, and organizational charts.

While tables, graphs, and figures certainly can help in the presentation of the results, much of the final report from a qualitative research study is in narrative form. Not surprisingly, too, qualitative research papers tend to be lengthier than quantitative ones—often appearing as monographs or even books rather than as journal articles. Good qualitative research papers are well documented, and enriched with many data-based descriptions and examples to illustrate and substantiate key points. Including actual quotations from participants, short segments from field notes, and other pieces of data help the researcher "tell the story" well. In addition to the descriptive narratives, of course, are the researcher's interpretations, presentations of new or changed theoretical positions, and conclusions. Glesne and Peshkin (1992), in describing the three roles of a writer of qualitative inquiry as those of an artist, a translator/interpreter, and a transformer, captured well the complexity of the task.

CRITIQUING QUALITATIVE RESEARCH

As Denzin and Lincoln (1994) pointed out, there is considerable debate about how qualitative research should be assessed, and just what constitutes "good" qualitative research. They summarized four positions on this issue. The "positivist" position holds that the same criteria should be used to judge qualitative research as is used to judge quantitative research; these criteria include internal and external validity, reliability, and objectivity. The "postpositivist" position is that unique criteria must be constructed and used to evaluate qualitative research. Although there is a lack of agreement on exactly what suitable criteria would be, they generally include the extent to which a qualitative study generates theory, is empirically grounded, is scientifically sound, and produces generalizable or transferable findings. Researchers who espouse a third position, "postmodernism," believe that it is inappropriate to judge qualitative research, and that there are no criteria: "This argument contends that the very idea of assessing qualitative research is antithetical to the nature of this research and the world it attempts to study" (p. 480). The fourth position, called "poststructuralism," argues that entirely different criteria—not connected to positivist or postpositivist traditions—must be developed for qualitative research. Examples include "subjectivity, emotionality, feeling, and other antifoundational factors" (p. 480).

Some of the methodologists who have written extensively on the topic of judging qualitative research tend to belong, generally, to the second—postpositivist—position (e.g., Goetz & LeCompte, 1984; Strauss & Corbin, 1990). As is true with any research study, a qualitative one can be evaluated only if its procedures are explicit. Goetz and LeCompte (p. 233) emphasized that a complete report should include the following components:

- goals and research questions
- conceptual and theoretical frameworks underlying the research
- overall design characteristics
- participants and others who provided data
- roles and experience of the researchers
- data-collection methods
- data-analysis strategies
- conclusions, interpretations, and applications of key findings.

To then judge the research, two themes emerge—authenticity and trustworthiness. Strauss and Corbin enumerated seven attributes that contribute to sound qualitative research: "significance, theory-observation compatibility, generalizability, consistency, reproducibility, precision, and verification" (1990, p. 250).

Following the pattern set in Chapter 3, we first list some questions pertinent to all qualitative research. Then separate lists are provided for ethnographic and historical research.

Questions Applicable to All Qualitative Research

In assembling the questions on qualitative research in general, we draw from Gay (1987), McMillan (1996), McMillan and Schumacher (1993), and Strauss and Corbin (1990).

1. Is the conceptual framework for the study clear?
2. Are the procedures used in the study well explicated?
3. Are the data sources–whether subjects or documents–well described, along with sampling methods used?
4. Are the data-collection methods well detailed?
5. Are the analyses used detailed, appropriate, and inductive?
6. Are concepts and constructs generated?
7. Are conceptual linkages between constructs explicated, along with the development of any derived categories?
8. Do the methods and findings appear to be free from bias?
9. Are the conceptual and theoretical findings significant?

Questions Specific to Types of Qualitative Research

We now consider questions relevant in critiquing ethnographic and historical research. The sources indicated above were again used. The questions below are representative rather than exhaustive.

Ethnographic Research

1. Is the research experience of the investigator sufficient for the study undertaken?
2. Is the role of the researcher, in terms of degree of involvement, well described and defended as appropriate?
3. Is the credibility of the study, and internal and external validity, addressed?
4. Is the reliability of multiple data collectors described and sufficient?
5. Are description and interpretation kept separate?
6. Are multiple methods used in the study?
7. Are multiple perspectives considered in the study?

8. Is generalization of findings well described and appropriately restrained?
9. Is the study sufficiently long to have credibility?

Historical Research

1. Are definitions of constructs specific and consistent?
2. Is the research topic well defined and studied in depth?
3. Are facts kept separate from inferences?
4. Are causation and correlation kept distinct?
5. Are primary sources prevalent, with a low reliance on secondary sources?
6. Are external criticism (authenticity) and internal criticism (accuracy) diligently applied to all data sources?
7. Are generalizations made reasonably, appropriately restrained, and logically related to the facts?
8. Are the findings and conclusions well organized and effectively synthesized?
9. Do the findings suggest multiple causes for complex events?
10. Are causal explanations clear, appropriately reasonable, and logically related to the facts and generalizations established in the study?

SUMMARY

Like quantitative researchers, qualitative researchers are urged to employ multiple methods of data collection or triangulation to better measure the phenomenon being studied. The strategies commonly used to acquire data in qualitative investigations include participant observation, interviewing, and document collection. Important questions for the researcher to answer are how active a participant to become in the matter being observed and how much structure to build into the interview protocols used—qualitative studies usually involve less structured, more informal interviews. Reliability in qualitative pursuits typically refers to the reproducibility of the results by other researchers, while validity asks the question of the accuracy of the findings. Threats to the internal and external validity of qualitative investigations have been identified; even when labeled the same as some quantitative internal validity threats, they are defined differently. Data analysis in all qualitative research is generative—that is, it commences early in the study process and, from it, key findings, principles, and sometimes even theories may emerge. The heart of qualitative analyses is coding, whereby the researcher organizes verbal and other output from all the data collected–field notes, interview responses, event records, documents–into meaningful categories. This complex and often tedious analysis process increasingly is being assisted by imaginative computer programs. Qualitative research reports are characterized mainly by rich, narrative descriptions, with some but usually limited use of tables and figures. Questions helpful in critiquing qualitative research are presented. With the understandings of qualitative and quantitative research presented previously in the book as a backdrop, the possible integration of these two research orientations is considered in Part IV, Chapter 7.

PART IV

SYNTHESIS

Chapter 7

Integrating Quantitative and Qualitative Research

In this concluding chapter, we more fully develop the position we declared in the opening chapter. That is, we sense no inherent incompatibility between quantitative and qualitative approaches to the generation of knowledge. In fact, we will attempt to explicate the foundation for our belief that the two major types of research, while different, have unique strengths and limitations that can render their combined use both logical and wise.

We begin by sketching the issue that educational researchers and others have debated for some time. Essentially, it is a double-sided debate about which approach, quantitative or qualitative, is better and about whether the two approaches can be integrated in a single research undertaking. We then briefly present our own views on the matter. A third section in the chapter contains material about the two approaches' similarities and complementary features. A fourth section includes an examination of possible designs for integrating quantitative and qualitative research. Finally, examples of research undertakings that integrated the two research orientations are considered.

QUALITATIVE VERSUS QUANTITATIVE OR QUALITATIVE AND QUANTITATIVE

By the early 1980s, qualitative research had become a more obvious part of the research landscape in education than had been true a decade earlier. That trend has continued (Eisner & Peshkin, 1990); one might guess that qualitative studies now represent perhaps 20% of the studies conducted in education. These investigations are unevenly distributed across different specialties. For example, qualitative research appears more common in reading and literacy journals than it does in those for special education. About 20 years ago, given the increased presence of qualitative research, vigorous debates about the merits of the two orientations began to be waged.

About a decade ago, we wrote an article entitled "Qualitative vs. Quantitative or Qualitative and Quantitative Research?" (Goodwin & Goodwin, 1984). In it, we noted the increasingly vociferous debate between proponents of qualitative and quantitative research. We presented three misunderstandings—for emphasis we termed them "myths"—that were very much in evidence at the time. The first myth was that quantitative and qualitative research strategies represented obviously different, mutually exclusive paradigmatic perspectives. As noted in Chapter 2, quantitative research methods tend to be seen as related to the logical-positivist paradigm, while qualitative methods are more frequently viewed as associated with a phenomenological paradigm. However, these do not represent rigid or mandatory rules; said differently, a linkage between paradigm and method is neither an inherent nor a consistent requirement. So while certain methods are usually associated with certain paradigms, these are not exclusive associations.

The second myth was that quantitative methods are always objective, controlled, and obtrusive, and that qualitative methods are always subjective, naturalistic, and unobtrusive. As you might imagine, the word "always" gets in the way of both truth and practice. While the myth generally might be defensible, there are a number of difficulties with it. For example, aspects of some quantitative research are quite subjective, experiments conducted "in the field" (such as the child care center or preschool) can clearly struggle at establishing a controlled situation, and numerous quantitative studies are done that appear as "the natural order of things" to the subjects. Conversely, aspects of certain qualitative studies can be objective and quantitative, not particularly naturalistic, and can have obtrusive overtones.

The third myth presented was that measurement-related validity and reliability were not important in qualitative research. Of course, as we saw in Chapter 6, both validity and reliability, while defined somewhat differently, have crucial roles in qualitative investigations. Our articulation of the three myths was intended to help the field move on to more productive pursuits (that is, in our view, more productive than debating the merits of each approach). Numerous authors then were attempting to promote the integration of qualitative and quantitative research or to define middle ground between them that could be productively planted and harvested.

A legitimate question to ask currently, then, is to what extent educational researchers have moved on to other issues and debates. There have been changes directed at the increasing legitimatization of qualitative research. Eisner and Peshkin (1990), for example, noted the increasing availability of qualitative research courses in universities, the growing supply of texts on qualitative investigation, and the practice of some universities to hire professors specifically prepared in qualitative methodology. At the same time, while they hoped new questions would emerge from a quarter century of discussion, they recognized the perspectives of four groups on the state of research methodology. One group thought that the research question should drive the selection of method, and that the available methods were complementary. A second group was distinctly quantitative-oriented, with qualitative procedures deemed worthwhile only for exploratory studies. The third group criticized the quantitative approach, and lauded the qualitative, for sensitivity in researching the human condition. The final group postulated no important differences between quantitative and qualitative research, and suggested that both should strive to meet the same criteria of adequacy.

Our review of the current scene causes us to believe that, while the debate is not currently raging, the first three groups identified by Eisner and Peshkin (1990) certainly exist and possibly the fourth does also. We believe that it is possible to identify fairly recent written materials that strongly suggest that the debate and its inherent issues have never been resolved. For example, let us note some of the articulations of the "opposing" positions.

Hatch edited a book (1995b) that examined specific uses of qualitative methods in researching early childhood topics. In his introduction (1995a), he noted his experience a decade ago in defending his dissertation. His study had been primarily qualitative and apparently served to trigger a substantive paradigm war between the positivists and the constructivists; the resultant article about this experience articulated the positions of the Quantoids and the Smooshes (Hatch, 1985). Each of these two groups viewed themselves as quite distinct and argued that their approach to research was markedly superior. While Hatch (1995a) reported his belief that qualitative research had gained in stature from 1985 to 1995, a stated goal of his recent book was to add to a foundational base for qualitative investigators.

In a similar vein, Miles and Huberman (1994) reviewed the struggle, providing opinions of noted researchers on opposing sides of the paradigmatic fence. Thus, they noted Kerlinger's pronouncement to one of them that qualitative data did not exist, but that all data were either a 1 or a 0. On the flip side, they cited Berg's (1989) view that all data were basically qualitative, and Campbell's (1974) notion that all research had a qualitative foundation. Rather than Quantoids and Smooshes, they noted the existing stereotypes of number crunchers and navel-gazers. While not endorsing the rift, Miles and Huberman documented its existence, noting, among other things, Gherardi and Turner's (1987) analysis of the disagreement in an article titled "Real Men Don't Collect Soft Data." (While recognizing those authors' attempt to capitalize on a parody of a popular book of that time, we believe using "Researchers" in the title rather than "Men" might have been just as effective.)

Opinions bearing directly on the issue can also be cited. For example, Leininger (1994) examined nursing research and voiced opposition to the use of a "mixing and matching" approach wherein methods typical to qualitative and quantitative research were used in the same study. Her view was that researchers following such a course did not understand the philosophical foundations underlying each research paradigm. The result, she believed, was an eroding of each paradigm and the generation of noncredible research. To resolve the situation, she recommended advance study and better understanding of the qualitative paradigm: "The 'mix and match syndrome' will continue to be an issue until qualitative nurse researchers learn through advanced seminars and experts in qualitative research the philosophic roots and purposes of each paradigm" (p. 103).

A similar position in the field of education has been taken by Bogdan and Biklen (1992). While allowing that using the approaches together might at times result in good research, they considered that such combinations most often were unwise. Like Leininger, they noted that the two approaches were based on different assumptions. They thought it inappropriate, particularly for novices, to attempt a study combining the two orientations.

> Researchers, especially novices, trying to combine good quantitative design and good qualitative design have a difficult time pulling it off, and rather than producing a superior hybrid, usually produce a piece of research that does not meet the criteria for good work in either approach. . . . While it is useful to have an interplay of competing data, often such studies turn out to be studies in method rather than in the topic the research originally started out to study. (p. 43)

They concluded that a single researcher attempting to conduct sophisticated quantitative and qualitative studies simultaneously was likely to experience a big headache.

We consider, therefore, the issue of which method is "better," and its corollary of whether the approaches can be combined productively, to be current and unresolved. We do not take this position in any way to reignite the debate—quite the contrary. Rather, we have presented the material above to place in context much of what follows and to document the reality that the integration we opt for has a very steep and difficult route to negotiate. To this end, the next section contains a brief statement of our own position on such matters.

QUALITATIVE AND QUANTITATIVE RESEARCH: TO BE OR NOT TO BE COMBINED

We continue to be dismayed by the considerable time consumed by methodological disputes in educational research without much evidence of progress. To some extent, we believe that we bring this unfortunate state of affairs on ourselves. For example, in our doctoral preparation programs, too often we ask our students to become proficient in either qualitative or quantitative methods, rather than seeking their balanced preparation and expertise in both types of method.

We fully acknowledge the heartfelt and strongly held views of the authors already cited and the scores of others with similar positions. At the same time, we believe it is time for the field to move on. In our view, both qualitative and quantitative research have great merit and separately can generate knowledge of considerable importance for education. Further, we consider it wise often to combine qualitative and quantitative methods in a single study—that is, their strengths are complementary so that their use in tandem will generate balanced, in-depth understandings and outcomes.

We realize that the philosophical bases of the two paradigms are distinct and quite different. We believe that each philosophical base has merit and that the knowledge sought via each has potential value in both the short and the long run. At the same time, granting one of the philosophical bases legitimacy and not the other seems counterproductive and foolish in that it is likely to preclude the generation of an important segment of knowledge. Focusing on the philosophical differences between qualitative and quantitative approaches seems, to us, to polarize the research community and to reduce the likelihood of addressing on a timely basis many important research topics.

Further, we believe that if researchers can recognize and respect both philosophies for what they are, they can proceed to select research methods most germane to a given topic and, quite often, bring both approaches to bear on that topic. Cause-and-effect questions about a given topic might be better examined via quantitative experimental or single-subject methods. Other aspects of the very same topic—let's say its current nature and evolution over time—could well be more profitably addressed in depth using qualitative ethnographic procedures. To send a researcher into the investigation of a selected topic with preset givens, such as Method X must be used and Method Y cannot, surely constricts the generation of knowledge about that topic.

Why do we endorse such a pragmatic position? There are three principal reasons. First, we believe a combination of methods is likely to best serve the goals of generating knowledge and attaining diverse research purposes. Greene, Caracelli, and Graham (1989) noted that in evaluative inquiry up to five purposes could be served by combining quantitative and qualitative approaches in a single design. One purpose was *triangulation*, as discussed in Chapter 6. That is, the separate methods could be used to measure the same phenomenon and, given convergence of the results of each, to more definitively and more credibly establish accuracy. A second purpose was *complementarity*, whereby the results from one method, say quantitative, are used to enhance, elaborate, or illustrate the results of the other method (qualitative in this case). The third purpose cited was *development*; via it, one method is initiated first with findings used to guide the implementation of the other method subsequently. Via an *initiation* purpose, the researcher deliberately seeks paradox or contradiction. Thus, areas highlighted by the nonconvergence of qualitative and quantitative approaches might yield reformulations or areas for additional study. The fifth purpose denoted was *expansion*, that is, the combined methods were used to extend the scope and depth of inquiry. A common pattern was to use quantitative methods to research outcomes and qualitative procedures to assess implementation.

Second, we believe that the multiple-method researcher is the researcher best prepared to conduct credible and high-quality research. In this belief, we take a position very similar to that of Patton (1990). He opted for pragmatism over one-sided allegiance to a single paradigm and provided the following rationale:

> My own purpose in writing about alternative inquiry paradigms has been to *increase* the options available to evaluators, not to replace one limited paradigm with another limited, but different, paradigm. The importance of understanding alternative research paradigms is to sensitize researchers and evaluators to the ways in which their methodological prejudices, derived from their disciplinary socialization experiences, may reduce their methodological flexibility and adaptability. The purpose of describing how paradigms typically operate in the real world of research is to free evaluators from the bonds of allegiance to a single paradigm. (p. 38)

A third reason for this pragmatic position is possibly the most important one. We believe that the time has long since come for educational researchers to move away from waging methodological wars, diverting energy thus freed up to conducting research per se. We realize that the end of the debate, if that does materialize, in no way guarantees more resources for research—possibly the field will simply move on to other debates. Nonetheless, we believe we have hoed the field of qualitative versus quantitative research again and again—and quite enough—across the past quarter century. In general, in adopting a pragmatic position on this issue, we are far from alone. Others (e.g., Borg, Gall, & Gall, 1993, Creswell, 1994, Glesne & Peshkin, 1992, Miles & Huberman, 1994, Patton, 1990, and Shulman, 1988) offered similar positions. Shulman, for example, put it this way:

> We must avoid becoming educational researchers slavishly committed to some particular method. The image of the little boy who has just received a hammer for a birthday present and suddenly finds that the entire world looks to him like a variety of nails, is too painfully familiar to be tolerated. We must first understand our problem, and decide what questions we are asking, then select the mode of *disciplined inquiry* most appropriate to those questions. If the proper methods are highly quantitative and objective, fine. If they are more subjective or qualitative, we can use them responsibly as well. (p. 15)

SIMILARITIES AND COMPLEMENTARITIES BETWEEN QUALITATIVE AND QUANTITATIVE RESEARCH

Another tack to resolving this issue—and to advocating the use of both qualitative and quantitative methods in a single study—is to examine the ways the two approaches are similar and complementary. We do this to be illustrative rather than exhaustive; that is, there are probably additional similarities and complementarities not considered here. We first examine the similar and then the complementary features.

Similarities

We find a number of similarities between the two research approaches including the following:

- *Both approaches generate knowledge.* This knowledge, of course, takes different forms. As Patton (1990) noted, quantitative research generates knowledge that focuses on outcomes, generalizations, predictions, and causal explanations. Qualitative research, on the other hand, generates knowledge that puts emphasis on processes, extrapolation, understanding, and illumination. Patton also wisely pointed out that these different types of knowledge could well appeal to different audiences. We also view the knowledge generated as quite different. In the quantitative case, the hallmark characteristic of the knowledge produced could well be generalizability. With the knowledge emanating from qualitative inquiry, the central feature could well be meaning or meaningfulness. In either case, though, the similarity remains that knowledge is generated, thus creating a significant bond between the approaches. Salomon (1991) provided an important introspective thought that knowledge was being sought either analytically by controlling a few preselected variables or systemically by examining and attempting to understand the variables' interaction in the complex, real world.

- *Both approaches are rigorous.* Another way to state this similarity might be to note that both orientations stress extensive preparation in how to conduct inquiry; further, each expects a disciplined and professional execution of the researcher role. Part of this rigor involves the researcher's being knowledgeable about previous inquiry on the topic of study. With the quantitative investigator, this knowledge is crucial in planning the research and in interpreting the findings. In the qualitative case, knowledge of prior research helps define the foreshadowed problem, fortifies the researcher's intuitions during fieldwork, enhances the researcher's inductive processes while considering data, and aids in shaping the study's conclusions. Again, this shared emphasis on rigor, deep training, and prior research outcomes serves as an important link between the approaches.
- *Both approaches share findings with the field.* It is important that all research be examined by professional colleagues and others for critique and comment. Both qualitative and quantitative researchers use publications such as journal articles or books, present papers at professional meetings, and use electronic networks to offer their research for the review of colleagues. In terms of sharing knowledge with practitioners, both approaches have similar responsibilities. For reasons mentioned in Chapter 5, this task might well be more expeditiously performed in terms of qualitative outcomes, given their emphasis on narration and meaning. Nonetheless, this dissemination of one's finding with colleagues and practitioners serves as another shared value across the two research orientations.
- *Both approaches utilize measurement.* In both research orientations, measurement serves as a crucial element in the endeavor's credibility. We have noted substantive differences in this area—such as the quantitative researcher's love affair with numbers or the view of some that the qualitative researcher is *the* measuring instrument (since so much of what is "measured" is filtered through the researcher). At the

same time, both orientations at times make substantial use of observation and interviews, and to a lesser extent questionnaires varying in their degree of structure or open-endedness. This mutual allegiance to measurement, while not always of the same form, provides a good reason to combine such approaches in a given study. Via triangulation, for example, the researcher noting convergence can add to the credibility of findings, while divergence can serve to highlight surprises in the outcomes or additional areas in need of clarification or investigation.

Complementarities

Some complementary features of qualitative and quantitative research orientations are now presented. Pertinent definitions of complementary in this case are making full and complete or supplying each other's lack. As we will see, these features link rather directly to the similarities already presented.

- *The knowledge generated by each approach is complementary.* Throughout the book, we have noted that *if* one is able to reach the position that both quantitative research and qualitative research produce legitimate forms of knowledge, then one can celebrate their differences. That is, when both orientations are employed in the same investigation, the study's outcomes should be more complete and informative than they would have been if only one orientation guided the effort. There are, of course, resource implications—utilizing both orientations rather than one most likely will mean greater costs in terms of researcher time and expenditures (e.g., for materials, data collection, data analysis).

  We consider this complementary feature to be of particular importance for research in general, and for research in early childhood education in particular. Why? In our view, simultaneously planning a coordinated qualitative and quantitative inquiry focused on aspects of the same topic is likely to result in more complete and comprehensive knowledge of the topic than otherwise would be possible. Further, the multifaceted knowledge generated supports full understanding of the topic. The quantitative focus can address, for example, the extent of child care and preschools for children birth to 5 years old in this and other countries, as well as parents' attitudes toward them and their apparent effects; the degree of generalizability of such findings can also be examined. The qualitative focus, on the other hand, can round out the knowledge produced by humanizing and personalizing the topic to increase the understanding of it. Thus, case studies of a few children in child care and preschools, and the attitudes and behaviors of their families related to that experience, would bring to life and extend the quantitative outcomes also realized in the investigation. As noted by Walsh, Tobin, and Graue (1993), a qualitative and interpretive orientation in case studies and ethnographies generates knowledge both important and persuasive because the focus is on the human element so important in matters involving children and their families.

- *The measurement methods of each approach are complementary.* Related to the first feature, this characteristic emphasizes the complete "package" of measures that might be fashioned when quantitative and qualitative orientations are used in tandem in a specific study. Material we presented in Chapters 4 and 6 makes it obvious that while there is some overlap between measurement strategies in the two orientations (e.g., questionnaires and interviews, although of different types), there also are fairly distinct strategies (e.g., pre- and posttesting in quantitative pursuits, participant observation in qualitative endeavors). Having all sorts of measure available for potential use in a combined study obviously would give the researcher a wonderful opportunity to fully measure and explore the topic of interest and to answer the research questions posed.

  Patton (1990) provided several examples of the use of this complementarity. For example, he noted how quantitative measures might be appropriate to establish the extent of developmental change in children by their use in a pre- and post-measure fashion. At the same time, he opined that the dynamics of the developmental change process and an in-depth understanding of its nature might well be better assessed via qualitatively oriented observations or interviews. Together, the two sets of measures—one addressing *how well* and the other *how* and *why*—would paint a much fuller picture of the development occurring. He also discussed the "advantage" of qualitative methods and measures for *rapid reconnaissance,* that is, getting into the field quickly to initiate a study of opportunity without needing to do all the preplanning typical in a deductive, quantitative undertaking. While we agree with him, we also see that this characteristic of qualitative research has the potential to serve as an important first phase of a more rounded, complete combined study. That is, the quantitative aspects of the study could be planned and finalized while qualitative data collection was taking place and, very likely, also was providing guidance for aspects of the quantitative effort to follow. Another aspect of this complementary feature could involve using qualitative measures for outcomes as yet not measured well quantitatively; Patton cited creativity as an example. Further, it would seem that quantitative measures would generally provide a breadth of assessment, while qualitative measurement methods would add depth and detail to the assessment. Patton also pointed out that certain situations do not lend themselves to measures distinctly quantitative or, in other cases, qualitative. For example, he noted his preference for interviews over questionnaires in much cross-cultural research; at the same time, he observed that cultural mores and values had to be honored in terms of which topics were suitable to pursue, whose permission was needed prior to interviewing significant subjects, and the like.

- *Each approach can inform and assist the other approach.* There are a number of other important linkages that can operate when the two approaches are used together. Miles and Huberman (1994) paraphrased the work of Sieber (1973), which examined these possible links:

> Quantitative data can help with the qualitative side of a study during *design* by finding a representative sample and locating deviant cases. It can help during *data collection* by supplying background data, getting overlooked information, and helping avoid "elite bias" (talking only to high-status respondents). During *analysis* quantitative data can help by showing the generality of specific observations, correcting the "holistic fallacy" (monolithic judgments about a case), and verifying or casting new light on qualitative findings. . . . Qualitative data can help the quantitative side of a study during *design* by aiding with conceptual development and instrumentation. They can help during *data collection* by making access and data collection easier. During *analysis* they can help by validating, interpreting, clarifying, and illustrating quantitative findings, as well as through strengthening and revising theory. (Miles & Huberman, 1994, p. 41, emphasis in original)

In all, we consider the similarities and complementarities presented to bolster the legitimacy of conducting combined investigations. The comprehensive portrayal of the topic of interest that results—in both breadth and depth—seems to us to warrant the active consideration of a combination of qualitative and quantitative approaches when initiating a research investigation. This is not to say, by any means, that all investigations should utilize a combined format, as a distinctly quantitative or distinctly qualitative approach may make excellent sense for certain topics and certain questions. Rather, we see the foregoing as a foundation for considering a combined approach and evaluating it as one possibility for the research that is to follow. We now turn to a consideration of some more formal notions about the character of research designs using both qualitative and quantitative orientations.

COMBINED QUALITATIVE AND QUANTITATIVE RESEARCH DESIGNS

Several authors have presented their notions of what forms combined quantitative and qualitative designs might take. We now briefly review three such schemes, those by Creswell (1994), Miles and Huberman (1994), and Patton (1990).

Creswell (1994) came at the task of detailing combined designs by suggesting three models. In the two-phase model, either a qualitative phase precedes a quantitative phase or vice versa. While Creswell viewed the phases as quite distinct, so that the researcher could follow one set of foundational assumptions at a time, he noted that the consumer might not perceive the connection between the study's two phases. The second model was termed the dominant–less dominant design. In it, the researcher identifies and for the most part follows a dominant paradigm. Then, during the course of the inquiry, the researcher conducts one small component or side study using the alternative paradigm. Creswell termed the third model the mixed-methodology design. As conceptualized, it represents the most integrated of his proposed designs for the researcher mixes aspects of each approach in many or even all of the methodological steps encountered. While complex, difficult, and requiring an excellent working knowledge of both approaches, this model, in Creswell's opinion, would involve a nice exchange between inductive and deductive ways of studying a problem.

Miles and Huberman (1994) endorsed combined designs and portrayed four representative schematics. To our way of thinking, their models in general were substantially more integrated than those of Creswell. In the first, the quantitative and qualitative aspects of the study were fully integrated and occurred concurrently and continuously; thus, conceptually it was similar to Creswell's mixed-methodology design. In the second or multiwave design, qualitative fieldwork occurred continuously while quantitative survey phases took place intermittently. Thus a quantitative survey might inform the fieldwork by highlighting things to watch for, the field data collected might cause revisions in the next wave of surveys given, and so forth. The third design variation involved sequencing the two approaches, first qualitative, then quantitative, then qualitative again. The example given cast the first qualitative segment in an exploratory role, followed by a quantitative questionnaire, with the final phase characterized by the use of qualitative procedures to deepen and test the questionnaire findings. The fourth design reversed the order of the third. In the example given, an initial quantitative phase used a survey, the intermediate qualitative phase extended and added meaning to the survey's findings via fieldwork, and the final quantitative phase consisted of an experiment informed by the earlier two phases.

Patton (1990) endorsed combined models but thoughtfully visualized their nature somewhat differently than either Creswell or Miles and Huberman. Initially, he described "pure" approaches: hypothetical-deductive or quantitative typically featured by experimental design, quantitative data, and statistical analysis; and, conversely, qualitative usually characterized by naturalistic inquiry, qualitative data, and content or case analysis. Then he recombined these three elements—design, data, and analysis—in four manners he titled "mixed forms." The first mixed form utilized experimental design, qualitative data, and content analysis. The second variation also began with experimental design and qualitative data, but then turned to statistical analysis. As an example of this, Patton visualized subjects randomly assigned to treatment and control groups with both groups interviewed in-depth prior to and at the end of a special program received only by the treatment group; the interviews were rated on several dimensions by judges, and the ratings were then statistically analyzed (note that content analysis of these interviews, rather than ratings by judges, would have been an example of the first mixed form). The third mixed form combined naturalistic design, qualitative data, and statistical analysis. The final mixed approach featured naturalistic inquiry, quantitative data, and statistical analysis. As an example, Patton pictured a program underway with an observer present, but with no preset categories of interest or variables for study. After several weeks in the field, the observer derives a system of categories to represent several variables for investigation, and uses a structured observation system to generate numerical data on the categories. The resultant data are then statistically analyzed.

From the work of Creswell (1994), Miles and Huberman (1994), and Patton (1990), as well as others, it is clear that there are a great number of ways to combine qualitative and quantitative approaches in a single study or highly related studies. We believe that this is an excellent strategy to consider when planning how to best research a given topic, especially when an adequate base of resources for the research is available. As aptly noted by Miles and Huberman (1994), we need both words and numbers to understand our world. While our view is pragmatic, we consider effective research most likely to result if, given the topic of interest, the researcher is free to select and implement a host of methods, unshackled by a permanent allegiance to this or that approach. We now turn to examples of integrated qualitative–quantitative research studies.

RESEARCH EXAMPLES COMBINING QUALITATIVE AND QUANTITATIVE APPROACHES

We now examine four sample research studies that, in our view, combine qualitative and quantitative approaches. In the first two studies, the intent to approach the topic utilizing both orientations may not have been quite as deliberate as in the last two examples.

In the first case, Pedersen, Faucher, and Eaton (1978) seem to have planned a quantitative study, but ended up with aspects that were qualitative. As many researchers of that time period, they had been influenced by studies on teacher expectations. They began by examining third- and sixth-grade IQ test scores in the archives for past students of a given elementary school that, in general, had a majority of students who did not finish high school. During this process, they decided to group the IQ data by which first-grade teacher the students had had. They were struck by the fact that students who had had "Miss A" as a first-grade teacher were more likely to have experienced an increase in IQ score from third to sixth grade, even though assignment of children to different first-grade teachers appeared matched and equal. It was then decided to interview 60 former students, now adults—20 who experienced IQ increases, 20 with decreases, and 20 with little change—using a semi-structured set of questions, some with closed responses and some that were open-ended.

Part of the interview involved classifying the sample on adult status variables: highest grade completed, amount of rent paid, type of housing, state of repair of the housing, personal appearance, and occupational level. Once again, the adult status scores of Miss A's former students were dramatically higher than those of students having other teachers. Further, via the open-ended questions, it was learned that Miss A was remembered by all her students (not the case for other teachers), and most of them rated both her teaching and effort as good or excellent. Responses of former students to other open-ended questions described Miss A's warmth and her consistent message of the importance of schooling. In her grading (data pulled from the archives), Miss A gave her students much higher marks than other first-grade teachers in achievement, effort, leadership and initiative, and cooperation. These high marks for these students persisted in subsequent grades with other teachers. The authors concluded, through examining the data and using both deductive and inductive processes, that an individual teacher could have a profound effect on students.

The next study also seemed to use both qualitative and quantitative methods to investigate storybook reading in homes of New Zealand families (Phillips & McNaughton, 1990). The families of 10 3- and 4-year-olds were asked to keep a log of all the storybook reading in the home for 28 days. A quantitative analysis of this data revealed that 87 books were read on average across the period, predominately narratives with animal characters rather than informational, knowledge-linked books. The log data also informed a second phase of the study in which the mother and child in each family were audiotaped as they "read" together 9 storybooks provided by the researchers. Comments made during reading of 3 of the books were coded and analyzed inductively. Over 85% of the comments involved identifying meaning—for clarification, anticipation, or integration—related to the narrative of the story, and were equally likely to be made by the mother or the child, especially during re-readings of the books, when the child's participation picked up. The authors speculated that early storybook reading might assist children in constructing meaning about written language, preparing them for subsequent high achievement in school.

Another study with combined features examined low socioeconomic children's success or failure at early literacy learning (Purcell-Gates & Dahl, 1991). Children in three inner-city schools using traditional, skills based instruction were pre and posttested at the beginning of kindergarten and the end of first grade on six written language measures, and they also took two standardized achievement tests as first grade concluded. Thirty-five of the children were observed at school across the 2 years of this longitudinal, multisite study. Four types of learners were identified inductively with regard to their literacy paths: independent explorers who actively investigated print and early on visualized the links between written language and the skills-based instruction; curriculum-dependent children who had a much more circumscribed concept of print and relied greatly on instruction; passive nonweavers who were minimally involved in reading and tended not to weave understandings of literacy concepts into meaningful processes; and deferring learners, who started as active learners but became passive once confused by mismatches between their knowledge of print and the curriculum. Among other findings, the authors argued that individual instruction was crucial for students following the less productive paths to literacy learning. This combination of pre-data, process paths, and outcome data served to generate considerable knowledge, quantitative and qualitative, about the development of literacy in a skills-based environment.

Our final example is the most extensive early childhood study we found that deliberately set out to examine a topic—in this case, student retention—wearing both qualitative and quantitative glasses. In terms of design, implementation, analysis, and reporting, both research orientations were represented (Shepard & Smith, 1987, 1989; Smith & Shepard, 1988). The quantitative elements in the study included a quasi-experimental design to assess the effects of kindergarten retention on first-grade achievement and adjustment (Shepard & Smith, 1987). Of seven outcome measures, retained children were significantly ahead on a standardized reading achievement test by about one month; there were no differences on a standardized mathematics test or on teacher ratings of reading achievement, math achievement, attention, social maturity, or student self-concept. Parent interview data suggested that retained children were somewhat more negative about school. In all, these results were comparable to the majority of research on the topic.

The principal qualitative elements of the investigation centered on kindergarten teachers' belief systems (Smith & Shepard, 1988). Data consisted of participant observation of a purposeful sample of kindergarten classes and decision-making meetings; documents such as school policies, curriculum objectives, and test results; audiotaped interviews with a sample of parents; and, especially, semi-structured interviews with over 90% of the district's kindergarten teachers. Data collection extended across a one-year time period. Extensive data coding and analysis took place. One major finding was that teachers' beliefs about school readiness fell along a continuum from "nativism" (readiness is an internal, organismic process relatively unaffected by intervention) to "environmentalism" (readiness is a process that can be influenced by interventions from teachers, parents, and other environmental factors). Based on interviews and confirmed by classroom observations, about half the teachers were considered nativists, while the other half were environmentalists of three types: remediationists, diagnostic-prescriptives, and interactionists. The retention rates of the teachers by and large matched these belief systems—that is, nativists recommended the retention of significantly more children than did the environmentalists. Another provocative finding was that kindergarten teachers within the same school tended to have similar belief systems on this issue. In all, the numerous and integrated qualitative and quantitative focuses of this research endeavor generated substantive knowledge—both narrative and numerical—about retention. Although we have provided only a brief description of the retention study's outcomes, we hope enough information has been provided to illustrate the wonderful blending and complementarity that can occur utilizing the two orientations on a given topic.

EPILOGUE

As we conclude this book, three matters seem important: to remind the reader of our original purpose; to provide a general descriptive statement of the current research enterprise in society; and to make some predictions about what the future might hold in terms of research and early childhood education.

The stated purpose for this book was to provide the reader with an understanding of the research endeavor, its processes, and its products. We hope that we have been successful in this regard. "We are wild about research!" may be a bit of an overstatement, but it is obvious to us that we hold the generation of knowledge through research in very high regard—and having readers adopt this same attitude is important to us. The progress of early childhood education, and indeed the progress of society itself, seems to depend in large measure on the production of knowledge about all aspects of the human condition.

In describing the status of the current research enterprise in this society and many others, we truly are impressed by its scope and strength. From the material presented here, it should now be obvious that society is truly fortunate to have such a wide range of complementary research methods available—essentially an impressive methodological arsenal. Well conceptualized and well executed, research using this arsenal holds great promise for bettering the human condition. Recall too, from Chapter 1, that we never think of particular research methods as good or bad; rather, the different methods have varying capabilities for addressing a given research problem.

Three predictions come to mind that relate more or less directly to early childhood education and research. *First*, we believe that there will be a significant increase in the number of educators, including those working with very young children, who will at times be wearing their researcher hats as they fulfill their teaching roles. Quite possibly more user-friendly computer programs for data analysis will help this prediction materialize. *Second*, we believe that society will increase its use of research to help resolve important issues, including many issues that would impact early childhood education. For example, research seems a fruitful avenue to travel in trying to resolve policy issues related to determining appropriate government support for various segments of society in times of scarce financial resources. A related issue could be determining through evaluation research which early childhood programs and practices are most effective for achieving specified outcomes. Both of these predictions imply a continuing emphasis on developing stronger measures and assessment practices for use with young children and in their programs. *Third*, we believe that individual topics or problem areas increasingly will be researched by using both quantitative and qualitative approaches in single, integrated investigations, in order to better and more fully know the topic studied. To our mind this probably will require the preparation of many more individuals who are equally adept at conducting quantitative or qualitative research.

Some among our readers might view our three predictions as wishful thinking, rather than as outcomes likely to eventuate from current conditions and emerging forces. After all, did we not lament early in this chapter that too often today's researcher-in-training is virtually forced to select either quantitative or qualitative methods to master? And, practically in the same breath, did we not imply that many persons continue to be strongly biased toward the use of quantitative methods, with others equally attracted to qualitative procedures? Well, maybe we did. At the same time, we would like to recall for you Lesser's (1972) response when he was criticized for departing from reality in his presentation of a courteous New York City bus driver on "Sesame Street":

> Now, we all know that a bus driver often is not society's best example of someone who is kind and courteous. But on *Sesame Street*'s bus trip, the driver responds to the passengers' hellos and thank yous, tells a child who cannot locate his money, "That's all right, you can pay me tomorrow," and, when seeing a young woman running after the bus just as it has left the curb, actually stops to let her on. Why present . . . such an outrageous misrepresentation of the realities of a city transportation system? . . . Our basic position was to show the child what the world is like when people treat each other with decency and consideration. . . . even if we stretch familiar reality a bit in order to do so. . . . But, even at the risk of sugar-coating these realities, perhaps we can suggest a better vision of things. (pp. 246–247)

So, if you consider our predictions wishful thinking (and we do admit their very positive tone), perhaps you can at least accept them under Lesser's "better vision of things" philosophy.

We truly do hope that the complementary use of quantitative and qualitative research in individual investigations increases in coming years. As noted earlier, numbers and narratives are both needed to better understand our world. Certainly this dictum applies to research in early childhood education, a vital enterprise for societies everywhere. Further, early childhood education seems an ideal breeding ground for the greater use of a combined quantitative-qualitative methodology. For example, quantitative research outcomes can produce verifiable effects caused by our infant and preschool programs for at-risk children or by our interventions for exceptional children and their families. Used in tandem, qualitative research can richly depict the "heart" of the programs and interventions, by describing in narrative the human and affective side of their implementation. Our view is that this complementary use of quantitative and qualitative procedures can yield valuable knowledge for advancing early childhood education.

References

Adkins, D. C., & Ballif, B. L. (1973). *Animal Crackers: A Test of Motivation to Achieve: Examiner's manual.* Monterey, CA: CTB/McGraw-Hill.

Adler, P. A., & Adler, P. (1994). Observational techniques. In N. K. Denzin and Y. S. Lincoln (Eds.), *Handbook of qualitative research* (pp. 377–392). Thousand Oaks, CA: Sage.

American Educational Research Association, American Psychological Association, National Council on Measurement in Education. (1966). *Standards for educational and psychological tests and manuals.* Washington, DC: APA.

American Educational Research Association, American Psychological Association, National Council on Measurement in Education. (1985). *Standards for educational and psychological testing* (3rd ed.). Washington, DC: APA.

Anderson, S. B., & Bogatz, G. A. (1979). *Circus manual and technical report.* Monterey, CA: CTB/McGraw-Hill.

Aries, P. (1962). *Centuries of childhood: A social history of family life.* New York: Knopf.

Axtman, A. (1992). Infant assessment: Issues and glossary. In L. R. Williams & D. P. Fromberg (Eds.), *Encyclopedia of early childhood education* (pp. 300–302). New York: Garland.

Aylward, E. (1991). *Understanding children's testing.* Austin, TX: Pro-Ed.

Ayres, A. J. (1980). *Southern California Sensory Integration Tests: Manual* (rev. ed.). Los Angeles: Western Psychological Services.

Ball, S. (1971). *Assessing the attitudes of young children toward school.* Princeton, NJ: Educational Testing Service.

Baratz, D. (1983). How justified is the "obvious" reaction? *Dissertation Abstracts International, 44/02B,* 644B. (University Microfilms No. DA 8314435)

Barnett, S. (1990). Developing preschool education policy: An economic perspective. *Educational Policy, 4,* 245–265.

Beery, K. E. (1989). *Revised administration, scoring, and teaching manual for the Developmental Test of Visual-Motor Integration.* Cleveland: Modern Curriculum Press.

Bennett, R. E. (1982). The use of grade and age equivalent scores in educational assessment. *Diagnostique, 7,* 139–146.

Berg, B. L. (1989). *Qualitative research methods for the social sciences.* Boston: Allyn & Bacon.

Berliner, D. C. (1992). Telling the stories of educational psychology. *Educational Psychologist, 27,* 143–161.

Best, J. W., & Kahn, J. V. (1993). *Research in education* (7th ed.). Boston: Allyn and Bacon.

Blinco, P. M. A. (1992). A cross-cultural study of task persistence of young children in Japan and the United States. *Journal of Cross-Cultural Psychology, 23,* 407–415.

Boehm, A. E. (1986a). *Manual for the Boehm Test of Basic Concepts—Preschool Version.* San Antonio, TX: Psychological Corporation.

Boehm, A. E. (1986b). *Manual for the Boehm Test of Basic Concepts-Revised.* San Antonio, TX: Psychological Corporation.

Boehm, A. E. (1992). Glossary of assessment instruments. In L. R. Williams & D. P. Fromberg (Eds.), *Encyclopedia of Early Childhood Education* (pp. 293–300). New York: Garland.

Bogdan, R. C., & Biklen, S. K. (1992). *Qualitative research for education* (2nd ed.). Boston: Allyn and Bacon.

Borg, W. R., Gall, J. P., & Gall, M. D. (1993). *Applying educational research: A practical guide* (3rd ed.). New York: Longman.

Bredekamp, S., & Shepard, L. A. (1989). How best to protect children from inappropriate school expectations, practices, and policies. *Young Children, 44*(3), 14–24.

Browning, P. C., & Hatch, J. A. (1995). Qualitative research in early childhood settings: A review. In J. A. Hatch (Ed.), *Qualitative research in early childhood settings* (pp. 99–114). Westport, CT: Praeger.

Bruininks, R. H. (1978). *Bruininks-Oseretsky Test of Motor Proficiency.* Circle Pines, MN: American Guidance Service.

Bruner, J. S. (1961). The act of discovery. *Harvard Educational Review, 31,* 21–32.

Buchler, J. (Ed.). (1955). *Philosophical writings of Peirce.* New York: Dover.

Campbell, D. T. (1974, August-September). *Quantitative knowing in action research.* Kurt Lewin Award Address, Society for the Psychological Study of Social Issues, presented at the annual meeting of the American Psychological Association, New Orleans.

Campbell, D. T., & Fiske, D. W. (1959). Convergent and discriminant validity in the multitrait-multimethod matrix. *Psychological Bulletin, 56,* 81–105.

Campbell, D. T., & Stanley, J. C. (1963). *Experimental and quasi-experimental designs for research.* Chicago: McNally.

Chandler, M., Fritz, A. S., & Hala, S. (1989). Small-scale deceit: Deception as a marker of two-, three-, and four-year-olds' early theories of mind. *Child Development, 60,* 1263–1277.

Child, D. (1970). *The essentials of factor analysis.* New York: Holt, Rinehart and Winston.

Ciupryk, F. A., Fraser, B. J., Malone, J. A., & Tobin, K. G. (1989). Exemplary grade 1 mathematics teaching: A case study. *Journal of Research in Childhood Education, 4,* 40–50.

Cole, N. S., & Moss, P. A. (1989). Bias in test use. In R. L. Linn (Ed.), *Educational measurement* (3rd ed., pp. 201–219). New York: American Council on Education and Macmillan.

Conoley, J. C., & Impara, J. C. (Eds.). (1995). *The twelfth mental measurements yearbook.* Lincoln: University of Nebraska Press.

Cook, T. D., & Campbell, D. T. (1979). *Quasi-experimentation: Design and analysis issues for field settings.* Chicago: McNally.

Coopersmith, S., & Gilberts, R. (1982). *Behavioral academic self-esteem* (Exper. ed.). Monterey, CA: CTB/McGraw-Hill.

Cost, quality, and child outcomes in child care centers: Executive summary. (1995). Denver: Economics Department, University of Colorado at Denver.

Creswell, J. W. (1994). *Research design: Qualitative & quantitative approaches.* Thousand Oaks, CA: Sage.

Crocker, L., & Algina, J. (1986). *Introduction to classical and modern test theory.* Chicago: Holt, Rinehart and Winston.

Cronbach, L. J. (1980). Validity on parole: How can we go straight? *New directions for testing and measurement: Measuring achievement, progress over a decade,* No. 5 (pp. 99–108). San Francisco: Jossey-Bass.

Cronbach, L. J. (1988). Five perspectives on validity argument. In H. Wainer & H. I. Braun (Eds.), *Test validity* (pp. 3–17). Hillsdale, NJ: Lawrence Erlbaum.

Cronbach, L. J. (1990). *Essentials of psychological testing* (5th ed.). New York: Harper and Row.

Cronbach, L. J., Gleser, G. C., Nanda, H., & Rajaratnam, N. (1972). *The dependability of behavioral measurement.* New York: Wiley.

Cronbach, L. J., & Meehl, P. E. (1955). Construct validity in psychological tests. *Psychological Bulletin, 52,* 281–302.

CTB/McGraw-Hill (1985). *California Achievement Test.* Monterey, CA: Author.

Davis, F. (1973). The Martian and the convert: Ontological polarities in social research. *Urban Life, 2,* 333–334.

Dawe, H. C. (1934). An analysis of two hundred quarrels of preschool children. *Child Development, 5,* 139–157.

Denzin, N. K. (1988). *The research act* (rev. ed.). New York: McGraw-Hill.

Denzin, N. K. (1989). *Interpretive interactionism.* Thousand Oaks, CA: Sage.

Denzin, N. K., & Lincoln, Y. S. (Eds.). (1994). *Handbook of qualitative research.* Thousand Oaks, CA: Sage.

Dorsey, A. G. (1992). Professional journals related to early childhood education. In L. R. Williams & D. P. Fromberg (Eds.), *Encyclopedia of early childhood education* (pp. 443–444). New York: Garland.

Dreisbach, M., & Keogh, B. K. (1982). Testwiseness as a factor in readiness test performance of young Mexican-American children. *Journal of Educational Psychology, 74,* 224–229.

Dunn, L. M., & Dunn, L. M. (1981). *Manual for Peabody Picture Vocabulary Test—Revised.* Circle Pines, MN: American Guidance Service.

Dyson, A. H. (1987). The value of "time off task": Young children's spontaneous talk and deliberate text. *Harvard Educational Review, 57,* 396–420.

Edson, C. H. (1988). Our past and present: Historical inquiry in education. In R. R. Sherman & R. B. Webb (Eds.), *Qualitative research in education: Focus and methods* (pp. 44–58). London: Falmer.

Eisenhart, M., & Borko, H. (1993). *Designing classroom research: Themes, issues, and struggles.* Boston: Allyn and Bacon.
Eisner, E. W., & Peshkin, A. (1990). Introduction. In E. W. Eisner & A. Peshkin (Eds.), *Qualitative inquiry in education: The continuing debate* (pp. 1–17). New York: Teachers College Press.
Elam, S. M., Rose, L. C., & Gallup, A. M. (1992). The 24th annual Gallup/Phi Delta Kappa poll of the public's attitudes toward the public schools. *Phi Delta Kappan, 74,* 41–53.
Elam, S. M., Rose, L. C., & Gallup, A. M. (1993). The 25th annual Phi Delta Kappa/ Gallup poll of the public's attitudes toward the public schools. *Phi Delta Kappan, 75,* 137–152.
Elder, G. H., Jr., Modell, J., & Parke, R. D. (Eds.). (1993). *Children in time and place: Developmental and historical insights.* Cambridge, England: Cambridge University Press.
Erickson, F. (1986). Qualitative methods in research on teaching. In M. C. Wittrock (Ed.), *Handbook of research on teaching* (3rd ed., pp. 119–161). New York: Macmillan.
The ETS test collection. Volume 5: Attitude tests. (1991). Phoenix, AZ: Oryx Press.
Farley, F. (1993). Street science. *Psychological Science Agenda, 6*(4), 11.
Fetterman, D. M. (1989). *Ethnography: Step by step.* Thousand Oaks, CA: Sage.
Fontana, A., & Frey, J. H. (1994). Interviewing: The art of science. In N. K. Denzin & Y. S. Guba (Eds.), *Handbook of qualitative research* (pp. 361–376). Thousand Oaks, CA: Sage.
Frankenburg, W. K., Dodds, J. B., Fandal, A. W., Kazuk, E., & Cohrs, M. (1975). *Denver Developmental Screening Test: Revised reference manual.* Denver: LADOCA Foundation.
Friedrich, L. K., & Stein, A. H. (1973). Aggressive and prosocial television programs and the natural behavior of preschool children. *Monographs of the Society for Research in Child Development, 38* (4, Serial No. 151).
Fulghum, R. (1988). *All I really needed to know I learned in kindergarten.* New York: Ivy.
Gage, N. L. (1991). The obviousness of social and educational research results. *Educational Researcher, 20*(1), 10–16.
Gay, L. R. (1987). *Educational research: Competencies for analysis and application* (3rd ed.). Columbus, OH: Merrill.
Geisinger, K. G. (1992). The metamorphosis of test validation. *Educational Psychologist, 27,* 197–222.
Genishi, C. (1988). Kindergartens and computers: A case study of six children. *Elementary School Journal, 89,* 185–201.
Gesell, A. (1928). *The mental growth of the pre-school child.* New York: Macmillan. (Original work published 1925)
Gherardi, S., & Turner, B. A. (1987). Real men don't collect soft data. *Quaderno 13.* Dipartimento di Politica Sociale, Universita di Trento, Italy.
Ginsburg, H. P., & Baroody, A. J. (1983). *Test of Early Mathematical Ability.* Austin, TX: Pro-Ed.

Glaser, B. G., & Strauss, A. L. (1967). *The discovery of grounded theory: Strategies for qualitative research.* Chicago: Aldine.

Glaser, R. (1963). Instructional technology and the measurement of learning outcomes. *American Psychologist, 18,* 519–521.

Glass, G. V. (1978). Standards and criteria. *Journal of Educational Measurement, 15,* 237–261.

Glass, G. V. (1988). Quasi-experiments: The case of interrupted time series. In R. M. Jaeger (Ed.), *Complementary methods for research in education* (pp. 445–461). Washington, DC: American Educational Research Association.

Glass, G. V., & Hopkins, K. D. (1984). *Statistical methods in education and psychology* (2nd ed.). Englewood Cliffs, NJ: Prentice-Hall.

Glass, G. V., McGaw, B., & Smith, M. L. (1981). *Meta-analysis in social research.* Thousand Oaks, CA: Sage.

Glesne, C., & Peshkin, A. (1992). *Becoming qualitative researchers: An introduction.* White Plains, NY: Longman.

Goetz, J. P. (1976). Configurations in control and autonomy: A microethnography of a rural third-grade classroom. *Dissertation Abstracts International, 36,* 6175A. (University Microfilms No. 76-6275)

Goetz, J. P., & LeCompte, M. D. (1984). *Ethnography and qualitative design in educational research.* San Diego: Academic Press.

Gold, R. L. (1969). Roles in sociological field observations. In G. J. McCall & J. L. Simmons (Eds.), *Issues in participant observation: Text and reader.* Reading, MA: Addison-Wesley.

Goodwin, L. D., & Goodwin, W. L. (1984). Qualitative vs. quantitative or qualitative and quantitative research? *Nursing Research, 33,* 378–380.

Goodwin, L. D., & Goodwin, W. L. (1991a). Estimating construct validity. *Research in Nursing and Health, 14,* 235–243.

Goodwin, L. D., & Goodwin, W. L. (1991b). Using generalizability theory in early childhood special education. *Journal of Early Intervention, 15,* 193–204.

Goodwin, W. L., & Driscoll, L. A. (1980). *Handbook for measurement and evaluation in early childhood education: Issues, measures, and methods.* San Francisco: Jossey-Bass.

Goodwin, W. L., & Goodwin, L. D. (1989). The use of nonreactive measures with preschoolers. *Early Child Development and Care, 41,* 173–194.

Goodwin, W. L., & Goodwin, L. D. (1993). Young children and measurement: Standardized and nonstandardized instruments in early childhood education. In B. Spodek (Ed.), *Handbook of research on the education of young children* (pp. 441–463). New York: Macmillan.

Gravetter, F. J., & Wallnau, L. B. (1988). *Statistics for the behavioral sciences* (2nd ed.). St. Paul, MN: West.

Graziano, A. M., & Raulin, M. L. (1993). *Research methods: A process of inquiry* (2nd ed.). New York: Harper Collins.

Greene, J. C., Caracelli, V. J., & Graham, W. F. (1989). Toward a conceptual framework for mixed-method evaluation designs. *Educational Evaluation and Policy Analysis, 11,* 255–274.

Gresham, F. M., & Elliott, S. N. (1990). *Social Skills Rating System.* Circle Pines, MN: American Guidance Service.

Guba, E. G., & Lincoln, Y. S. (1981). *Effective evaluation: Improving the usefulness of evaluation results through responsive and naturalistic approaches.* San Francisco: Jossey-Bass.

Guilford, J. P. (1946). New standards for test evaluation. *Educational and Psychological Measurement, 6,* 427–438.

Hair, J. F., Jr., Anderson, R. E., Tatham, R. L., & Black, W. C. (1992). *Multivariate data analysis* (3rd ed.). New York: Macmillan.

Harlow, H. F. (1958). The nature of love. *American Psychologist, 13,* 673–685.

Harlow, H. F. (1959). Love in infant monkeys. *Scientific American, 200*(6), 68–74.

Haskins, R. (1989). Beyond metaphor: The efficacy of early childhood education. *American Psychologist, 44,* 274–282.

Hatch, J. A. (1985). The quantoids versus the smooshes: Struggling with methodological rapprochement. *Issues in Education, 3,* 158–167.

Hatch, J. A. (1995a). Introduction. In J. A. Hatch (Ed.), *Qualitative research in early childhood settings* (pp. xi–xvii). Westport, CT: Praeger.

Hatch, J. A. (Ed.). (1995b). *Qualitative research in early childhood settings.* Westport, CT: Praeger.

Henson, K. T. (1995). Writing for publication. *Phi Delta Kappan, 76,* 801–803.

Hieronymus, A. N., Hoover, H. C., & Lindquist, E. F. (1986). *Iowa Tests of Basic Skills.* Chicago: Riverside.

Hills, T. W. (1987). Children in the fast lane: Implications for early childhood policy and practice. *Early Childhood Research Quarterly, 2,* 265–273.

Holmes, R. M. (1991). Categories of play: A kindergartner's view. *Play & Culture, 4,* 43–50.

Holmes, R. M. (1992). Play during snacktime. *Play & Culture, 5,* 295–304.

Hopkins, D. (1993). *A teacher's guide to classroom research* (2nd ed.). Bristol, PA: Open University Press/Taylor & Francis.

Hopkins, K. D., & Glass, G. V. (1986). *Basic statistics for the behavioral sciences* (2nd ed.). Englewood Cliffs, NJ: Prentice-Hall.

Hopkins, K. D., Stanley, J. C., & Hopkins, B. R. (1990). *Educational and psychological measurement and evaluation* (7th ed.). Englewood Cliffs, NJ: Prentice-Hall.

Hubbard, R. S., & Power, B. M. (1993). *The art of classroom inquiry: A handbook for teacher researchers.* Portsmouth, NH: Heinemann.

Isaac, S., & Michael, W. B. (1981). *Handbook in research and evaluation* (2nd ed.). San Diego: Edits.

Jaeger, R. M. (1988). Survey methods in educational research. In R. M. Jaeger (Ed.), *Complementary methods for research in education* (pp. 303–387). Washington, DC: American Educational Research Association.

Jaeger, R. M. (1989). Certification of student competence. In R. L. Linn (Ed.), *Educational measurement* (3rd ed., pp. 485–514). New York: Macmillan.

Jennings, C. M., Jennings, J. E., Richey, J., & Dixon-Krauss, L. (1992). Increasing interest and achievement in mathematics through children's literature. *Early Childhood Research Quarterly, 7,* 263–276.

Jones, E., & Reynolds, G. (1992). *The play's the thing: Teachers' roles in children's play.* New York: Teachers College Press.
Kachigan, S. K. (1991). *Multivariate statistical analysis: A conceptual introduction.* New York: Radius Press.
Kaestle, C. F. (1993). The awful reputation of educational research. *Educational Researcher, 22*(1), 23–31.
Kagan, S. L. (1990). Readiness 2000: Rethinking rhetoric and responsibility. *Phi Delta Kappan, 72,* 272–279.
Kane, M. T. (1994). Validating the performance standards associated with passing scores. *Review of Educational Research, 64,* 425–461.
Karnes, M. B., Johnson, L. J., & Beauchamp, K. D. F. (1989). Developing problem-solving skills to enhance task persistence of handicapped preschool children. *Journal of Early Intervention, 13,* 61–72.
Kaufman, A. S., & Kaufman, N. L. (1983). *Interpretive manual for the Kaufman Assessment Battery for Children.* Circle Pines, MN: American Guidance Service.
Kerlinger, F. N. (1979). *Behavioral research: A conceptual approach.* New York: Holt, Rinehart and Winston.
Kerlinger, F. N. (1986). *Foundations of behavioral research* (3rd ed.). New York: Holt, Rinehart and Winston.
Keyser, D. J., & Sweetland, R. C. (Eds.). (1994). *Test critiques* (Vol. 10). Austin, TX: Pro-Ed.
Kirk, J., & Miller, M. L. (1986). *Reliability and validity in qualitative research.* Thousand Oaks, CA: Sage.
Langhorst, B. H. (1989). *Assessment in early childhood education: A consumer's guide.* Portland, OR: Northwest Regional Educational Laboratory.
Laursen, B., & Hartup, W. W. (1989). The dynamics of preschool children's conflicts. *Merrill-Palmer Quarterly, 35,* 281–297.
Leininger, M. (1994). Evaluation criteria and critique of qualitative research studies. In J. M. Morse (Ed.), *Critical issues in qualitative research methods* (pp. 95–115). Thousand Oaks, CA: Sage.
Lesser, G. S. (1972). Learning, teaching, and television production for children: The experience of Sesame Street. *Harvard Educational Review, 42,* 232–272.
Levy, A. K., Wolfgang, C. H., & Koorland, M. A. (1992). Sociodramatic play as a method for enhancing the language performance of kindergarten age students. *Early Childhood Research Quarterly, 7,* 245–262.
Lewis, M., & Brooks-Gunn, J. (1979). *Social cognition and the acquisition of self.* New York: Plenum.
Lichtenstein, R. (1982). New instrument, old problem for early identification. *Exceptional Children, 49,* 70–72.
Lincoln, Y. S., & Guba, E. G. (1985). *Naturalistic inquiry.* Thousand Oaks, CA: Sage.
Linn, R. L. (1994). Performance assessment: Policy promises and technical measurement standards. *Educational Researcher, 23*(9), 4–14.
Linn, R. L., & Gronlund, N. E. (1995). *Measurement and assessment in teaching* (7th ed.). Englewood Cliffs, NJ: Prentice-Hall.

Livingston, S. A., & Zieky, M. J. (1982). *Passing scores: A manual for setting standards of performance on educational and occupational tests.* Princeton, NJ: Educational Testing Service.

Lofland, J., & Lofland, L. H. (1984). *Analyzing social settings: A guide to qualitative observation and analysis* (2nd ed.). Belmont, CA: Wadsworth.

Lomax, R. G. (1992). *Statistical concepts: A second course for education and the behavioral sciences.* White Plains, NY: Longman.

Lubeck, S. (1985). *Sandbox society.* Philadelphia: Farmer.

Lubeck, S. (1995). Policy issues in the development of child care and early education systems: The need for cross-national comparison. In J. A. Hatch (Ed.), *Qualitative research in early childhood settings* (pp. 79–98). Westport, CT: Praeger.

Lukasevich, A., & Summers, E. G. (1986). Characteristics of the journal literature in early childhood education. In L. G. Katz & K. Steiner (Eds.), *Current topics in early childhood education* (Vol. 6. pp. 280–296). Norwood, NJ: Ablex.

Maclean, M., Bryant, P., & Bradley, L. (1987). Rhymes, nursery rhymes, and reading in early childhood. *Merrill-Palmer Quarterly, 33,* 255–281.

Malinowski, B. (1922). *Argonauts of the Western Pacific.* New York: Dutton.

Martin, R. P. (1988). *The Temperament Assessment Battery for Children—Manual.* Brandon, VT: Clinical Psychology Publishing.

Martin, R. P. (1991). Assessment of social and emotional behavior. In B. A. Bracken (Ed.), *The psychoeducational assessment of preschool children* (2nd ed., pp. 450–464). Boston: Allyn and Bacon.

McCarthy, D. (1972). *Manual for the McCarthy Scales of Children's Abilities.* San Antonio, TX: Psychological Corporation.

McCarthy, D. (1978). *Manual for the McCarthy Screening Test.* San Antonio, TX: Psychological Corporation.

McGee-Brown, M. J. (1995). Multiple voices, contexts, and methods: Making choices in qualitative evaluation in early childhood education settings. In J. A. Hatch (Ed.), *Quantitative research in early childhood settings* (pp. 191–211). Westport, CT: Praeger.

McMillan, J. H. (1996). *Educational research: Fundamentals for the consumer* (2nd ed.). New York: Harper Collins.

McMillan, J. H., & Schumacher, S. (1993). *Research in education: A conceptual introduction* (3rd ed.). New York: Harper Collins.

Meeker, M., & Meeker, R. (1979). *S.O.I. Learning Abilities Test: Examiner's manual* (rev. ed.). El Segundo, CA: S.O.I. Institute.

Mehrens, W. A., & Lehman, I. J. (1991). *Measurement and evaluation in education and psychology* (4th ed.). Chicago: Holt, Rinehart and Winston.

Meisels, S. J. (1985). A functional analysis of the evolution of public policy for handicapped young children. *Educational Evaluation and Policy Analysis, 7,* 115–126.

Meisels, S. J. (1987). Uses and abuses of developmental screening and school readiness testing. *Young Children, 42*(2), 4–6, 68–73.

Meisels, S. J. (1989a). *Developmental screening in early childhood: A guide* (3rd ed.). Washington, DC: National Association for the Education of Young Children.

Meisels, S. J. (1989b). High-stakes testing in kindergarten. *Educational Leadership, 46*(7), 16–22.

Meisels, S. J. (1992). Doing harm by doing good: Iatrogenic effects of early childhood enrollment and promotion policies. *Early Childhood Research Quarterly, 7,* 155–174.

Meisels, S. J., & Wiske, M. S. (1983). *Early Screening Inventory.* New York: Teachers College Press.

Melton, G. B. (1987). The clashing of symbols: Prelude to child and family policy. *American Psychologist, 42,* 345–354.

Messick, S. (1980). Test validity and the ethics of assessment. *American Psychologist, 35,* 1012–1027.

Messick, S. (1988). The once and future uses of validity: Assessing the meaning and consequences of validity. In H. Wainer & H. I. Braun (Eds.), *Test validity* (pp. 33–45). Hillsdale, NJ: Lawrence Erlbaum.

Messick, S. (1989). Validity. In R. L. Linn (Ed.), *Educational measurement* (3rd ed., pp. 13–103). New York: American Council on Education and Macmillan.

Messick, S. (1995). Validity of psychological assessment. *American Psychologist, 50,* 741–749.

Miles, M., & Huberman, M. (1984). *Qualitative data analysis: A sourcebook of new methods.* Thousand Oaks, CA: Sage.

Miles, M., & Huberman, M. (1994). *Qualitative data analysis: An expanded sourcebook* (2nd ed.). Thousand Oaks, CA: Sage.

Miller, L. J. (1982). *Miller Assessment for Preschoolers–Manual.* San Antonio, TX: Psychological Corporation.

Mischler, E. G. (1979). Meaning in context: Is there any other kind? *Harvard Educational Review, 49,* 2–10.

Morse, J. M. (1994). Designing funded qualitative research. In N. K. Denzin & Y. S. Lincoln (Eds.), *Handbook of qualitative research* (pp. 220–235). Thousand Oaks, CA: Sage.

Moss, P. A. (1992). Shifting conceptions of validity in educational measurement: Implications for performance assessment. *Review of Educational Research, 62,* 229–258.

Moss, P. A. (1994). Can there be validity without reliability? *Educational Researcher, 23*(2), 5–12.

National Association for the Education of Young Children. (1988). NAEYC position statement on standardized testing of young children 3 through 8 years of age. *Young Children, 43*(3), 42–47.

Newman, L. S. (1990). Intentional and unintentional memory in young children: Remembering vs. playing. *Journal of Experimental Child Psychology, 50,* 243–258.

Nurss, J. R., & McGauvran, M. E. (1986). *Metropolitan Readiness Test* (5th ed.). San Antonio, TX: Psychological Corporation.

Odom, S. L. (1988). Research in early childhood special education. In S. L. Odom & M. B. Karnes (Eds.), *Early intervention for infants and children with handicaps: An empirical base* (pp. 1–21). Baltimore, MD: Brookes.

Patton, M. Q. (1990). *Qualitative evaluation and research methods* (2nd ed.). Thousand Oaks, CA: Sage.

Peck, C. A., Carlson, P., & Helmstetter, E. (1992). Parent and teacher perceptions of outcomes for typically developing children enrolled in integrated early childhood programs: A statewide survey. *Journal of Early Intervention, 16,* 53–63.

Pedersen, E., Faucher, T. A., & Eaton, W. W. (1978). A new perspective on the effects of first-grade teachers on children's subsequent adult status. *Harvard Educational Review, 48,* 1–31.

Peet, S. H. (1995). Parental perceptions of the use of internal sources of information about children's development. *Early Education and Development, 6,* 145–154.

Phillips, G., & McNaughton, S. (1990). The practice of storybook reading to preschool children in mainstream New Zealand families. *Reading Research Quarterly, 25,* 196–212.

Pinon, M. F., Huston, A. C., & Wright, J. C. (1989). Family ecology and child characteristics that predict young children's educational television viewing. *Child Development, 60,* 846–856.

Popham, W. J., & Husek, T. R. (1969). Implications of criterion-referenced measurement. *Journal of Educational Measurement, 6,* 1–9.

Purcell-Gates, V., & Dahl, K. L. (1991). Low-SES children's success and failure at early literacy learning in skills-based classrooms. *Journal of Reading Behavior, 23,* 1–34.

Rist, R. C. (1980). Blitzkrieg ethnography: On the transformation of a method into a movement. *Educational Researcher, 9*(2), 8–10.

Robson, C. (1993). *Real world research: A resource for social scientists and practitioner-researchers.* Oxford, England: Blackwell.

Roethlisberger, F. J., & Dickson, W. J. (1941). *Management and the worker.* Cambridge, MA: Harvard University Press.

Rosenthal, R. (1966). *Experimenter effects in behavioral research.* New York: Appleton-Century-Crofts.

Rothlein, L., & Brett, A. (1987). Children's, teachers', and parents' perceptions of play. *Early Childhood Research Quarterly, 2,* 45–53.

Salomon, G. (1991). Transcending the qualitative–quantitative debate: The analytic and systemic approaches to educational research. *Educational Researcher, 20*(6), 10–18.

Sanford, A. R. (1974). *A manual for the use of the Learning Accomplishment Profile.* Winston-Salem, NC: Kaplan School Supply.

Sax, G. (1980). *Principles of educational and psychological measurement and evaluation* (2nd ed.). Belmont, CA: Wadsworth.

Schenk, V. M., & Grusec, J. E. (1987). A comparison of prosocial behavior of children with and without day care experience. *Merrill-Palmer Quarterly, 33,* 231–240.

Schmidt, F. L. (1988). Validity generalization and the future of criterion-related validity. In H. Wainer & H. I. Braun (Eds.), *Test validity* (pp. 173–189). Hillsdale, NJ: Lawrence Erlbaum.

Seekins, T., Fawcett, S. B., Cohen, S. H., Elder, J. P., Jason, L. A., Schnelle, J. F., & Winett, R. A. (1988). Experimental evaluation of public policy: The case of state legislation for child passenger safety. *Journal of Applied Behavior Analysis, 21,* 233–243.

Seidman, I. E. (1991). *Interviewing as qualitative research: A guide for researchers in education and the social sciences.* New York: Teachers College Press.

Shavelson, R. J., Webb, N. M., & Rowley, G. L. (1989). Generalizability theory. *American Psychologist, 44,* 922–932.

Shepard, L. A. (1979). Norm-referenced vs. criterion-referenced tests. *Educational Horizons, 57,* 26–32.

Shepard, L. A. (1984). Setting performance standards. In R. A. Berk (Ed.), *A guide to criterion-referenced test construction* (pp. 169–198). Baltimore, MD: Johns Hopkins University Press.

Shepard, L. A. (1993). Evaluating test validity. *Review of Research in Education, 19,* 405–450.

Shepard, L. A. (1994). The challenges of assessing young children appropriately. *Phi Delta Kappan, 76,* 206–212.

Shepard, L. A., & Graue, M. E. (1993). The morass of school readiness screening: Research on test use and test validity. In B. Spodek (Ed.), *Handbook of research on the education of young children* (pp. 293–305). New York: Macmillan.

Shepard, L. A., & Smith, M. L. (1987). Effects of kindergarten retention at the end of first grade. *Psychology in the Schools, 24,* 346–357.

Shepard, L. A., & Smith, M. L. (1989). *Flunking grades: Research and policies on retention.* London: Falmer.

Sherman, R. R., & Webb, R. B. (1988). Qualitative research in education: A focus. In R. R. Sherman & R. B. Webb (Eds.), *Qualitative research in education: Focus and methods* (pp. 1–21). London: Falmer.

Shulman, L. S. (1988). Disciplines of inquiry in education: An overview. In R. M. Jaeger (Ed.), *Complementary methods for research in education* (pp. 3–17). Washington, DC: American Educational Research Association.

Sieber, S. D. (1973). The integration of fieldwork and survey methods. *American Journal of Sociology, 78,* 1335–1359.

Siegel, D. F., & Hanson, R. A. (1991). Kindergarten education policies: Separating myth from reality. *Early Education and Development, 2,* 5–31.

Silverman, D. (1993). *Interpreting qualitative data.* Thousand Oaks, CA: Sage.

Smith, M. L., & Glass, G. V. (1987). *Research and evaluation in education and the social sciences.* Englewood Cliffs, NJ: Prentice-Hall.

Smith, M. L., & Shepard, L. A. (1988). Kindergarten readiness and retention: A qualitative study of teachers' beliefs and practices. *American Educational Research Journal, 25,* 307–333.

Sparrow, S. S., Balla, D. A., & Cicchetti, D. V. (1985). *Vineland Adaptive Behavior Scales.* Circle Pines, MN: American Guidance Service.

Spatz, C. (1993). *Basic statistics: Tales of distributions* (5th ed.). Pacific Grove, CA: Brooks/Cole.

Spodek, B. (Ed.). (1993). *Handbook of research on the education of young children.* New York: Macmillan.

Sprinthall, R. C. (1990). *Basic statistical analysis* (3rd ed.). Englewood Cliffs, NJ: Prentice-Hall.

Stark, L. J., Collins, F. L., Jr., Osnes, P. G., & Stokes, T. F. (1986). *Journal of Applied Behavior Analysis, 19,* 367-379.

Stipek, D., Feiler, R., Daniels, D., & Milburn, S. (1995). Effects of different instructional approaches on young children's achievement and motivation. *Child Development, 66,* 209–223.

Strauss, A., & Corbin, J. (1990). *Basics of qualitative research: Grounded theory procedures and techniques.* Thousand Oaks, CA: Sage.

Symonds, P. M. (1956). A research checklist in educational psychology. *Journal of Educational Psychology, 47,* 101–109.

Tesch, R. (1990). *Qualitative research: Analysis types and software tools.* New York: Falmer Press.

Thompson, B. (1992). Two and one-half decades of leadership in measurement and evaluation. *Journal of Counseling & Development, 70,* 434–438.

Thomson, J. A., Ampofo-Boateng, K., Pitcairn, T., Grieve, R., Lee, D. N., & Demetre, J. D. (1992). Behavioural group training of children to find safe routes to cross the road. *British Journal of Educational Psychology, 62,* 173–183.

Thorndike, E. L. (1918). The nature, purposes, and general methods of measurements of educational products. In G. M. Whipple (Ed.), *The measurement of educational products* (17th Yearbook, Part 2, National Society for the Study of Education, pp. 16–24). Chicago: University of Chicago Press.

Thorndike, R. L., Hagen, E. P., & Sattler, J. M. (1986). *Technical manual: The Stanford Binet Intelligence Scale* (4th ed.). Chicago: Riverside.

Torrance, E. P. (1974). *Norms-technical manual: The Torrance Tests of Creative Thinking.* Bensenville, IL: Scholastic Testing Service.

Torrance, E. P. (1981). *Thinking Creatively with Action and Movement.* Bensenville, IL: Scholastic Testing Service.

Torrance, E. P., & Caropreso, E. J. (1991). Assessment of preschool giftedness: Intelligence and creativity. In B. A. Bracken (Ed.), *The psychoeducational assessment of preschool children* (2nd ed., pp. 430–449). Boston: Allyn and Bacon.

Trawick-Smith, J. (1992). A descriptive study of persuasive preschool children: How they get others to do what they want. *Early Childhood Research Quarterly, 7,* 95–114.

Varga, D. (1991). The historical ordering of children's play as a developmental task. *Play & Culture, 4,* 322–333.

Vaughn, B. E., & Langlois, J. H. (1983). Physical attractiveness as a correlate of peer status and social competence in preschool children. *Developmental Psychology, 19,* 561–567.

Venn, J. J., Serwatka, T. S., & Anthony, R. A. (1987). *Scales of Social Development.* Austin, TX: Pro-Ed.

Walsh, D. J., Tobin, J. J., & Graue, M. E. (1993). The interpretive voice: Qualitative research in early childhood education. In B. Spodek (Ed.), *Handbook of research on the education of young children* (pp. 464–476). New York: Macmillan.

Webb, E. J., Campbell, D. T., Schwartz, R. D., Sechrest, L., & Grove, J. B. (1981). *Nonreactive measures in the social sciences* (2nd ed.). Boston: Houghton Mifflin.

Wechsler, D. (1989). *Manual for the Wechsler Preschool and Primary Scale of Intelligence–Revised.* San Antonio, TX: Psychological Corporation.

Werner, E. E., & Smith, R. S. (1982). *Vulnerable but invincible: A longitudinal study of resilient children and youth.* New York: McGraw-Hill.

Wien, C. A. (1991). *Developmentally appropriate practice and the practical knowledge of day care teachers.* Unpublished doctoral dissertation, Dalhousie University, Halifax, Nova Scotia, Canada.

Wien, C. A. (1995). *Developmentally appropriate practice in "real life": Stories of teacher practical knowledge.* New York: Teachers College Press.

Williams, L. R., & Fromberg, D. P. (Eds.). (1992). *Encyclopedia of early childhood education.* New York: Garland.

Winterer, C. (1992). Avoiding a "hothouse system of education": Nineteenth-century early childhood education from the infant schools to the kindergartens. *History of Education Quarterly, 32,* 288–314.

Wirt, R. D., Lachar, D., Klinedinst, J. K., & Seat, P. D. (1984). *Multidimensional description of child personality: A manual for the Personality Inventory for Children* (rev. ed.). Los Angeles: Western Psychological Services.

Wittrock, M. C. (Ed.). (1986). *Handbook of research on teaching* (3rd ed.). New York: Macmillan.

Wolcott, H. F. (1988). Ethnographic research in education. In R. M. Jaeger (Ed.), *Complementary methods for research in education* (pp. 187–249). Washington, DC: American Educational Research Association.

Wolcott, H. F. (1994). *Transforming qualitative data: Description, analysis, and interpretation.* Thousand Oaks, CA: Sage.

Wong, L. (1987). Reaction to research findings: Is the feeling of obviousness warranted? *Dissertation Abstracts International, 48/12,* 3709B. (University Microfilms No. DA 8801059)

Woodill, G. A., Bernhard, J., & Prochner, L. (Eds.). (1992). *International handbook of early childhood education.* New York: Garland.

Woolner, R. B. (1966/1968). *Preschool Self-Concept Picture Test,* Memphis, TN: Memphis State University, Department of Curriculum and Instruction.

Wortham, S. C. (1995). *Tests and measurement in early childhood education* (2nd ed.). Englewood Cliffs, NJ: Merrill/Prentice-Hall.

Worthen, B. R., & Sanders, J. R. (1987). *Educational evaluation.* New York: Longman.

Wrigley, J. (1989). Do young children need intellectual stimulation? Experts' advice to parents, 1900–1985. *History of Education Quarterly, 29,* 41–75.

Zigler, E. F. (1970). Raising the quality of children's lives. *Children, 17,* 166–170.

Zigler, E. F., & Finn-Stevenson, M. (1989). Child care in America: From problem to solution. *Educational Policy, 3,* 313–329.

Index

NAMES

SUBJECTS

About the Authors

WILLIAM L. GOODWIN received his Ph.D. in Educational Psychology from the University of Wisconsin–Madison (1965). While on leave from Bucknell University, he was an AERA-USOE Postdoctoral Fellow in Early Childhood Education at Harvard University's Laboratory of Human Development (1969–1970). He was also a Fellow in the USOE Leadership Training Institute for Early Childhood Education (1970–1972). He has been a faculty member at the University of Colorado at Denver since 1970 and is now Professor and Coordinator of the Educational Psychology Division. He teaches courses in early childhood education, educational psychology, measurement, and research methodology. His previous publications include books in both educational psychology and early childhood education as well as numerous articles.

LAURA D. GOODWIN received her Ph.D. in Research Methodology, Evaluation, and Measurement through the Laboratory of Educational Research at the University of Colorado, Boulder (1977). After six years at the University's Health Sciences Center, she joined the faculty of the School of Education at the University of Colorado at Denver in 1983. There, she is now Professor and Associate Dean, and is also a Presidential Teaching Scholar for the University of Colorado system. She teaches courses in statistics, measurement, and research methods. She has published extensively, often on methodological issues, in both nursing and education journals.